THIS STRANGE STRANGE WORLD
REAL or UNREAL?

Danger in the Night

Something big . . . something bad . . . was coming through the dark woods . . . coming straight toward Kenny and his father 2

"Get It Away From Me!"

Cindy screamed, "Why is it doing these things to me? Help me!" 6

Lost Over the Bermuda Triangle

The big airplane was lost . . . somewhere over the Bermuda Triangle . . . and something was pulling it down . . . straight into the sea! 10

The Girl Who Lived Twice

Karen cried, "I am not Karen! I am Anne Lancaster!" But Anne Lancaster had been dead for 100 years 16

The City That Disappeared

Zena and Alex sat looking over the beautiful city of Atlantis. How could they know it was the very last day 20

Editor-in-chief: Jean Robbins • Reading Editor: Beverly Riskin • Visuals: Victoria Productions, inc. • Photographer: William T. Martin • Atlantis art: Kinuko Craft • Writer: Nina B. Link • Designer: The Studio, Herb Blumenthal • Cover: Walter Smith, Jr. • Research: Kathryn Seeth.

Something big…something bad…
was coming through the dark woods
…coming straight toward
Kenny and his father….

DANGER IN THE NIGHT

It was night. Kenny and his father had hiked in the Oregon mountains all day. They were having fun on their camping trip, but today it rained and was muddy. They were glad to put up their tent and crawl into their sleeping bags.

Kenny listened to the night sounds of animals and insects outside the tent. Every bone in his body seemed to hurt from the long hike. He was tired but sleep would not come.

He turned to look at his father. Slowly his father's sleeping bag rose and fell with his even breathing.

WORD BOX

hiked. Took a long walk.

Kenny thought back to what had happened that afternoon. He and his father were looking for a dry place to stop for lunch.

Suddenly, his father bent down to look at the ground. He shook his head. Kenny bent down beside him and drew in his breath sharply.

There were four giant-size footprints in the soft mud.

"A bear?" Kenny whispered.

"No. These aren't bear prints. They look like a person's footprints, but they're too big and they have only four toes. Look! They're two times bigger than my own foot!"

"Should we follow the tracks?" Kenny asked.

"I don't know what's at the other end. The thing that made these prints must be eight feet tall. I've never seen anything like it."

When they looked around, they could see branches broken off some of the trees. They followed the trail for a few minutes. Then they lost it.

For the rest of the afternoon, they tried to figure out what could have left those footprints. Was it an animal? A person? They were still talking about the prints when they crawled into their sleeping bags for the night. Kenny's father went right to sleep. But Kenny could not get those strange, giant footprints out of his mind.

His thoughts were broken by the sudden cracking of a branch. Then there was a heavy footstep. Another branch broke. Another footstep sounded in the night. Some birds cried out loudly and flew away. Kenny wanted to shout, but he could not find his voice. ⟶

WORD BOX

footstep (foot • step). The sound of a step.

More branches cracked off. The footsteps grew louder. His father still slept.

A tall figure appeared near the fire. Kenny could not move. He felt goose bumps all over his body. The thing moved closer. By the light of the fire, Kenny could see it more clearly. It looked part human and part ape. It stood about seven feet high and was covered with reddish-brown hair. The hands and feet looked almost human. Its arms hung down to its knees. Its head seemed to sit on its shoulders because it had a very short neck. It had a strong, bad smell.

It took another step closer. Then it let out a loud, high scream. Kenny began to shake.

The thing screamed again. Kenny looked toward his father and saw that he was wide awake. His father's eyes were big and scared. The thing began to tear through their packs, pulling out food. Pans went flying and crashing to the ground.

Then it stopped. It looked at the tent. It started to walk toward Kenny and his father. The smell got stronger and stronger. Kenny held himself very still. He waited.

Slowly, the smell began to disappear. Kenny heard his father's voice. "Kenny, it's gone. Are you all right?"

"What was it?" Kenny asked in a shaky voice.

"I don't know. It looked like something that's called a Bigfoot. I read about it in a book. But I thought it was some kind of joke."

"This was no joke," Kenny said quietly.

Kenny and his father did not go back to sleep. They sat up all night, watching the dark woods and listening for footsteps until the morning light spread over the mountain. They quickly packed up their things. They did not look at the giant footprints near the fire. They did not follow the trail of broken branches. They did not stop to rest until they were miles away from the spot where they had spent the night. ■

WHAT ARE THE FACTS?

- Could this story be true?

- Are there really hairy giants walking the earth today?

There are thousands of reports from people who have seen these giants or their footprints. These reports come from all over the world. In the Himalaya mountains in Asia the giant is called a *Yeti*. In Canada it is called *Sasquatch*. In South America it is called *Mono Grande*. And in the United States we call it *Bigfoot*.

No matter which name is used, it is described pretty much the same way. These giants look part human and part ape. They are tall and very wide and have a strong, bad smell. They are covered with long hair. They walk like humans, on two legs. They are most often found in the mountains.

Stories of wild, hairy men living in the mountains go way back in time. Are these stories true or are they just made up? If any of the stories are true, are hairy giants still living today?

Some people believe that since stories about these giants have been around for so long, and so many people have seen them in so many different places, Bigfoot must be real. They feel that maybe, long ago, there were many of these strange giants, but most of them died out or were killed by early men. Maybe a few of the hairy giants stayed alive by hiding out in the mountains.

WORD BOX

human (hu • man). A person, or very much like a person.

Here are some of the stories told by people who say they have seen Bigfoot:

In 1924, Albert Ostman says a Bigfoot family grabbed him and carried him away. He was kept for six days by this family of four before he was able to run away.

In the same year, Fred Beck says he and a group of miners killed a Bigfoot in the state of Washington. That night, hairy giants threw large rocks at the miners' cabin.

In 1967, Bob Gimlin and Roger Patterson were out trying to track down a Bigfoot in California. They finally came across one, and Mr. Patterson took pictures of Bigfoot with his camera. The color pictures clearly show a hairy giant that looks very much like those described by other people.

Many casts have been made of Bigfoot prints which do not fit the prints of any other known animal. Still, a lot of people do not believe in these hairy giants. They say the stories from long ago are not true, but are just tales that were passed along through the ages.

Many of the Bigfoot stories have been fakes. In 1958, a circus had a hairy giant frozen in ice. They called it the Iceman. Later, it was found that the Iceman was really a man-made monster. Many of the Bigfoot prints have been made by fake feet worn by people as a joke. Some of the people who thought they saw a Bigfoot were really seeing men dressed up in monkey suits.

It does seem strange that no Bigfoot has ever been caught. Why have no Bigfoot bones been found? Why are there no Bigfoot pictures except for the ones taken by Patterson? Yet, Bigfoot stories have been around for a long time, and there are more and more reports every year. Not all the footprints can be explained by fake feet.

What do you think?

IS THERE REALLY A BIGFOOT?

WORD BOX

casts. Copies of the footprints made by putting soft material such as clay into the print and letting the clay get hard.

monster (mon • ster). A very big animal or thing.

Cindy screamed, "Why is it doing these things to me? Help me!"

"GET IT AWAY FROM ME!"

It's over. After two weeks it has finally stopped. I keep thinking it is going to happen again. I am still afraid. No one in my family will talk about it now. They are trying to forget. But it is always on my mind. If I tell you about it, maybe I'll feel better.

* * * * *

Two weeks ago, on a Monday night, I was in bed just about to fall asleep. I heard a knocking sound. At first I thought it was my brother, Billy, in the next room. I yelled to him to stop fooling around. The knocking got louder. Billy came to my door.

"Will you cut it out, Cindy," he said. "How am I supposed to sleep if you keep banging on the wall?"

"I thought it was you," I answered. "I'm not doing anything."

"Maybe it's a ghost," Billy laughed.

After he went back to his room, I heard the knocking three more times. I looked in Billy's room. He was sleeping. No one else was in the house. My parents were visiting my uncle. I stayed awake for a long time, listening. But there was no more knocking, and I finally fell asleep.

The next morning was bright and sunny. The knocking seemed like a bad dream. Billy and I even joked about it at breakfast. But deep inside me, I was still a little scared.

I had a good day at school, and by the time I got home, I had forgotten about it. I was on my bed, doing my homework, when a loud crash made me jump. I looked up quickly. A glass on my desk had smashed to pieces!

I started to get up for a closer look, then stopped cold. My chair was tipping back and forth — all by itself!

My notebook flew off the bed and into the air. Papers fell all over the room. What was going on? I felt as if something were out to get me. My heart was pounding. For a moment, I couldn't move. Then I ran out the bedroom door and down the stairs.

"Mom," I yelled. "Help me! Things are flying all over my room, breaking — coming after me!"

"Things just don't fly around and break all by themselves, Cindy," Mom said.

Before she could say another word, a jar of jelly came sailing across the room and crashed against the wall.

"Did you see that?" I screamed. "I'm not imagining things!"

"I'm not sure what I saw." My mother looked worried.

"That jar moved all by itself!" I yelled.

Mom didn't say anything. Her hands were shaking as she cleaned up the jelly and broken glass.

I would not go back to my room. I was afraid to be alone. I stayed in the kitchen, waiting for my father to come home for dinner. As soon as I heard him at the door, I ran to tell him what had happened. "Billy is just playing some kind of joke," he laughed.

"Billy was at school when the jelly jar flew off the table," my mother pointed out.

"He could have set up a trick." Dad didn't believe us. He thought it was a big joke.

We sat down to dinner. I wasn't very hungry, but I tried to eat. Suddenly, the plate of meat slid across the table and crashed to the floor. A glass flew up in the air, then landed on the floor and broke. I jumped out of my chair and began to cry. We all looked at each other, scared. We didn't finish dinner that night. No one was laughing now.

As the days went by, more and more strange things happened. We heard knocking sounds

→

again and again. Windows closed by themselves. Pictures fell off the walls. Tables and chairs moved across the room. My shoes even flew through the air and slammed against a window.

It got so bad, I couldn't eat or sleep. Mom sent me to stay at my friend Beth's house. I was so happy to go there. I thought I was away from it all. But my first night at Beth's, there was a knocking on *her* walls. A chair fell over. A bottle of soda opened by itself, fell on its side, and spilled all over the table. The strange happenings were following me!

"Oh, no!" I cried. "What's happening to me? Can't I get away from all this?"

We didn't get much sleep at Beth's house that night. Next day at school, I couldn't think about my work. After school, I went home. I couldn't stay at Beth's house again.

Billy was in the kitchen with my mother when I got home. "It was nice and quiet while you were away," he said.

"What do you mean, Billy?" I started to shake.

"All those noises and things moving only happen when you're around," he answered.

"Oh, no, no! Mom, help me! What's happening to me?" I was crying and screaming at the same time.

Mom put her arms around me and held me close. But all the time she was holding me, I knew that she too thought it was my fault. And she was scared.

Dad called the police. They called in some scientists. They all heard noises. They all saw things move by themselves. But no matter how hard they looked, they could not find out why these things were happening.

Then five days ago, it all stopped as suddenly as it started. The house is quiet now. Nothing flies through the air. Nothing moves by itself. I don't sleep much. I keep wondering if it is going to happen again. ■

WHAT ARE THE FACTS?

For the past one thousand years, there have been reports of strange noises and objects that moved by themselves. Many people think that these strange happenings are caused by *poltergeists.*

The word *poltergeist* means "noisy ghost." But some scientists say that people like Cindy are really making the strange things happen themselves. How can this be, when Cindy herself did not know she was causing the problem?

Here's how scientists explain it. The strange things usually happen around a child or teenager. The scientists think that a very few young people may have a lot of extra energy that needs to be used up. Because of this, their minds may have special powers. These special powers may be strong enough to use the extra energy to make things move and to cause noises. In the story, Cindy's mind was acting as a poltergeist.

Poltergeists are not reported very often. There are only about three new cases every year. But three things always seem to be true. A young person is in the middle of the problem. Objects move by themselves and strange noises are heard when that person is around. These things start suddenly, last a few days or weeks, then stop suddenly.

WORD BOX

objects (ob • jects). Things that can be seen or felt; for example, chairs, tables, apples, jars.

scientists (sci • en • tists). People who are trained to know a lot about the facts and laws of nature and the universe. A scientist usually works in one kind of science. For example, he or she may know a lot about the stars or the oceans or how people think and act.

energy (en • er • gy). As used in the story, the power of the body or mind to do things.

Some people say it is all done by tricks. Sometimes, people have used rubber bands and string to make things look as if they moved by themselves. They have used records and tapes to make noises. But a lot of cases cannot be explained by tricks. Here are some of these cases:

In 1960 in Scotland, a girl named Virginia Campbell was very scared by what was happening around her. Furniture in her house lifted and moved. There were knocking and sawing sounds. Her desk top in school lifted and fell when nobody was near it. A doctor came to find out what was making these things happen. He could not find out why the strange things were going on around Virginia.

That same year, two scientists studied the strange case of Betty Ruth. They stayed on her family's farm in Missouri. A pot lifted off the stove and fell to the floor. A can of shoe polish came flying through the air. Every day, something happened that could not be explained. Suddenly, one day it all stopped.

The Bottle-Popping Case happened in Long Island, New York, in 1958. Bottles popped open all over the house. Strange noises were heard at night. Sixty-seven different things happened in about a month. Scientists and police were called in to find out why these things were happening. They did not find any tricks. They did not find anything wrong with the house. All they found was that the noises and moving objects seemed to be going on around a twelve-year-old boy named James.

Someday, we may know more about poltergeists. We may learn that our minds do have strange powers. Maybe even strange enough to make things move.

The big airplane was lost . . .
somewhere over the Bermuda Triangle . . .
and something was pulling it down . . .
straight into the sea!

LOST OVER THE BERMUDA TRIANGLE

"Thirty more minutes and we land in sunny Bermuda," I said to Dan, my co-pilot. "I'm heading straight for a swim."

Dan smiled. Then he looked worried. "Say, isn't this the part of the ocean they call the Bermuda Triangle? The place where all those planes and ships disappeared? I've never been over the Bermuda Triangle before. It gives me the creeps."

I smiled. Just then, Mary, the flight attendant, opened the heavy cockpit door. "Last chance for you two to have a cup of coffee. Want one?"

Before we could answer, there was a loud roar, and the plane tipped sideways. It felt as if we had hit something big out there in the sky. Then, suddenly, we were caught in a strong wind that bumped our big jet around like a rubber ball.

Mary fell against the door. I grabbed the controls and reached for the mike.

"Please fasten your seat belts," I told the passengers. "We have run into some bad weather. Stay in your seats. We'll fly out of this in a few minutes."

I called the control tower on the radio. "This is Sunways Flight 215. We've run into some bad weather. Please tell us where the storm is. We need to know how to fly out of it."

I could see Mary trying to stand up and falling again. I couldn't help her. I had to try to fly the plane. But the plane had gone crazy. The controls felt as if they were being pulled out of my hands, as if somebody or something else were flying the plane.

"Hey, what's going on?" I yelled. Before I could say another word, the plane shook hard and rolled over. Passengers screamed. Some of them hadn't closed their seat belts, and they were thrown across the plane. I could hear their cries. Mary was hurt, but I could not help.

"Sunways Flight 215 to control tower," I yelled. "The instruments aren't working. The plane is turning over. I cannot stop it! Can

you help? Can you help?"

Now it felt as if someone had picked us up and was throwing us around like a baseball. I pulled on the controls as hard as I could. Nothing happened for a moment. Then, suddenly, the plane turned right side up.

→

WORD BOX

co-pilot (co-pi • lot). The second pilot on an airplane. The pilot is the person who "drives" the plane; the co-pilot helps the pilot.

flight attendant (flight at • ten • dant). The person who takes care of the passengers on the airplane.

cockpit (cock • pit). The room in the plane where the pilot and co-pilot sit.

controls (con • trols). The wheel the pilot uses to steer the plane.

control tower (con • trol tow • er). The building at an airport from which people give the pilot directions over a radio.

instruments (in • stru • ments). The devices that tell the pilot where the plane is, how high it is, how fast it is going, and so on.

I could hear the passengers screaming. Now the plane was falling fast. We were heading straight for the water!

"Dan," I yelled. "Radio the control tower that I'm going to try to make a sea landing!"

I could hear the control tower on the radio. "Where are you? Where are you? Sunways Flight 215, please answer," they asked over and over.

Dan could only say, "I don't know. The instruments aren't working." Then I heard him say, "I can't see the sun. I can't find it. Everything out there looks wrong . . . strange. Even the ocean doesn't look right."

I pulled my eyes away from the instruments and looked out the window. I could not believe what I saw. The blue water and the blue sky seemed to meet and become one. I couldn't tell what was ocean and what was sky. Everything outside looked silver.

I felt as if the plane were sitting in a big blue balloon that was falling fast.
Just as I thought we were going to hit the water, the plane straightened out. Then it began to go up again. The higher we got, the more the strange silver color disappeared. The wind stopped as suddenly as it had started. In a few minutes, we were once again flying smoothly through a clear, sunny sky. Whatever it was, it was all over.

I radioed the control tower. "Landing in five minutes. Send help. We have hurt people on board."

We landed without any problems. I don't remember much about it. But one thing I do remember. After we landed, Dan asked me, "What time do you have?"

I looked at my watch. "It's three-thirty," I said.

"My watch says three-thirty, too," Dan said. "But look at the clock over there."

I looked. It said four-thirty.

I couldn't think about that right away. I had too many other things to wonder about. But now, when I think back, I feel cold all over. Somehow, somewhere, on that strange flight, we had lost an hour.

Where had we been in that lost hour? What had happened to us over the strange Bermuda Triangle? What did it mean? ■

WHAT ARE THE FACTS?

What is the Bermuda Triangle? It is part of the Atlantic Ocean that goes from Bermuda to Puerto Rico to Florida and back to Bermuda. The map on this page shows where it is.

A legend, or story, has grown about the Bermuda Triangle. The story is that a lot of ships and airplanes have strangely disappeared here. Some people say that more than one hundred ships and planes have been lost. They say the weather was usually good, the ships and planes were on course — yet they suddenly disappeared. Later, no bodies were found and no parts of broken planes and ships were seen. Strangest of all, sometimes a ship was found — but all the people were gone!

These stories go back over 500 years. Christopher Columbus and his men sailed through the Bermuda Triangle. They told about miles of seaweed, worms that ate through the wooden ships, a ball of fire, and a strange light on the water. Their stories made many people afraid to sail through that part of the Atlantic Ocean.

A lot of people began to believe the legend of the Bermuda Triangle when five Navy planes disappeared in 1945. A plane that was sent to find them also disappeared. Some writers added to the legend by saying that the last thing one of the pilots said was, "Everything is wrong . . . strange. We can't be sure of any direction. Even the ocean doesn't look right."

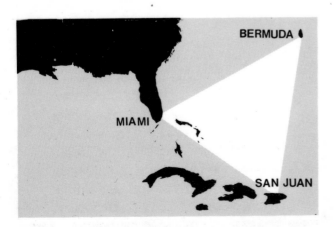

There is a long list of ships and planes that have been lost in the Bermuda Triangle. But ships and planes sometimes disappear in other parts of the world, too. Why do some people think the Bermuda Triangle is so unusual?

There are a lot of reasons. Some say that creatures from outer space come and take our planes and ships so they can see what the people of our world are like. Maybe that is why some ships have been found with no one on them. That would also explain why a lot of UFOs (Unidentified Flying Objects) have been reported around the Bermuda Triangle.

Other people believe there is a kind of hole in the sky through which planes might fly by mistake and get lost in outer space.

Another reason people sometimes give for the lost ships is that there might be cities under the sea, like Atlantis, that were once above the water thousands of years ago. Lost cities in the Bermuda Triangle might have some kind of power stations that pull ships and planes under. Or perhaps there are strange creatures under the sea that are taking our ships, planes, and people.

These are pretty strange stories, and they make a good legend. But a lot of people say that the facts are very different. One man, Lawrence David Kusche, found out all he could about sixty Bermuda Triangle cases. He looked at Navy records, ships' records, newspaper reports, and talked with many →

WORD BOX

legend (leg • end). A story passed down through the years that may or may not be true.

seaweed (sea • weed). Plants that grow in the sea.

creature (crea • ture). A living person or animal.

UFOs, Unidentified Flying Objects (Un • i • den • ti • fied Fly • ing Ob • jects). "Flying saucers"; ships from outer space or flying objects. Nobody knows where they come from or what they are.

power stations (pow • er sta • tions). Places that make or send out power such as electricity.

people. He decided that some of the cases really happened in other parts of the world. And some of them never happened at all. They were made-up stories.

Kusche was able to explain most of the others. Even though the legend does not say so, bad weather probably caused many of the accidents. Instruments that broke down might have caused others. Pilots probably got lost or made mistakes about where they were; then they ran out of fuel and crashed. Kusche was able to explain most of the cases. But there are always some disappearances that are never explained.

Kusche also explained why the planes and ships and people were often not found. In the ocean bottom of the Bermuda Triangle, there are many deep holes. A plane or ship could disappear into such a hole and never be found. Also, many of the accidents happened at night, and search parties could not set out until the next day. By that time, the ocean could have washed away all signs of the ships or planes and the people.

Kusche gave very good reasons for the Bermuda Triangle accidents. But he was not able to explain all the accidents. Maybe he could not find out enough about these cases. Or maybe something strange does sometimes happen.

What do you think?

Would you fly over the Bermuda Triangle?

Here is a list of some of the airplanes that have disappeared in the Bermuda Triangle:

1. December 5, 1945: five TBM Navy Avenger bombers on training flight from Fort Lauderdale, Florida; total crew of 14; two-hour normal flight; lost about 225 miles northeast of base.

2. December 5, 1945: PBM Martin bomber; sent with crew of 13 to help the TBM patrol; twenty minutes later radio contact was lost and plane disappeared.

3. January 29, 1948: *Star Tiger,* four-engine Tudor IV; lost radio contact after last contact 380 miles northeast of Bermuda; plane lost with 31 passengers and crew.

4. February 2, 1952: York Transport (British); disappeared north of Triangle on course to Jamaica; 33 aboard.

5. June 5, 1965: C-119 Flying Boxcar; ten aboard; lost in the southeast Bahamas.

6. January 11, 1967: Chase YC-122; four aboard; lost in the Gulf Stream between Palm Beach, Florida, and Grand Bahama.

Listed below are some of the ships that disappeared or were found with no one on board in the Bermuda Triangle:

1. March 4, 1918: U.S. Navy supply ship U.S.S. *Cyclops,* 500 feet; sailed from Barbados to Virginia with 309 people; no bad weather; no radio messages; no wreckage ever found.

2. March 1938: *Anglo-Australian,* freighter with crew of 39; last message received west of Azores: "All well."

3. October 22, 1944: Cuban freighter *Rubicon;* found by Coast Guard in Gulf Stream off Florida coast; deserted except for a dog.

4. December 1967: *Revonoc,* all-weather 46-foot racing yacht; disappeared within sight of land.

5. December 24, 1967: *Witchcraft,* cabin cruiser; passenger and owner disappeared while boat was at harbor buoy one mile from Miami.

6. March 1973: *Anita,* 20,000-ton freighter with crew of 32; sailing from Newport News to Germany.

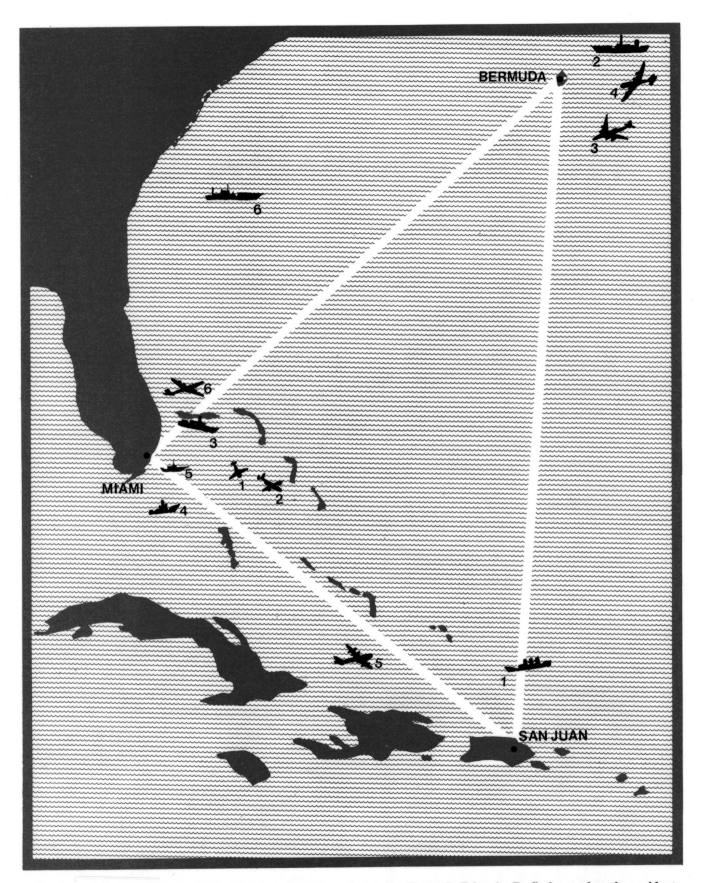

This map shows where some of the ships and planes were lost in the Bermuda Triangle. To find out when the accidents happened, look at the lists of missing planes and ships on the opposite page. Match the numbers on the map to the numbers on the lists to learn more about them.

Karen cried, "I am not Karen! I am
Anne Lancaster!" But Anne Lancaster
had been dead for 100 years . . .

THE GIRL WHO LIVED TWICE

Karen was halfway up the big tree in her back yard. She stopped climbing to let her friend Larry catch up to her. As she waited for him, she looked out over the bushes around the yard. The sun was shining on the roofs of the cars that passed by on the busy street below her. Her friend Betsy rode by on her bike, and Karen yelled hello.

Suddenly, the yard, the street, and the cars began to disappear from her sight. Instead, she saw a big, white house with beautiful, green lawns all around it.

"Oh, no," Karen thought. "It's happening to me again."

She began to feel as if she were someone else, a girl who had lived long ago. It was that girl who was in the tree. Karen could see the girl falling. She could hear her screaming. Now the girl was on the ground, crying. Her left leg and arm were broken. Oh, how she hurt! She cried out, "Help! Help me!"

"Are you all right?" Larry yelled.

The picture of the hurt girl went away. Karen found that she was holding tight to the tree branch. She was shaking with fear. She could not get that poor, hurt girl out of her mind. She could almost feel how much the broken leg and arm hurt.

"I'm getting down," Karen cried. She held onto the tree tightly as she climbed down. Larry gave her a strange look as she ran into her house.

"Mom, Mom, where are you?" she yelled, running through the rooms.

"Why, Karen, what's the matter?" her mother asked as she came out of the bedroom.

"Oh, Mom, it happened again. I was in our yard one minute, and the next minute I was that other girl. I was in another place. It was a long time ago. And I fell out of a tree. I got hurt. I cried and screamed. Oh, Mom, I was so scared."

Karen's mother was worried. She remembered how it had all started.

Karen had been watching her mother sew a patch on her jeans. "I'll do that," Karen said suddenly.

"Why, Karen, you don't know how to sew," her mother answered.

"I know I can do it. You'll see." Karen took the jeans, needle, and thread from her mother's hands.

"Well, okay, give it a try. It will give me a chance to go to the store," her mother said as she left the room.

16

Karen started sewing. She watched her hands doing things she had never learned. They seemed to move by themselves, taking tiny, perfect stitches.

"Where did you learn to sew like that?" her father asked.

He picked up the jeans and took a closer look. "I can't believe you did this so well."

"I can't either," Karen whispered. "Daddy, my hands seemed to do it all by themselves. I don't know what's happening to me. I'm so frightened. I keep seeing these pictures. There's a girl in the pictures in a long, beautiful dress. She's the one who can sew. I've seen these pictures for a long time. But lately, they come every day. And I hear people talking. One of the people is me. But I'm not Karen in the pictures."

"What are you talking about, Karen? It all sounds so strange!"

"Don't you understand? I'm someone else. I even know my name. I'm Anne Lancaster. My parents are named Frank and Laura. And I live in a big house in Lee, Massachusetts. And it's a long time ago, in the 1800s!"

"How old are you in these pictures?"

"All different ages. Sometimes I'm a baby and sometimes I'm a teenager. Today I could see myself in a long, blue dress. I looked different, but I still knew it was me."

Her father put his arms around her. "Maybe you're just dreaming," he said.

Karen pushed him away, shouting, "I am Anne Lancaster, don't you see? I want to go back to the big house and see my other parents and my brother and little sisters!"

Karen began to cry loudly. Her father led her to her bed and covered her with a blanket. She fell asleep quickly.

For the next few weeks, Karen talked about Anne Lancaster all the time. She told her parents about the big, white house she used to live in. She named Anne's brother and sisters, friends and neighbors. She talked about the parties in that beautiful house and the games she played with her friends. She believed that once, over one hundred years ago, she lived a different life. ⟶

Karen's parents did not know what to make of the way she was acting. They were afraid to tell people about the strange things Karen was saying. They asked themselves over and over again if her story could be true. They could not figure out how Karen could know so much about the 1800s. Sometimes when Karen talked about her "other" family, she spoke the way people did a long time ago.

One morning Karen came running to her mother. "How did I get this mark on my back?" she asked.

"You were born with it," her mother answered.

"That's the very same spot where I was shot when I was fifteen years old!"

"Karen, we've had enough of this kind of talk!" her father shouted.

"My brother was out hunting, and he shot me by accident. I died two days later. This is the spot!" Karen cried.

Slowly, Anne Lancaster began to take over Karen's life. Karen asked her parents to take her back to Lee, Massachusetts. She talked of nothing else. At last, her worried parents decided to try and see if what she was saying could in any way be true. They drove from their home in Maryland to Lee.

"It all looks so different," Karen said. "I know I've been here before, but there are so many buildings and cars and stores."

They went to the Town Hall to look through the records of people who lived in Lee during the 1800s.

"Look at this!" her father shouted late on the second afternoon. "Here is a record of Frank and Laura Lancaster. They had a son Seth, born in 1858. Twin daughters Mary and Alice were born in 1863, and a daughter Anne was born in 1860!"

Karen said quietly, "Come with me. I will show you where I am buried."

She led them to an old churchyard not far away. She took them past gravestones that had fallen over and broken. She led them straight to a gravestone in the corner of the churchyard. They bent down to read the writing on the old, worn stone. And here they saw:

Anne Lancaster
Born 1860   Died 1875
Beloved daughter of
Frank and Laura Lancaster
A terrible accident took her from us.
May she rest in peace. ∎

WHAT ARE THE FACTS?

Could Karen have lived before? Could she have once been Anne Lancaster?

The idea that a person lives more than one life is called *reincarnation*. The word *reincarnation* means "to be born again."

It is the idea that we return to earth again and again after we die, each time as a different person. This idea goes way back thousands of years. Many people believe in it. In places like India, it is part of the people's religion. Eskimos believe in it, too.

Many people in this country learned about reincarnation because of a man named Edgar Cayce. He would tell people about lives they had lived before. A lot of people believed these stories.

Now, scientists have started to study people who feel they lived before. Often, the scientists cannot explain how someone could know so much about another life. Some of the things people have told the scientists about "other lives" have been found to be true.

Dr. Ian Stevenson is the best known of the scientists who study reincarnation. He has been all over the world to study more than six hundred people who say they have lived before. He questions these people. He tries to learn if their stories of other lives are true. He tries to find out why they think they have lived before.

Dr. Stevenson works most often with young children. Sometimes, these children tell him about people and places they have never seen or heard about. When a child's story turns out to be true, Dr. Stevenson feels that the child may really know these things from another life. He thinks that young children don't know enough about the world to make up these stories. Some of the people Dr. Stevenson has seen even have a mark on their skin in the same place in which they had been cut or hurt in their other life.

Reincarnation might help explain why we sometimes feel that we have been someplace before or know someone well even though we never saw them before. Maybe we lived in that place in another life. Maybe the person was a friend in that other life — or even someone in our other family.

Reincarnation might also explain why some children can do things that only grown-ups can usually do. Maybe they can play the piano, write fine stories, or paint beautiful pictures because they learned to do those things in another life.

Many people feel there is no such thing as reincarnation. They say we have only one life on earth. The things people seem to remember about other lives are only dreams or secret wishes. Many times, the places and names people remember do not turn out to be true. Maybe they have read about other times, and these stories have stayed in their minds. People who do not believe in reincarnation ask why we all can't remember our other lives if we have lived before.

Do you think you may have lived another life? Who were you? Who would you like to be if you could be born again?

WORD BOX

churchyard (church • yard). The ground around a church.

gravestone (grave • stone). A flat stone, with a dead person's name written in it, that is placed on top of a grave.

beloved (be • lov • ed). Very much loved.

religion (re • li • gion). Belief in a god or gods.

scientists (sci • en • tists). People who are trained to know a lot about the facts and laws of nature and the universe. A scientist usually works in one kind of science. For example, he or she may know a lot about the stars or the oceans or how people think and act.

THE CITY THAT DISAPPEARED

Zena threw a grape into the air, and Alex caught it in his mouth. Zena laughed out loud and threw another grape. They did not notice the strange, low sound like thunder that came from under the mountain they were playing on.

"I have to go back to the shop now," Alex said. "I'll see you tonight, when you dance at the temple."

Zena watched Alex head down the mountain. The mountain was in the middle of the island she lived on. Below her was the beautiful city of Atlantis, with its wide streets and big buildings. Zena felt lucky to live there. She knew from stories told by sailors that in the rest of the world, people lived in dark caves like animals.

But here, the red, black, and white stones of the city buildings were bright in the sun. There were many great sailing ships at the docks. People stood near the ships, their bright-colored clothes making a pretty picture against the blue sky.

Zena began walking to meet the other dancers. She thought she felt the ground shake a little under her feet. She stopped for a minute, but when nothing more happened, she went on. She met the other girls, and they started to practice their dance.

The ground shook again. There was no mistake this time.

"Did you feel that?" one girl cried.

"Could it be an earthquake?" another asked.

"Maybe our dancing is too heavy for the earth," a third girl said, laughing.

"It's not funny!" Zena said. "I felt the ground shake before!"

* * * * *

Alex ran to his father's shop to tell him about the shaking of the earth. People were standing outside the shop, trying to find out what was happening. They saw a thick fog spreading over the mountain top.

Then a sound like thunder came from under the ground. People all over Atlantis stopped what they were doing to listen to the strange noise. They did not know that they lived on top of a volcano.

Then it happened. The earth gave a great shake, and red-hot, melted rock broke through the top of the mountain. Zena saw a river of this lava start to creep down the mountain. She screamed and began running with her friends. People in the city were pouring out of their houses. The ground was shaking badly now. The walls of the houses started to break up and fall.

Zena raced to her house to find her mother and father, but there was only a deep hole where the house had been.

"Mother! Father! Where are you?" she cried as she ran through the screaming crowds and falling buildings.　　　　　　　→

WORD BOX

temple (tem • ple). A building, like a church, used for praying to a god or gods.

earthquake (earth • quake). A shaking or sliding of the ground, caused by changes under the earth.

volcano (vol • ca • no). A mountain with an opening through which steam, ashes, melted rock, and dust come out.

lava (la • va). Hot, melted rock that comes out of a volcano.

Zena looked for Alex. She found him in the shop with his father. They were packing everything they could carry with them.

"I was afraid I wouldn't find you," she screamed. "My house is gone! I can't find my mother and father!"

"They must be at the docks," Alex said. "All the people are trying to get away from Atlantis before it blows up. Come with us to the ships. We'll take care of you."

Zena held onto Alex's hand, and together they pushed their way through the screaming crowds. Babies were crying. People were looking for their families and friends. One ship after another filled up with people. The white sails of the boats dotted the water as people tried to row to a safe place. Twenty rowers on each side of the boats pulled the oars as hard and fast as they could. Behind them, the great buildings of Atlantis were breaking apart.

Alex pushed Zena into a boat with his mother and father. Even before Zena sat down, people started rowing.

"I see them!" Zena yelled. "My mother and father! They are in the boat in front of us."

Zena and Alex called to them. But their voices could not be heard over the noise of the earthquake and the screams of the people. Suddenly, a great roar made the people in the boats look back at their island.

A moment later, the mountain blew apart. The sky grew dark as night as stones and dust and lava rained from the sky. Alex threw himself on top of Zena to try to protect her. A large stone hit him on the head and he fell into the sea. Zena stretched her hands over the side of the boat, but she could not reach him.

Atlantis began to sink into the sea. Giant waves two hundred feet high spread out from

the sinking island and rushed toward the ships.

Zena felt her boat lift high up and turn over. Above her own screams, she heard the screams of the thousands of people in all the boats. Water washed over her again and again. She couldn't breathe. She had nothing to hold onto. She felt the water closing over her head. Seconds later, she was gone.

Soon, the whole island of Atlantis, with its great mountain and beautiful cities, had disappeared into the sea. ■

Some people think this could be a true story. They believe there really was a beautiful city called Atlantis ten thousand years ago. Atlantis, they say, now lies somewhere under the Atlantic Ocean.

But most scientists do not think there ever was an Atlantis. They say that as far as we have been able to find out, there were no great cities at that time — because people were still living in caves!

Many people say the scientists are wrong. Why do they believe in Atlantis? Because the story of a city that blew up or sank has been told for thousands of years by people all over the world. The story we know best was told four thousands years ago by a man called Plato.

A lot of strange ideas go along with the Atlantis story. A few people believe that Atlantis was the most beautiful place there ever was, and that the people of Atlantis knew more things than we know today. Maybe the first people of Atlantis even came from outer space.

Some people who believe in the Bermuda Triangle stories (see the story, *Lost Over the Bermuda Triangle*) think a power station from Atlantis may be pulling planes and ships into the sea.　　　　⟶

— WORD BOX —

scientists (sci•en•tists). People who are trained to know a lot about the facts and laws of nature and the universe. A scientist usually works in one kind of science. For example, he or she may know a lot about the stars or the oceans or how people think and act.

Bermuda Triangle (Ber•mu•da Tri•an•gle). A part of the Atlantic Ocean where airplanes and ships are said to disappear in some strange way.

power station (pow•er sta•tion). A place that makes or sends out power such as electricity.

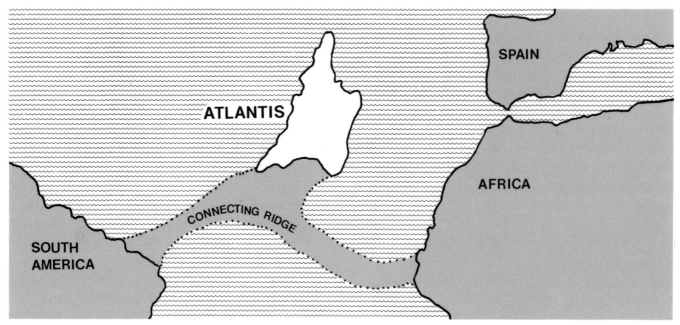

Those who believe in reincarnation (see the story, *The Girl Who Lived Twice*) say the people of Atlantis are being born again. They are coming back to teach us all about such things as outer space.

Even without these strange ideas, there is a lot of mystery in the Atlantis story.

One question is: If there was an Atlantis, where was it? The usual answer is that it was somewhere in the Atlantic Ocean. It may have been a big island, or it may have been a land bridge — a piece of land that reached from the old world to the new world, as shown on the map.

Can a big island or land bridge sink into the sea? Earthquakes or volcanoes might sink such a place. Mountains have been found far under the Atlantic Ocean. One of these mountains may even be the volcano that blew up Atlantis.

Or maybe Atlantis could have been covered by a great flood. Long ago, the earth was covered with ice. When the ice melted, the oceans got higher, and Atlantis could have been covered by water.

There is a bird mystery that goes along with the Atlantis story. Some birds that fly to warm places in winter stop every year at the same place over the Atlantic Ocean. They fly around and around in circles before they fly away again. Could it be that thousands of years ago,

birds like these used to go to Atlantis in the winter? Even though Atlantis is gone, maybe the birds are trying to find the place where they spent the winters long ago.

Will we ever find Atlantis? Edgar Cayce thought so. He was a man who said he could tell about things years before they were going to happen. In 1940 he said that we would find Atlantis in 1968 in the ocean near the Bermuda Triangle. In 1968, people found a building showing through the water just where Cayce said it would be. Some people say they also found a stone road under the sea, and that the road is ten thousand years old. Are the building and the road part of Atlantis? If they are, that could mean there really was a city ten thousand years ago, in cave-man days!

People have many different ideas about the Atlantis story. Even though most scientists say there never was an Atlantis, people still keep looking for the lost city.

Do you think there could have been a beautiful city in cave-man days? Do you believe we will ever find the answer to this mystery?

WORD BOX

mystery (mys • ter • y). Something that is not explained or that people do not understand.

GLOBAL JOURNEY'S BEGINNING: The Gannett/USA TODAY Gulfstream IV used for JetCapade takes off from San Diego for Acapulco, Mexico, on Feb. 1, 1988.

WINDOW ON THE WORLD

Faces, Places and Plain Talk from 32 Countries

ALLEN H. NEUHARTH

B O O K S

GANNETT CO. INC.

WASHINGTON, D.C. 20044

Printed and bound for USA TODAY Books by Arcata
Graphics Co. in Kingsport, Tennessee, the United States of
America.
Other books by Allen H. Neuharth: *Truly One Nation,
Profiles of Power: How the Governors Run Our 50 States*
and *Plain Talk Across the USA.*

Library of Congress Cataloging-in-Publication Data

Neuharth, Allen.
   Window on the world : faces, places and plain talk from
32 countries / Allen H. Neuharth.
     p.   cm.

   1. History, Modern — 1945-   2. Interviews.   I. Title.
D848.N48   1988   909.82—dc19   88-30708
                                        CIP

ISBN 0-944347-16-9

CONTENTS

Introduction ix
JetCateers at work xiii

ARGENTINA

*Don't cry for Evita,
but 'Tina needs help*

Close-up: The Falklands

1

AUSTRALIA

*Sophisticated blokes
and Crocodile Dundees*

Close-up: South Pacific islands

9

BRAZIL

*Rio, a romantic refuge;
Brazil, a tranquil giant*

17

CANADA

*Giant, genteel neighbor:
'A camp for grown-ups'*

23

CHINA

*Bicycles, brains
move 1 billion-plus pioneers*

Close-up: Taiwan

29

COSTA RICA

*A peaceful pearl prospers
in troubled waters*

37

CUBA

*30 years under Fidel:
How Cuba has changed*

Close-up: Guantanamo Bay

43

EGYPT

*Egypt is everlasting:
Age-old, up-to-date*

51

FRANCE

*Wine, women, song:
Oui, and new self-esteem*

57

GREECE

*Their Dukakis dream:
'Flowers, not weeds'*

63

HONG KONG AND SINGAPORE

*Two Asian mighty mites:
Pragmatic, prosperous*

69

INDIA

*Poverty with dignity;
continuity amid change*

77

IRELAND

*Their Irish is up
and that's no blarney*

83

ISRAEL

*How to settle score
in 'world's stress lab'*

89

ITALY

*The pope and pasta,
plus an awesome past*

95

JAPAN

*Unconditional surrender,
unparalleled prosperity*

Close-up: U.S. military

101

CONTENTS

KENYA

*Can Mother Nature
survive 'progress'?*

109

MEXICO

*Our image of Mexico
not quite the way it is*

115

PHILIPPINES

*Love, hate, jealousy:
All here for the USA*

Interview: Ferdinand Marcos
121

POLAND

*Best is yet to come,
but when is tomorrow?*

129

SAUDI ARABIA

*Written in oil:
Saudis' rags-to-riches saga*

135

SOUTH AFRICA

*Hope and hopelessness;
apartheid solid, and soft*

Close-up: Zimbabwe
141

SOUTH KOREA

*Olympics: Showoff time;
will tension ease?*

149

SOVIET UNION

*What does it all mean
to Ivan and Katrina?*

Close-ups: Foreign relations, space program, news media
155

SPAIN

*Old tree, new branches
greening for '92 showoff*

167

SWEDEN

*A smooth playing field,
stiff admission price*

173

SWITZERLAND

*A peaceful cubbyhole
that's rich and ready*

179

UNITED KINGDOM

*Our Mother Country
is a proud Mom again*

Close-up: Northern Ireland
185

VIETNAM

*Victory but no winners;
wounds healing slowly*

193

WEST GERMANY

*U.S. roots in Europe;
a reunion at Rumbach*

Close-ups: U.S. military; the Berlin Wall
199

BACK IN THE USA: *Eureka! I found it, all around the world* **209**

Views on the USA 212

Appreciation 214

About the Author 217

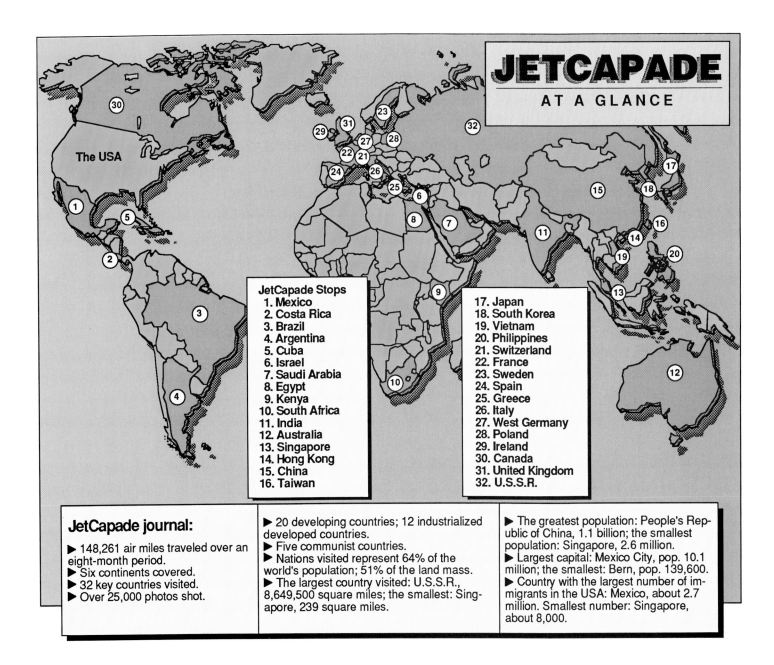

JETCAPADE
AT A GLANCE

The USA

JetCapade Stops
1. Mexico
2. Costa Rica
3. Brazil
4. Argentina
5. Cuba
6. Israel
7. Saudi Arabia
8. Egypt
9. Kenya
10. South Africa
11. India
12. Australia
13. Singapore
14. Hong Kong
15. China
16. Taiwan

17. Japan
18. South Korea
19. Vietnam
20. Philippines
21. Switzerland
22. France
23. Sweden
24. Spain
25. Greece
26. Italy
27. West Germany
28. Poland
29. Ireland
30. Canada
31. United Kingdom
32. U.S.S.R.

JetCapade journal:

▶ 148,261 air miles traveled over an eight-month period.
▶ Six continents covered.
▶ 32 key countries visited.
▶ Over 25,000 photos shot.

▶ 20 developing countries; 12 industrialized developed countries.
▶ Five communist countries.
▶ Nations visited represent 64% of the world's population; 51% of the land mass.
▶ The largest country visited: U.S.S.R., 8,649,500 square miles; the smallest: Singapore, 239 square miles.

▶ The greatest population: People's Republic of China, 1.1 billion; the smallest population: Singapore, 2.6 million.
▶ Largest capital: Mexico City, pop. 10.1 million; the smallest: Bern, pop. 139,600.
▶ Country with the largest number of immigrants in the USA: Mexico, about 2.7 million. Smallest number: Singapore, about 8,000.

❝ *We're going to tell our readers about these key countries by talking to the real experts — the people who live and work every day of their lives there.* ❞

David Mazzarella, JetCapade director, describing the aim of JetCapade's news coverage.

Journey's goal: Understanding our global village

The JetCapade goal was simple: Help the USA better understand its friends — and adversaries — around the world.

The method wasn't as simple: Visit 32 key countries on six continents in eight months and talk with the mighty and the meek, bankers and beggars, lawmakers and law breakers, preachers and teachers, students and shopkeepers. Interview them about their lives, their families, their hopes, their desires, their fears.

We traveled 148,261 air miles. Talked with more than 2,000 people. Shot thousands of photos.

We chose the countries because they are particularly important to the USA or are representative of their regions. These key countries also help put world issues into perspective.

We visited the giants of international power and population — the Soviet Union and China; the small dynamos of international trade — Singapore and Hong Kong. The European countries that hold the roots of nearly 200 million of the USA's 243 million citizens — England, Germany, Ireland, France and Italy. Africa and Asia, where the roots of other important parts of the USA's population can be found. Our closest neighbors — Canada and Mexico.

JetCapade was a new twist to the job Gannett journalists do every day: Go to the source for news and information, and then share it with readers, viewers and listeners.

Thirty Gannett journalists were involved in gathering information, taking photographs, writing and editing JetCapade stories, both for USA TODAY and for Gannett News Service. (See pages 214-216 for contributors.)

What did we discover on JetCapade?

Canadian writer Marshall McLuhan was right.

The world is becoming a global village. Not all the globe's nations are united, but they are linked — electronically. And many of those links come from the USA. We freely export sports, entertainment, media and politics.

▶ We saw the 1988 Super Bowl re-run on wide-screen TV in Acapulco, the day after we watched it live in San Diego.

▶ We spotted former major leaguers from the USA playing alongside Japanese teammates at a domed baseball stadium in Tokyo.

▶ We talked about U.S. politics with day laborers living in mud huts in India. One of them mentioned Gary Hart and all of his friends erupted in laughter.

▶ We saw Bruce Springsteen and Michael Jackson trouping through Europe for concerts every bit as lively as in the USA.

In short, interest in the USA looms large everywhere. And nations we once viewed as bitter enemies now share some common bonds.

NEWSROOM IN THE AIR: Using a 1926 Royal typewriter, Allen H. Neuharth works on a JetCapade column.

We believe you'll find the people we encountered as interesting as we did. To help you get to know them, we've devoted a chapter to each of 28 of the countries we visited. Four other countries — China and Taiwan and Hong Kong and Singapore — are combined in two chapters. Several chapters also include close-ups — visits to important neighboring countries, or extra coverage about specific topics, such as the U.S. military communities in Japan and West Germany.

In each chapter you'll find:

▶ My column — plain talk about the country, how it compares to and affects the USA. How the country fits into the USA's and the world's past, present and future.

▶ An interview with one or more top leaders.

▶ Photographs and quotes from residents.

▶ A map and almanac-style information about the country.

▶ A reproduction of the national flag.

Jetting the globe put us in the middle of some breaking news events. The stories we developed sometimes merited the front page of USA TODAY because our news team was aggressive enough to be in the right place at the right time.

We were there when:

▶ West German Chancellor Helmut Kohl predicted the European Economic Community will become the strongest economic power in the world after 1992 when barriers between the countries — trade laws, taxes and currencies — end. We spoke with Kohl just after he had talked with Britain's Prime Minister Margaret Thatcher.

▶ Wojciech Jaruzelski, Poland's president and chairman of the Communist Party, confided he wants closer ties with the USA and the Western world.

▶ The Philippines' ill, exiled former President Ferdinand Marcos warned that if he returned to his country in a pine box, a civil war could be expected. Just hours after meeting with the JetCapade news team, Marcos was hospitalized with chest pains. He later recovered. His successor, Corazon Aquino, told us she would stand firm in her decision to block his return to the Philippines.

▶ After a day and a half wait, Cuban President Fidel Castro agreed to one of his rare interviews. A late-night, but lively, talk with him lasted nearly six hours. The communist leader, who has reigned there since his revolutionary takeover in 1959, provided a look at his Cuba from his perspective.

We also learned that exporting USA-style journalism is controversial.

In some countries, the U.S. press provokes strong negative reactions from government leaders. Those include charges that some in our media manipulate the news and stage and incite incidents.

In the eyes of some leaders, the "ugly American" is no longer the wealthy camera-laden tourist in Bermuda shorts. He or she is the arrogant Nikon-carrying reporter from a big USA newspaper.

Unless we journalists are sensitive to different political systems and philosophies, unless we try to report international issues from all perspectives, not just ours, we run the risk of perpetuating worldwide the same image of arrogance some of us suffer from here in the USA.

For years, I've been suggesting that here in the USA we should practice a journalism of hope, not a journalism of despair. I've advocated reporting the good and the bad, the glad and the sad. That's called balance or fairness. The First Amendment doesn't guarantee it, but the public — around the world — wants it.

It's extremely important that the media from the USA practice informational journalism, not confrontational journalism. We should inform, not indict.

That's basically what JetCapade was all about — information about the world, not confrontation with it. That's the kind of coverage that appeared on USA TODAY's JetCapade pages from February through September 1988, and it's the kind of coverage that appears in this book. It's also the kind of coverage that will make the world's powerful and poor more likely to share their problems and their hopes with us.

Allen H. Neuharth
Founder, USA TODAY

Highflying news team covered the globe

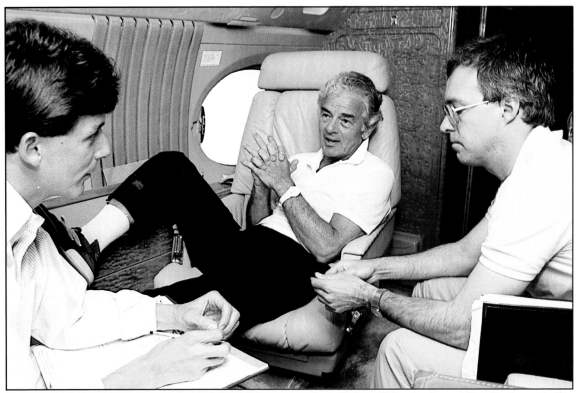

PLANNING IN THE AIR: From left, USA TODAY reporter Jack Kelley, Al Neuharth and Ken Paulson, JetCapade managing editor, discuss Neuharth's JetCapade column for Japan while flying to Taiwan.

PLANNING ON THE GROUND: In a hotel suite in Mexico City, the advance reporting team plans for JetCapade's first stop, Mexico. Clockwise from bottom: Gaynelle Evans, Gannett News Service reporter; Martha T. Moore, USA TODAY reporter; Laurence Jolidon, USA TODAY reporter; John Simpson, JetCapade advance team editor; Juan Walte, USA TODAY reporter; and Ramon Bracamontes, a reporter for Gannett's *El Paso* (Texas) *Times.*

SHOOTING IN KENYA: Callie Shell, a photographer at Gannett's paper in Nashville, *The Tennessean,* shoots an overview of downtown Nairobi.

A.M. INTERVIEW: Cuban President Fidel Castro makes a point during a discussion with Al Neuharth, David Mazzarella, JetCapade director, and Ken Paulson. An interpreter sits at Castro's right. The nearly six-hour interview ended at 3:55 a.m.

HISTORICAL BACKDROP: Jack Kelley talks with camel driver Hajy Kamel Abubasha at the Pyramids in Egypt.

GLOBAL GIFT: Al Neuharth points out the JetCapade route on a crystal globe to Israel Prime Minister Yitzhak Shamir. Globes were given to all top leaders visited by JetCapade.

SHOOTING IN TAHITI: Kathleen Smith Barry, a photographer at Gannett's *The Tennessean,* shoots a South Pacific sunset.

FINDING A FEATURE: Marilyn Greene, an editor for the USA TODAY International Edition, interviews a museum worker at the Nilometer (an ancient device on a rock to measure Nile river levels) at Aswan in Egypt.

HIGH WRITER: At 45,000 feet above the Persian Gulf, Andrea Redding, one of Al Neuharth's secretaries, works at typewriter.

KENYA CONVERSATION: USA TODAY reporter Mireille Grangenois Gates interviews a Masai village resident.

RIYADH REPORTING: Gannett News Service Senior Reporter Bill Ringle walks a road at Riyadh, Saudi Arabia, in search of a story.

GETTING THERE: Pilots Chuck Thomas, left, and Chuck Hanner in the cockpit of the JetCapade Gulfstream IV.

ARGENTINA

Featured in USA TODAY: Feb. 15, March 11

ARGENTINA
AT A GLANCE

Bolivia

Brazil

Chile

Paraguay

Argentina

Pacific Ocean

Uruguay

Hurlingham →

Mar del Plata

Atlantic Ocean

Capital/ largest city
Buenos Aires
Pop. 2,922,829

Language
Spanish.
Major products
Wheat, corn, oilseed, hides, wool.

Ushuaia

Falkland Islands

Argentina

0   700

miles

N

Population and land
▶ 31,186,000 people. 1,068,302 square miles; 8th largest country; 29% of U.S. size; about twice the size of Alaska.

Government
▶ Democratic republic. President elected to six-year term.

The USA and Argentina
▶ About 83,000 Argentine-born people live in the USA.

▶ U.S. rock music is very big in Argentina. Among the top stars: Tina Turner and Michael Jackson.

▶ The most popular U.S. TV program in Argentina is *Miami Division* – also called *Miami Vice*.

Don't cry for Evita, but 'Tina needs help

"Don't cry for me Argentina." *Evita* made that line famous in the USA when it played Broadway from 1979 to '83 — one of the longest-running foreign musicals ever.

Evita — **Maria Eva Duarte Peron**, second wife of strongman **Juan Domingo Peron**. Rich and poor, natives and foreigners visit her tomb in Buenos Aires as a popular shrine.

She died of cancer in 1952, at age 33. Peron took her body with him when he went into exile in Spain in 1955. Brought back and interred in La Rocelata cemetery in 1976.

EVITA: Heroine died at 33.

"People come to see Evita's grave because she did great things for the poor. She's buried among the rich, but most people know where her heart is," says cemetery caretaker **Fermin Allegre**, 55.

Whether they loved her or hated her, most agree her heart was in Argentina. Now, her beloved 'Tina is troubled.

▶ High inflation: 181.6% last year.

▶ Huge foreign debt: $55 billion.

President Raul Alfonsin, 61, acknowledges those problems. But the first democratically elected head-of-state here since seven years of military rule points to people progress.

"What we have done in the field of human rights has never been done before in any country or continent," says the former journalist turned politician.

Human rights is an immense issue here. Memories are vivid and signs still very visible of the many years of misuse of personal freedoms under military regimes.

EVITA'S TOMB: Popular shrine for fans.

The Mothers of Plaza de Mayo provide regular reminders of 8,900 people who were whisked away by the military in the 1970s and haven't been seen since. Led by **Juana de Pargament**, 72, whose son Alberto is among the missing, the mothers march around the main square every Thursday. Imprinted on their white head scarves are names of their missing relatives.

The Peronist party is still active. Leaders say they are moving it toward the political center.

DE PARGAMENT: Leads mothers of missing.

Despite memories, good and bad, of Peron, of other military regimes, and present economic woes, Buenos Aires by outward appearances is placidly prosperous.

This capital city (pop. 2,922,829) is squeaky clean, almost like Salt Lake City. Parks and parkways are beautifully maintained. Shops are filled with high-priced merchandise.

Home to nearly 10% of the country's population, Buenos Aires offers much of the cosmopolitan culture of New York, Paris, Montreal.

Out in the country, it's different. There people live modestly. But they eat well.

Argentines are meat eaters. Average annual beef consumption per person: 168 pounds. In the USA, 91. Soviet Union 57. Japan 13.

Those who raise and herd the cattle are "gauchos," like our cowboys. **Santiago Luis Medina**, 63, proudly wears his black hat, red scarf, dagger on his back, at Las Palmas Estancia ranch near Zarate (pop. 65,504) 100 miles northwest of Buenos Aires.

Beef raising and cutting is considered an

MEDINA: Colorful gaucho.

art. **Sergio Claudio Mendeta**, 24, is a butcher. He explains why Argentina's beef is butter-knife tender:

"Since we have a lot of lush pasture for the cattle to graze on, they don't have to walk far to eat. Since they don't walk, their muscles don't get hard. That makes for a tender piece of meat."

Next time you order steak, insist on a cut from a cow that didn't walk much.

That's Plain Talk from Argentina.

TWO WHO TANGO: Juan Carlos Copes and Maria Neves perform in *Tango Argentina* at the Casa Blanca nightclub in Buenos Aires. The troupe has toured Europe and the USA.

GAUCHO-IN-TRAINING: Walter Campodonico, 5, is learning the life of a gaucho at a ranch near Zarate.

SUNRISE ON THE RIVER: Sun peeks over the horizon on the Rio de la Plata, the world's widest river. In the foreground is the Sarmiento frigate at the Puerto Nuevo docks.

POLO IN BUENOS AIRES: Fernando Merlos, 79, began playing polo at age 58.

MAY I SEE YOUR LICENSE? Liliana Mabel Tricarico, 34, a traffic police officer in Ushuaia, is one of four women on the force. There are no parking meters in Ushuaia.

Erica Mafuchi, 38
Homemaker
Mar del Plata

"Sometimes it seems that we have all the open space in the world in Argentina. You see nothing but green in the pampas (grasslands). No trees, no hills, just a smooth blanket of unbroken green."

Julio Valdez Fillipe, 23
Policeman
Hurlingham

"There is an English neighborhood here with typical English houses, clean streets and manicured lawns. But besides the neighborhood and the name of this town, there is little of the English influence left."

Osvaldo Cesar Pereira, 27
Taxi driver
Ushuaia

"There is one semaphor (traffic light) here, but it is broken. That really doesn't make much difference, though. Nobody paid any attention to it when it was working."

Maria Alicia Pirosanto, 46
Sculptor
Buenos Aires

"While artists in this country aren't exactly getting rich, we are doing all right. There is an appreciation for art. With my work, I like to show people that Argentina has a lot of beautiful women."

We complain a lot, but life is better

On what image the people of the USA should have of Argentina:

"A very realistic image. We are a people who have undergone many years of political frustration, in regard to freedom and the dignity of man, and on the economic side. This is a people that struggles and sometimes feels very ill-tempered and is always complaining."

On whether there will be democratic elections in 1989:

"Undoubtedly. Democracy is consolidated in Argentina. This does not mean that we might not have some very unimportant incidents on the way. Years of frustration have created very small groups on the two extremes that can disturb but not interrupt this process."

On Argentina's economy:

"We have serious economic difficulties caused by the foreign debt and the fall of international prices. The USA, with great generosity, launched the Marshall Plan after World War II to help European democracies. Something similar is happening now in Latin America, where there is also a democratic revival taking place within the context of an extremely difficult economic situation. But instead of receiving the support of a Marshall Plan, in the last five years, Latin America has transferred wealth to the developed world."

On whether a Marshall Plan is needed:

"When I talk about a Marshall Plan, it's only as a metaphor. This gives you an idea for you to understand that the problem of the debt is not only a financial and economic one, but a political and social one. More than asking you for help, what we want you to understand is that we cannot go on helping any longer. The talk of curbing inflation in developed countries has been done at the expense of the fall of international prices."

On whether the USA should help with the debt problem:

"The USA government has accompanied us in the discussions we had with the IMF (International Monetary Fund). Most of the banks have already taken the first steps and made some provisions. Within the IMF, they are starting to understand our situation and the need for a non-conventional solution. The problem is that this solution is now urgent."

On whether the Reagan administration ignores South America:

"There is a very positive change in the policy of the USA in connection to all of Latin America. The idea that Latin America could be defended by supporting totalitarian governments has ended. We all know that the USA has stopped doing that and is really defending democracy in Latin America."

On British military maneuvers in the Falklands:

President Raul Alfonsin, 61, met with the JetCapade news team in the state-owned, ornate presidential residence, which sits on beautifully landscaped grounds. Alfonsin took office in December 1983 after seven years of military rule in Argentina. His election broke the hold of the Peronist party, which had dominated elections since 1945. Argentina's next election is scheduled for 1989.

"The U.K. has never considered us a democracy. Argentina will not try to take the Malvinas Islands — which belong to us — by force. We have tried to sit around a table. Up to now their response has been negative, and this attitude is going one step forward and is really an offense."

On other economic problems, including an underground economy:

"We have tax pressure that is the highest in Argentine history and at the same time we have low wages. There is a certain degree of underground economy. There is also tax evasion, which we are trying to prevent."

On the power of the Peronists:

"The Peronist party is trying to become democratized. An eventual victory by the Peronists — which I think is very doubtful — would not create a serious problem for Argentine democracy."

MUTTON MAJORITY: On the Falklands, sheep outnumber humans 700,000 to 2,000.

Falklanders are set in their British ways

The Falkland Islands — still snubbing neighbor Argentina in favor of faraway Britain, are thriving due to the 1982 war between their suitors.

Until 1982, few people could locate this sheep-rearing, wool-producing group of islands, which Argentina calls Islas Malvinas. That changed on April 2 of that year. Argentina, which had claimed the Falklands since 1820, invaded and dared the British to fight.

They did. Two months later, Argentina surrendered.

Falklanders rejoiced,

WAR REMINDER: Sign is a leftover from the 1982 war.

though the islands are 300 miles east of Argentina, compared to 8,500 miles southeast of London, England.

Many on the Falklands quickly point out they are more British than the British:

▶ They talk of "going home" when traveling to the United Kingdom.

▶ They drink tea at 5 p.m. with homemade pastries.

▶ They talk with pride about how many Falklanders have fought and died for the Union Jack.

Most Falklanders are descendants of British immigrants who came in the 19th century to ranch sheep.

"Last year, in a sort of referendum, 99.3% of the peo-ple decided to remain British or under the British sphere of influence," says Falklander Nick Hadden, 66, of Stanley.

The war has brought prosperity as well as attention to the Falklands, for 150 years a neglected and backward British colony.

Britain, as a result of the war, unilaterally declared a 150-mile fishing zone around the islands, effective Feb. 1, 1987. Now, payments for fishing licenses are flooding the islands with money. The world's fishing fleets are lured by the rich stocks of hake, blue whiting, cod and shellfish in the cold South Atlantic waters.

The islands' potential annual yield from fishing: more than 15 million British pounds ($27 million).

The fishing gains dwarf losses from a decline in tourism because of disrupted air travel.

Since Argentina cut off its flights to the Falklands during the 1982 war, the islands' only air connection is a 17-hour British Royal Air Force passenger jumbo jet route from London. Cost: $1,440 for an economy round-trip ticket. Before, 5,000 to 6,000 visitors per year came to the islands from South America; now only a few tourists visit.

AUSTRALIA

Featured in USA TODAY: May 6

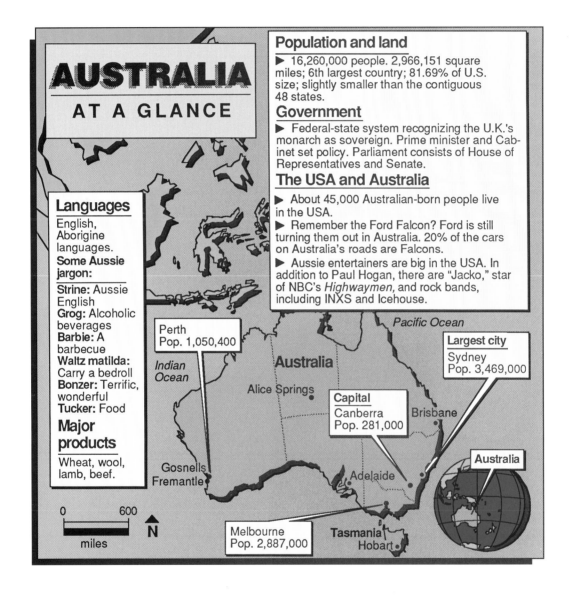

AUSTRALIA
AT A GLANCE

Population and land
▶ 16,260,000 people. 2,966,151 square miles; 6th largest country; 81.69% of U.S. size; slightly smaller than the contiguous 48 states.

Government
▶ Federal-state system recognizing the U.K.'s monarch as sovereign. Prime minister and Cabinet set policy. Parliament consists of House of Representatives and Senate.

The USA and Australia
▶ About 45,000 Australian-born people live in the USA.
▶ Remember the Ford Falcon? Ford is still turning them out in Australia. 20% of the cars on Australia's roads are Falcons.
▶ Aussie entertainers are big in the USA. In addition to Paul Hogan, there are "Jacko," star of NBC's *Highwaymen,* and rock bands, including INXS and Icehouse.

Languages
English, Aborigine languages.
Some Aussie jargon:
Strine: Aussie English
Grog: Alcoholic beverages
Barbie: A barbecue
Waltz matilda: Carry a bedroll
Bonzer: Terrific, wonderful
Tucker: Food

Major products
Wheat, wool, lamb, beef.

Perth
Pop. 1,050,400

Indian Ocean

Pacific Ocean

Australia

Alice Springs

Largest city
Sydney
Pop. 3,469,000

Capital
Canberra
Pop. 281,000

Brisbane

Australia

Gosnells
Fremantle

Adelaide

0   600
miles   N

Melbourne
Pop. 2,887,000

Tasmania
Hobart

Sophisticated blokes and Crocodile Dundees

"**D**own Under" conjures up sundry images in the USA and around the world. Many are genuine, what Aussies call "dinkum." Some are hokum.

▶ Dinkum: Pleasure-prone people. Prosperous. Happy. Hard drinking. Laid-back. Friendly.

▶ Hokum: A land overrun with rough and rowdy crocodile hunters and cowpokes.

The only country that also is an entire continent is celebrating its Bicentennial. As part of the celebration, **Queen Elizabeth II** dedicated the futuristic $1.1 billion new Parliament House in the capital city of Canberra.

Modern Australia began 200 years ago when the British shipped 570 male and 160 female convicts to establish a prison colony. That ancestry created an almost classless society.

Prime Minister Bob Hawke says, "Here the fellow who works the garbage truck is not socially inferior. He's just as good a bloke as the highflier in business."

Australia's profile:

▶ Prosperity. Per capita income $12,250, among the highest in the world. USA: $15,340. Great Britain: $10,132.

▶ Education. All free, including universities and technical schools. Illiteracy only 1.5%, among the lowest in the world.

▶ Urbanization. Among the highest in the world. 85% of the 16.3 million live in the cities.

Sailing is supreme. In the Perth/Fremantle area, site of the 1987 America's Cup, one-fourth of the people are registered boat owners. Countrywide, roughly 600,000 boats.

LEUNIG: America's Cup put Fremantle on map.

Despite watching their Kookaburra III lose to the USA's Stars and Stripes, memories of the Cup races are sweet. "Fremantle used to be just another port. Now it's world class," says **Kim Leunig**, 31, whose Evening Star chartered fans during the Cup.

Tennis tops individual competitiveness. The Bowreys of Sydney are the "first family of tennis." **Bill**, 43, was on the Aussie Davis Cup teams in '68 and '69. His wife, **Lesley Turner**, 48, won Wimbledon doubles titles in '62 and '64, and the French Open in '63 and '65.

Now their daughter **Michelle**, 17, two-time national junior champion, is about to join the international circuit. "Australians are definitely better tennis players than Americans," says Michelle. "Women are more competitive. Guys don't ask me to play anymore. I lost a friendship with a guy because I beat him six-love."

Happiness is pursued through sports and recreation:

▶ 1,149 golf courses, most of them public.

▶ 22,816 miles of coastline, most of it sunning and surfing beaches.

▶ Thousands of miles of plotted bushwalking trails and camps, many within two hours of major cities.

MICHELLE: Aussie tennis better than USA's.

▶ Exploration of the vast outback, home to some of the culture and tradition of the dark-skinned Aborigines whose ancestors came here from Southeast Asia 40,000 years ago.

Sydney, largest city, brings together old and new, Europe and Asia, in the setting and sophistication of San Francisco.

The landmark is the Sydney Harbour bridge, called the "Coat Hanger" because of its bowed appearance. That's where **Paul Hogan**, star of the hit movie *Crocodile Dundee* and its sequel, *Crocodile Dundee II*, worked as a rigger for 10 years.

Co-workers **Derek Quinn**, 60, and **Jim Turnbull**, 56, remember him fondly. Says Quinn:

"Hogan's very macho. Just like me. Like many Australians. Last Christmas he came back and brought us 200 cases of beer. What a bloke!"

That's Plain Talk from Australia.

SYDNEY'S "COAT HANGER": *Crocodile Dundee's* Paul Hogan worked here with Quinn, left, and Turnbull.

SYDNEY: A view of the largest city "Down Under" from the west shore of Sydney Harbour.

HEALTH WORKER: Jillie Nagamara, 45, of Yvenduma and grandson Geoffrey Spencer, 4, sit outside classroom of the Aboriginal Health Workers' Training Center in Alice Springs.

ORIGINAL INHABITANT: The koala is among Australia's famous native animals. Koalas feed on eucalyptus, the most common tree found in the dry areas of the continent.

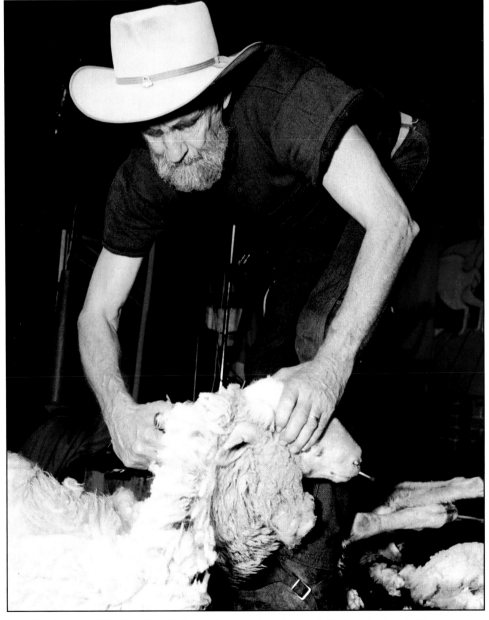

SHEEP SHEARING: Des De Belle performs at a show at Sydney's Argyle Tavern.

MAMMOTH MOUND: Ayers Rock in central Australia is the world's largest monolith and is one of two rocks sacred to several Aboriginal tribes. The caves at its base contain paintings believed to be part of their nomadic culture. Tourists visit daily to climb to its 1,143-foot crest or to peer into its clefts and caves.

Nick Kallas, 48
Restaurant owner
Fremantle

"*Australians have the reputation for being party people and they do drink a lot. The bars close so darn early, they have to hurry up if they're going to get any good drinking time in.*"

Lynne Bertram, 31
Schoolteacher
South Hobart

"*We (Tasmanians) are more countrified, more parochial, closer to the bush than people from the big island. Drugs are not a problem here, neither is crime. But the night life isn't so great.*"

Colin Dixon Tjapanunga, 30
Artist, Mt. Lebanuk

"*My father taught me to paint by drawing in the dirt on the ground. That is (our) traditional way. My subjects are my country and my father's stories.*"

Carl Swan, 53
Tennis coach
Sydney

"*The greatest quality Australians have is their ability to enjoy life. They're all having a bit of fun. They've got their grog, their barbie, their music. What else could they want?*"

U.S. protectionism: 'Recipe for disaster'

On free trade and U.S. protectionism:

"We live in a world where the principle of free trade between nations is at risk because of the increasingly complex economic environment. There are pressures, particularly where massive trade imbalances have built up between nations, to take the easy road of protectionism — which is a recipe for disaster!"

On what the USA should do about its trade deficit:

"The U.S. has to tackle the problem of its twin deficits. It's no good to only talk about its external imbalances, particularly with Japan. It has to tackle the problem of its internal deficit, because it will distort economic decision-making in the U.S. and, because of the size of the U.S. economy, it will affect the rest of the world."

On Australia's role in the Pacific:

"Our economy must become more outward looking, more export oriented. We have the capacity to be of assistance to a number of countries in the region. One of the most exciting countries in the region is China, and we have a better relationship with China than probably any other country. I mention China because of the changes that are taking place there. But it is an indication of the commitment we have to making sure that Australia is not isolationist."

On what residents should consider during Australia's Bicentennial celebration:

"Remember the past and take pride in the achievements, but also remember the weaknesses, the shortcomings of the past and try to regard 1988 as a period not just of pride, but of stock-taking in a sense. And to think about it in terms of saying to ourselves: 'Well, that's where we've been, that's what we've done, now what's the challenge and responsibility for the future?' Now obviously that's asking a lot, but I think the evidence is there to suggest that, in a significant way, that's what the Australian people are doing."

On how Australia's Aborigines fit into the Bicentennial celebration:

"This is 200 years of European settlement in this country, and it comes on top of 40,000 years of an Aboriginal civilization. It is undoubtedly the case that in the 200 years of European settlement, considerable injustices have occurred as far as the Aboriginal people are concerned. It is my hope that by the end of this Bicentennial year, we will have reached a basis upon which we, as a non-Aboriginal segment of Australia, will recognize the injustices and commit ourselves to a rectification of them. On the part of the Aboriginal people, I hope there will be a recognition of that commitment so that there can be a reconciliation."

On the Aussie character:

Robert "Bob" Hawke, 59, was first elected prime minister in 1983. He was re-elected in 1984 and again in 1987 — the first Labor prime minister to win a third term. Hawke met with the JetCapade news team in a small, informal interview room in the executive office building in Canberra.

"If I wanted to give you what I see as the fundamental elements to the Australian character, they are these: very friendly people, people not prone to, as we say, 'dip your lid,' that's 'doff your hat,' to others in a sense of recognizing a superiority in one class of people. There is a phrase we have in Australia — the 'fair go.' The fair go really means that all people are created with the right to develop and express themselves."

On his decision to stop drinking alcohol:

"The shareholders in the breweries are a bit annoyed. I think they respected I had a pretty healthy appetite for the pale brown amber liquid. I was no mean performer in its consumption. But I made a decision in 1980 that I was going to give it up. The simple fact is, if I hadn't made that decision, I wouldn't be talking to you in this capacity today."

TROPICAL TREAT: Calm South Pacific waters surround thatch beach huts along the shore in Tahiti. A lazy haze hovers over mountainous Moorea in the background. A warm, gentle breeze swaying through palm trees completes the Polynesian paradise.

American Samoa to Tahiti: South Pacific paradises

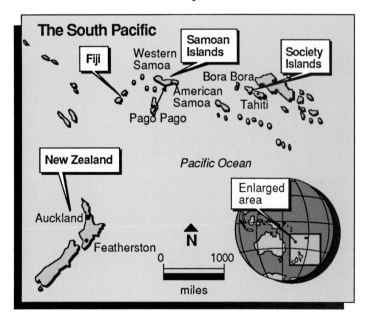

The South Pacific

Fiji
Western Samoa
Samoan Islands
Society Islands
Bora Bora
American Samoa
Tahiti
Pago Pago
New Zealand
Pacific Ocean
Auckland
Enlarged area
Featherston
N
0   1000
miles

▶ AMERICAN SAMOA

Gov. A.P. Lutali jokingly says that the seven islands that make up American Samoa are like TV's *Gilligan's Island.*

True, the islands are small — 76 square miles — blanketed in lush vegetation and surrounded by aqua blue water. And, from a continental USA perspective, they're remote: 4,800 miles from California.

But unlike *Gilligan's Island,* American Samoa, in its own way, is thriving. And it's certainly not deserted: Pop.: 37,000. Pago Pago (pronounced PAHNG oh PAHNG oh), capital and major city, has 3,592 people. A U.S. territory since 1900, it is administered by the Department of the Interior.

Pride runs deep here.

Pago Pago "has more boys in the military than any community its size in the U.S.," Lutali says.

"We don't have high crime, drugs," says Paul Salima, 17. "All the world should be as happy as Samoans."

▶ NEW ZEALAND

Tourists are helping the hard-pressed sheep industry in New Zealand (pop. 3.3 million) survive.

To raise money, more than 300 sheep farms now offer "farm holidays," giving visitors a chance to "have a go" at milking cows, cooking, and herding sheep.

Most visitors, however, opt not to work. They pay their $190 to $310 a night and "have a go" at hunting, riding horses, fishing.

▶ FIJI

Cannibalism may be dead in this group of 300 islands (pop. 714,548), but sales of cannibal eating instruments are thriving.

Replicas of wooden utensils once used by cannibals sell for $5 to $500. In the Fiji Museum, visitors can still find a handle with four sharp prongs labeled "Fork used in eating Rev. Baker."

Tourism, one of Fiji's main industries, is on the rise again after Fiji's two coups in 1987. Hotel occupancy rates, which had slipped to 35%, are back up to 50%.

▶ TAHITI

Come Friday, dozens of native Tahitians leave Papeete, Tahiti's main city, to escape the arrival of hundreds of tourists and job-seekers.

"We need the tourists who come looking for paradise, but Papeete is becoming too busy," says resident and longtime dancer Olga Perillaud, 40.

Tahiti (pop. 85,000 and 402 square miles) was made famous by the writers and artists who have lived there, including James Michener and Paul Gauguin.

Tahiti now attracts up to 150,000 tourists a year.

BRAZIL

Featured in USA TODAY: March 4

BRAZIL
AT A GLANCE

Atlantic Ocean

Pacific Ocean

Suriname
French Guiana
Venezuela
Guyana
Colombia
Ecuador
Manaus
Amazon
Brazil
Peru
Bolivia
Chile
Paraguay
Argentina
Uruguay
Recife
Salvador

Population and land
▶ 141,459,000 people. 3,286,488 square miles; 5th largest country; 90.5% of U.S. size; larger than the contiguous 48 states.

Government
▶ Federal republic. President elected to six–year term. National Congress consists of 72-member Senate and 479-member Chamber of Deputies.

The USA and Brazil
▶ About 54,000 Brazilian-born people live in the USA.
▶ The USA gets more of its coffee from Brazil than from any other country — roughly 518 million pounds in 1987. That's 27,652,640,000 cups of coffee.

Capital
Brasilia,
Pop. 1,178,908

0   N   700
miles

Largest city
Sao Paulo,
Pop. 7,032,547

Rio de Janeiro
Pop. 5,090,700

Brazil

Language
Portuguese.
Major products
Soybeans, coffee, transport equipment, iron ore, steel products, chemicals, orange juice, shoes and sugar.

Rio, a romantic refuge; Brazil, a tranquil giant

The song swept the world in 1963. First in Portuguese. Then Spanish. English. Won a Grammy in the USA as record of the year in 1964. Popular for years.

"Tall and tan, young and lovely
THE GIRL FROM IPANEMA goes walking . . .
She swings so cool and sways so gentle
And when she passes, each one she passes
Goes 'ah'."

ORIGINAL GIRL FROM IPANEMA: At 42, she's still stunning.

That girl from Ipanema Beach in Rio de Janeiro (pop. 5,600,000) was 16, single, and beautiful. She's now 42, married, has four children. Still beautiful.

Heloisa (Helo) Eneida Pinheiro. Now an actress, TV talk show hostess and model agency owner, she recalls those days:

"I lived two blocks from the beach. I went there almost every day. (Songwriters) **Vinicius de Moraes** and **Tom Jobim** used to drink at a place called Bar Veloso. They watched as I walked to and from the beach and whistled from the back of the bar."

De Moraes and Jobim wrote the song that made them rich and her famous. It also gave Rio its lasting worldwide image as a sanctuary for sensuous bathing beauties.

They're still here. On Copacabana, Ipanema, Leblon beaches. In the barest of bikinis — they call them "dental floss." They flirt and frolic.

While Rio and romance is the image most in the USA have of Brazil, it's only a small piece of a huge package. Like our beaches in Miami Beach. Or the bodies beautiful in Los Angeles. Or the revelry in New Orleans.

Carnival time in Rio each February is a five-day non-stop New Year's Eve. At a precarnival Bubble Ball the JetCateers attended, guests did indeed dance and play all night.

The rest of Brazil has a more serious, sometimes somber, reality of contrasts:

▶ Urban centers that match ours. Sao Paulo (pop. 7,032,547) is a lot like New York, Boston, Chicago. Fine restaurants. Chic shops. Cultural attractions. Huge factories.

▶ The infinite interior called the Amazon. Not as wild as its image, but unlike anything in the USA. Nearly 2 million square miles of mostly undeveloped land, rich with mineral deposits and other natural resources.

The potential of Brazil's vast interior was first focused on by **Pres. Juscelino Kubitschek** in the 1950s. Carved a controversial new capital out of the raw and rolling farm land 600 miles northwest of the centers of Rio and Sao Paulo.

I visited this site in 1959, covering **Pres. Dwight Eisenhower**'s "Operation Amigo" trip. Then Brasilia had fewer than 100,000 people, mostly construction workers.

Dedicated as the capital in 1960. Now, nearly 2 million people live in this planned city and its suburbs. Sparkling with distinctive architecture. Manicured parks and parkways. Landscaped lakes. An island of tranquility at the heart of Brazil.

Many say vision like Kubitschek's ultimately will stir this sometimes slumbering giant and make it a world leader.

Despite highly publicized high inflation and high debt, most Brazilians seem unworried about the future.

"Life here is peaceful, tranquil. We are happy people and quickly forget our problems," says Brasilia postal worker **Newton da Cunha**, 61.

Sergio Bondarovsky, 38, computer programmer and grandson of Russian immigrants, put it this way when interviewed on the volleyball court:

"Every time we worry that the economy is getting bad, suddenly it turns and goes up. This is a funny country. We are a lazy people. If we worked a little harder, it would be easier to get ahead."

That's Plain Talk from Brazil.

DA CUNHA IN BRASILIA: Tranquility and trees, statues and skyscrapers in capital dedicated in 1960.

MOVING MARKET: Fish, chicken and produce vendors like Nelson de Souza Neves, 40, set up shop in different areas along the streets of Rio daily.

PERCHED PAL: Maria Aparecida Hallack, 42, with her parrot Zaquinho, strolls streets of Rio de Janeiro as she shops at the free market. "The prices are better here because there's more to choose from and the produce is fresh."

RIO REVELRY: Festive partygoers don colorful costumes for the Pirate Ball at the Hippopotamus Club in Rio.

BEACH LIFE: Revelers swarm to Rio's beaches to swim in azure waters and soak up golden sunshine.

Roberto Resende, 31
Dentist
Brasilia

"We are proud of this city. Its architecture is unlike any in the world. It's shaped like an airplane. It's a shame our politicians are always out flying. They would enjoy this city."

Eugenia Cukier, 73
Retired
Rio de Janeiro

"These new swimsuits that show everything are nice, but there's no charm to them. Fifty-three years ago, we would ride the bus and men would go wild trying to get a glimpse of our ankles."

Boris Liberman, 48
Computer store owner
Sao Paulo

"The problem in our business is the import quota. It's time to review everything. Sure, a country like Brazil should keep out foreign competition for a few years. But it's been 10 years for computers. That's too long."

Joyce Camara, 24
Receptionist
Manaus

"In Rio, you find the street robbers. In the Amazon, you find the piranhas. But if you get bitten by a piranha, it doesn't hurt half as bad as a street robber. We know what we're stepping on and what to stay away from."

A poet who 'puts up with the political'

On Brazil's relationship with the USA:

"We have always had very good relations with the United States. We were allies in the two world wars. (But) I would be insincere if I said that our relations are going through a favorable period. We are the two great brothers in the continents of the North and South. But the U.S. is concerned more about internal policies than with external ones and political issues. Our trade relations are, in a way, contaminating our relationship, and we should avoid this."

On the major problems facing Brazil:

"We have several at the same time: institutional, economic, social, political. So far we have been able to negotiate our way through these problems and find peaceful solutions without violence."

On Brazil's $114 billion foreign debt — the largest in the Third World — and how it grew:

"Brazil was — and is — a country open for investments. There was an abundant amount of loan money available. We were not worried about the debt. We've been getting substantial support from the U.S. We want to assert ourselves in the financial community. I do believe we will be able to. We have the capacity to pay, and can give assurances that we will pay even though we have such a large debt."

On whether Brasilia has helped the interior of Brazil:

"This area has become one of the major centers of the country and provides jobs for many people. From the political point of view, I wonder if people went from big-city pressures to small-town pressures."

On what makes Brazil special:

"There are several Brazils. If we took Sao Paulo out of Brazil and considered it a country, it would rank perhaps fifth in the list of most-advanced countries. But the territories in the Amazon are underdeveloped."

On Brazil's new constitution:

"Our constitution is being drafted with a number of amendments that take into consideration today's problems. To quote Napoleon, a constitution should be somewhat ambiguous. Our constitution will allow changes to be made later."

On how he likes being president:

"I was never attracted by power. But in this life, there are two parallel paths, one of which is the path of politics, which brings you to power; the other is literature. I must accept fate and destiny as they are and put up with the political."

On his being a poet:

"Sometimes in politics you are writing bad poetry.

Jose Sarney Costa, 57, replaced Tancredo Neves, Brazil's first civilian president in 21 years, on April 22, 1985. Neves died before taking office, thrusting Sarney from the vice presidency to the presidency. A writer, Sarney has published a novel, short stories and poetry. After taking the presidential oath of office, Sarney said, "Here I stand, with the weight of a moment that I did not request and did not desire." Sarney's government is writing a new constitution. Sarney, over the objections of political opponents, is planning elections in 1989 instead of in 1988, as previously planned.

The critics can't say good things about my poetry, or they'll be accused of favoritism."

On the development and preservation of the Amazon:

"We have to look at the Amazon as if it's the first day of creation. We still haven't finished separating the waters. We don't think of any development of the Amazon without analyzing each project in relation to the ecological system, because we don't know what would happen if we treated it too harshly."

CANADA

Featured in USA TODAY: Aug. 26

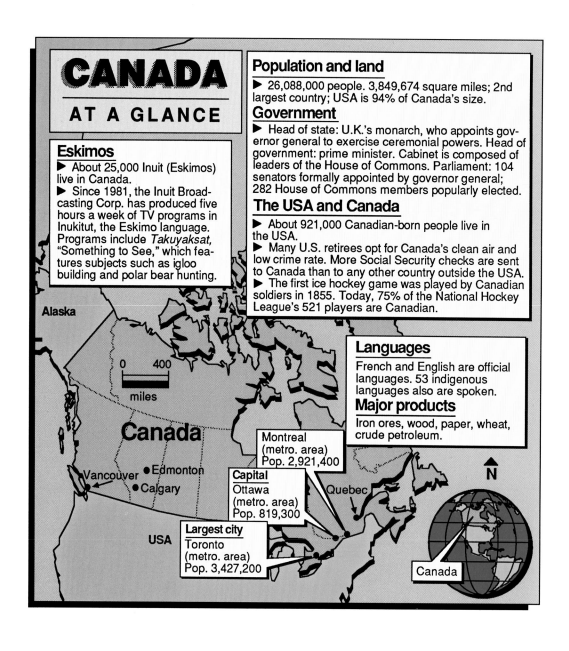

CANADA
AT A GLANCE

Eskimos
▶ About 25,000 Inuit (Eskimos) live in Canada.
▶ Since 1981, the Inuit Broadcasting Corp. has produced five hours a week of TV programs in Inukitut, the Eskimo language. Programs include *Takuyaksat,* "Something to See," which features subjects such as igloo building and polar bear hunting.

Population and land
▶ 26,088,000 people. 3,849,674 square miles; 2nd largest country; USA is 94% of Canada's size.

Government
▶ Head of state: U.K.'s monarch, who appoints governor general to exercise ceremonial powers. Head of government: prime minister. Cabinet is composed of leaders of the House of Commons. Parliament: 104 senators formally appointed by governor general; 282 House of Commons members popularly elected.

The USA and Canada
▶ About 921,000 Canadian-born people live in the USA.
▶ Many U.S. retirees opt for Canada's clean air and low crime rate. More Social Security checks are sent to Canada than to any other country outside the USA.
▶ The first ice hockey game was played by Canadian soldiers in 1855. Today, 75% of the National Hockey League's 521 players are Canadian.

Languages
French and English are official languages. 53 indigenous languages also are spoken.

Major products
Iron ores, wood, paper, wheat, crude petroleum.

Alaska

0   400
miles

Canada

Vancouver   ●Edmonton
          ●Calgary

USA

Montreal
(metro. area)
Pop. 2,921,400

Capital
Ottawa
(metro. area)
Pop. 819,300

Quebec

Largest city
Toronto
(metro. area)
Pop. 3,427,200

N

Canada

Giant, genteel neighbor: 'A camp for grown-ups'

It's the second largest country in the world, behind the Soviet Union. But it ranks only 31st in population, behind Colombia.

Next door to one of the world's two superpowers. Touches the USA across 3,987 miles from Maine to Washington, longest undefended border in the world.

How does life in this rugged, resource-rich neighbor compare to the USA? Some differences:

▶ Crime in Canada is like a Cub Scout camp by comparison. In Toronto, Canada's largest city, there were 1,118 crimes per 100,000 people in 1987; in New York City, the USA's largest, 2,036. Canada's 1987 murder rate: 2.5 per 100,000 people; the USA's: 8.3.

▶ Canada has an international reputation for fairness and neutrality among smaller nations. The USA is considered a bully by many.

"You have more prejudices and problems. You have a limited view of the world. Canadians tend to take a broader view," says **Vera Drobot**, 33, supervisor at Fort Edmonton Park in Alberta.

While most Canadians don't want to be a clone of the USA, they also don't want to go it alone.

Adds Drobot: "We also recognize your strong points as a neighbor."

Some similarities:

▶ A love of liberty.

Canada became a self-governing dominion within the British Empire in 1867, nearly 100 years after we declared our independence. It has been an autonomous member of the Commonwealth since 1931. While the queen is still the titular head, she exercises no power except on the advice of elected members of Canada's Parliament.

▶ Competition is cherished at work and at play.

Like those of us in the USA, Canadians prosper in the free marketplace. Per capita annual income for 1988: $14,100. The USA: $15,340.

While there is a political tug-of-war over it, **Prime Minister Brian Mulroney**'s government has completed a free trade agreement with the Reagan administration that sets Canada on a course of even greater competition.

In the area of fun and games, Canada considers itself increasingly competitive with the USA and the world. The Summer Olympics in Montreal in 1976 started the spirit. The 1988 Winter Olympics in Calgary added fuel.

And, the stunning defection of superstar **Wayne Gretzky** from the Edmonton Oilers to the Los Angeles Kings in August 1988 fanned the fire.

In Edmonton, hockey isn't just a sport. It's everything.

Says **Karen Bisch**, 33, homemaker: "Every parent here dreams of their child being NHL material. It becomes your whole life."

Adds her son, **Ryan**, 11, who plays for his fifth-grade Fultonvale Rink Rats: "I like Wayne Gretzky. ... No matter what team he plays for, he's still the greatest hockey player. I'd like to play in the U.S., too."

KAREN BISCH, SON RYAN: Producing a pro hockey player is family's dream.

In U.S.-Canadian competitiveness, hockey fans give no ground, for good reason. The Stanley Cup's home has been north of the border 46 out of 71 years.

Baseball is different. Montreal and Toronto are perennial contenders. But since their National and American league entries in 1969 and 1977, they have never been in the World Series.

That prompts people like Vera Drobot to say: "In Canada, those who can, play hockey. Those who can't, play baseball."

Popular as they are, spectator sports are subordinated here to participant play.

Canada's limitless acres of wilderness lure outdoor lovers from home and away. Canadians take pride in having thousands from the USA cross their borders to hunt and fish.

Terry Allen, 28, is co-owner of a company that arranges fishing trips in the wilderness of Northwest Canada. Many of his clients are from the USA. Says Allen:

"Fishing is our international language."

Allen's business partner adds: "Getting into the wilderness up here is an adventure. It's like a summer camp for grown people."

That's Plain Talk from Canada.

ALLEN: Speaks "international language" — fishing — well.

THE LEGEND LINGERS: Royal Canadian Mountie Tom Roy, 28, of Ponoka, Alberta, still uses his horse for some patrols. "Even though we have cars and computers, people still picture us coming to the rescue on horseback," Roy says. Mounties serve as the primary police force in remote areas. They are seldom used to patrol the provinces of Quebec and Ontario.

BASEBALL BUFFS: Ontario college students Craig Disero, 22, and Andrea Ucci, 20, cheer the Toronto Blue Jays at Toronto's Exhibition Stadium.

ART SHOWCASE: Debra Tunis, 37, is project coordinator for Canada's new $102 million National Gallery. The museum stands on a rise near downtown Ottawa and overlooks Parliament buildings.

TORONTO CONTRASTS: The bell tower of old City Hall is reflected in the mirrored walls of the contemporary Cadillac Fairview Tower near Eaton Center. The landmark still is used for court business and as the marriage license bureau.

MOUNTAIN METROPOLIS: The roof of the Olympic Saddle Dome frames the skyline of downtown Calgary. Home of the 1988 Winter Olympics, the arena also hosts concerts and shows every July during the Calgary Stampede, the world's largest rodeo.

Teresa Tobin, 26
Employee of National
Film Board, Montreal

"Prosperity is in the eyes of the beholder. Canadians seem happy and secure about themselves. Making money is not one of our main priorities. We think culture is more important."

Brian Houlihan, 46
Food services executive
Vancouver

"The Free Trade Agreement (with the USA) is good. Competition never did any harm. The USA has a far bigger market than we have, so there must be something there for us to go after."

Paul Mathias, 33
Sales supervisor
Calgary

"The Olympics created a worldwide awareness of Calgary and Canada. The games let a lot of people know what Canada is all about — its wide-open spaces . . . its feeling of freedom."

Linda Quick, 25
Marketing representative
Toronto

"Our closeness to the U.S. is always on people's minds. But we feel very Canadian. We have our identity, while at the same time we have a natural feeling toward Americans."

'We're indispensable to each other'

On the significance of the Free Trade Agreement:

"You have the two largest trading powers in the world. This is an exchange of $200 billion a year. It sets precedents in terms of investments, dispute settlements. We've just done the biggest deal in history. Already, the U.S. does more business with this province (Ontario) than it does with Japan. The U.S. does more business with Canada (as a whole) than it does with West Germany. Canada is indispensable to the economic well-being of the United States, and vice versa."

On the U.S. presidential election:

"The one thing I can't do is talk about the changing of the guard. I think that it would be insensitive. I've met George Bush, but I have not met Michael Dukakis. He is like George Bush on the question of free trade."

On his friendship with Reagan:

"Ronald Reagan has been a genuine friend of Canada and of freedom. He has accomplished historic things. The INF Treaty (Intermediate Nuclear Forces Treaty with the Soviet Union) and the economic resurgence of the United States will live on in history."

On Mulroney's re-election bid and his job:

"I'm looking forward to that. We do not have a set campaign. Being prime minister in a three-party parliamentary system is not easy. I have to be in the House of Commons every day for questions. I do not have the splendor of the Rose Garden to conduct press conferences. I have to be in the pit of the House of Commons. It's televised and that takes a toll. Great Britain will start televising this fall. Margaret Thatcher will have to slug it out. She and I have discussed the splendor of the television in the House of Commons."

On his accomplishments:

"We've had our share of difficulties, but we've come back. We kept to our goals in economic renewal, foreign policy and trade policy. Our deficit has declined, interest rates are down, economic growth is at record levels, we have a trade agreement with the U.S. The deficit had increased four years in a row before I took office, and now it's on the decline. We're going to have a record of accomplishments."

On hockey star Wayne Gretzky:

"It was a big loss. He certainly proved his star stature. I'm reminded of what my late father said, 'Brian, get yourself a good education because there's no money in sports.' It was a psychological thing for Canada. We're all proud of Gretzky. I know him well. The guy is probably the greatest hockey player of all time. If my dad were listening now, I'd say, 'Well, you're right on most things, but on this one...'"

Brian Mulroney, 49, Canada's 18th prime minister, is in the fourth year of his first term and looking forward to re-election. New balloting must be held by September 1989. Mulroney and his Progressive Conservative Party are thought to have a good chance at victory, especially if he succeeds in getting the Canadian Parliament to approve the Free Trade Agreement he signed with President Ronald Reagan in January 1988. The pact would create a sort of North American common market. Under the agreement, all trade barriers between the two nations would fall by 1999. Mulroney met with the JetCapade news team in his spacious second-floor office in the Langevin executive building in Ottawa. Its large windows look out across Parliament Hill to Canada's imposing, Tudor-style Parliament house. Mulroney, known for his rich baritone voice, fashionable clothes and good sense of humor, calls himself an "Irish optimist." In his dress, manner and looks, Mulroney gave the impression of a CEO of a successful company — the sort that climbed the ladder with a special knack for promotion and public relations. Tanned and relaxed-looking, he was extremely outgoing, mixing self-deprecating humor with forceful statements on trade and acid rain.

On baseball and prospects of a World Series:

"For 19 years, I've been following the Expos. I think they'll surprise everybody with a World Series. The Blue Jays franchise has been tremendously successful."

On acid rain:

"Acid rain (blamed on North American industrial plants) doesn't discriminate. It's killing lakes and streams in the Eastern United States and in Canada. We have to have a treaty with the United States to reduce this blight. People can't use beaches. Salmon rivers are being polluted. As your neighbor, you're my friend. I give you the benefit of the doubt. The test of our friendship is that I don't have the right to pollute your front lawn or dump garbage in your back yard. I told (the U.S.) Congress, 'We're your best friend. Why are you doing this to us?'"

CHINA

Featured in USA TODAY: May 9, 20

CHINA
AT A GLANCE

Languages
Chinese: 7 major dialects, Mandarin most common. Tibetan, Mongolian.

Literacy
80% of China's population was illiterate before communist takeover in 1949. Today, 80% are literate.

Military
2nd largest armed force in world: 2,950,000 serve in People's Liberation Army.

Major products
Rice, wheat, cotton, tin, steel, machine tools, chemicals.

Population and land
▶ 1.1 billion people — largest population in world. 3.7 million square miles; 3rd largest country; 101% of U.S. size.

Government
▶ Communist republic. Head of state: president. Head of government: premier, who presides over State Council. De facto leader: general secretary of the Communist Party. Legislature: National People's Congress. People's Liberation Army assists in carrying out party policies.

The USA and China
▶ About 543,000 Chinese-born people live in the USA.
▶ President Nixon reopened the door to China in 1972; full diplomatic relations were re-established in 1979.
▶ The Academy Award-winning movie *The Last Emperor* was filmed inside Beijing's Forbidden City using 19,000 extras.

China

0   500
miles

N

U.S.S.R.

Capital
Beijing
Pop. 5,970,000

Largest city
Shanghai
Pop. 7,100,000

Tianjin
Pop. 5,460,000

Japan

Mongolia

Xi'an
Pop. 2,390,000

China

Taiwan
Pop. 20 million
Capital
Taipei
Pop. 2,630,000

Guilin
Pop. 457,500

Sanming

Nepal

India

Vietnam

Taiwan

Burma

Bicycles, brains move 1 billion-plus pioneers

Eight years ago, when I last visited China, this giant was slumbering. Now, it's wide awake. Shedding its shyness and gaining confidence. Far from being a Shangri-La, it is a frontier.

▶ Then, bossman **Deng Xiaoping**, now 83 and semi-retired, had just begun his market-oriented reforms.

▶ Now, his successor **Zhao Ziyang**, 69, says "we will open China still wider and deeper and accelerate the reforms."

The policy under Deng and Zhao is to loosen the reins and stimulate the brains. What does it mean to China's overwhelming populace?

A unique perspective from inside and outside comes from **Bette Bao Lord**, 49, wife of **U.S. Ambassador Winston Lord**. Born in Shanghai, moved to Brooklyn at age 8. Returned for a tour of her homeland in 1978, on which she based her best-selling novel *Spring Moon.*

LORD: Spirit of the people bigger than the GNP.

The attractive, diminutive, demonstrative first lady of our embassy since 1985 says, "The spirit of the people here now is bigger than the GNP, bigger than the exports. They are confident of their culture and their future."

Modernizing this Communist Country does not mean abandoning Marxism, just adding at least a veneer of capitalism. Progress and problems:

▶ Per capita annual income only $300. But, double what it was 10 years ago.

▶ China-made television sets and radios in the homes have replaced the street-corner loudspeakers that provided news and information when I was last here.

Dozens of new hotels. 1.7 million foreign tourists here last year. Goal: 10 million annually by the year 2000.

▶ The country still moves on bicycles, an estimated 250 million of them. Only top officials and the most affluent own cars.

ZHANG: 2 cents to park your bike.

Zhang Shuming, 56, parks 700 bikes in her lot in Beijing. Charges 2 cents per bike per day. "We bicycle to get around and for exercise. That's how we stay so healthy and young."

The basics of the bike's importance were emphasized

recently, when **Ziao Guoqi**, 29, was executed after conviction for stealing 74 bicycles.

But Chinese are touring their country more, by bus, train, and plane. **Lu Chenghao**, 28, Shanghai boat worker, and his bride, **Xu Lili**, 26, nursery school attendant, came to the Great Wall on their honeymoon.

"When we have enough money, we want to visit the U.S.," says Xu hopefully.

Modernization has changed marriage and the family. In "Love Corner" of Beijing's downtown Working Peo-

XU, LU: Great Wall honeymooners.

ple's Cultural Palace Park, young couples mingle, many with parental supervision. But the legal age of marriage has been raised to 22 for men and 20 for women.

The government discourages more than one child per couple. **Pan Nai-mu**, associate professor of sociology at Beijing University, says this is producing a nation of "little emperors," the only child who is adored and spoiled.

U.S. businessmen here praise the Chinese workers. **Jon Nelson**, 55, quality control supervisor at Boeing Aircraft's Xi'an plant, says: "Once we teach the Chinese worker what we want done, their craftsmanship is much better than ours."

They are still struggling on the farms, where 79% of Chinese live.

Chen Shui Song, 30, farms six acres near Guilin in southeastern China. He and his wife plant and harvest — by hand — corn, sweet potatoes, rice, peanuts. Trade for other food and clothing.

FARMER CHENS: Can't read, write, but kids will.

Sell enough to make about 700 yuan ($189) a year.

Says Chen: "We can't read or write. We don't understand about the country's reforms. We have a boy, 4, and a girl, 5. They will go to school, so they will understand."

That's Plain Talk from China.

CHINA: PEOPLE AND PLACES

NO LONGER OFF-LIMITS: The Forbidden City, so named because only members of the emperor's household were allowed to enter, has been preserved as a museum. The complex includes palaces of former Chinese emperors.

COLLEGE LIFE: Students at Beijing University attend an outdoor English class.

HITCHING A RIDE: Child rides in the side-car of a bicycle during morning rush hour in Beijing. Though private citizens can own cars, few can afford them.

SUPERB SKILL: Members of The Acrobatic Troupe of China perform a balancing act in Beijing. Other acts include bicycling, juggling with feet, martial arts, dragon dancing.

4,000 MILES LONG: China's Great Wall is one of the country's top tourist attractions. Built as a defense against invaders from Central Asia, the wall is popular now with young Chinese honeymooners.

Chen Gen Bao, 30
Factory supervisor
Shanghai

"How much better off am I in today's China? When my parents were young, they lived in the dark ages. We own a color television, refrigerator, washing machine, radio and three bicycles."

Chen Hong, 19
Beijing U. student
Sanming

"I'm studying Japan and the Japanese language because China can use such knowledge. In terms of its economy, Japan is a strong country — well developed. I want to help our economy."

Sun Hong Bo, 40
Corporate executive
Xi'an

"American companies make good partners; they're honest, direct. Here at Xi'an Aircraft we have a good relationship with Boeing. China provides high technology with low labor costs."

Cai Ren Qiao, 30
Bicycle factory worker
Shanghai

"To Chinese people, owning a bicycle means freedom. You can go places. And it's so convenient. We think of our bicycles like Americans think of their automobiles."

We're non-aligned, but USA's friend

On China-U.S. relations:

"China attaches much importance to the development of China-U.S. relations, and President Reagan has done a lot to improve these relations. Naturally, there are also problems between China and the United States. One of them is the Taiwan issue. Another is restrictions on technology transfer to China. Although the United States regards China as a non-aligned, friendly country, actually, in terms of technology transfer, China is still being discriminated against. So the term 'non-aligned, friendly country' does not match what the United States is actually doing or trying to do."

On the impact of those relations on the world:

"China follows an independent foreign policy for peace. China is a major force in preserving peace. So China-U.S. friendship is in the interest of world peace. If China's economy benefits from this good relationship, so will the world economy. While visiting the United States in 1984, I told my American friends that the United States is the largest developed country in the world, while China is the biggest developing country in the world. This alone shows the tremendous significance of the friendship between China and the United States."

On the U.S. Congress:

"Some members of Congress often say things which irritate the Chinese people, and some of their statements are, as a matter of fact, actions interfering in China's international affairs."

On U.S.-Soviet relations:

"We welcomed the U.S.-Soviet summit, which led to an agreement on intermediate-range nuclear forces. We welcomed this development. But we don't think the international situation has really relaxed. In order to achieve that, we need to do a lot of work. Sometimes, some very difficult work is necessary over a long period of time, and we have to allow for twists and turns in the course of achieving that objective. The two leaders have talked about relaxation of international tension and arms reduction. They've also talked a lot about improving East-West relations. Our attitude is, first, we welcome this development. Second, we have to verify. We have to watch how they act."

On mainland China's relationship with Taiwan:

"Relations across the Taiwan Strait have relaxed quite a bit, and many people from Taiwan have come to visit their relatives and friends on the mainland. Indirect trade between the mainland and Taiwan is having considerable development."

On reunification of China and Taiwan:

"I see the situation moving toward relaxation. The return of Taiwan and the reunification of the country are

General Secretary Zhao Ziyang, leader of China's 1 billion-plus people, says he often sits around his dinner table debating China's domestic problems with his sons — but with little success. "I think my family is typical of the Chinese family today: The older generation cannot convince the younger generation, and the younger generation cannot convince the older generation," laughed the scholarly Zhao. But one thing he and his sons can agree on: China, formally called the People's Republic of China, is changing. Zhao, 69, warmly received the JetCapade news team at the Zhongnanhai government complex in Beijing. The mood was upbeat, the discussion cordial during the one-hour, 10-minute interview.

more and more possible. Our hopes are higher and higher every day. If you ask me when will the mainland and Taiwan be reunited, I can't answer that. But I think the situation is improving steadily."

On advice he would give U.S. business people:

"We think our friends in the United States have a lot to do. They can try to create the necessary conditions to improve China-U.S. economic and technological cooperation. Although we welcome the relaxation of restrictions on U.S. technology exports to China, still we think that the U.S. government's policies for restricting technology transfer to China have hurt many U.S. firms. Although U.S.-made products are very good in quality, the prices are much higher than Japanese goods."

On reaction in China to the expansion of the economy and to inflation:

"There have been lots of complaints, and these complaints have been quite strong. But I have told my people very frankly that, on one hand, they want a pay raise. On the other hand, they need a high rate of economic development. Third, they hope prices will remain stable. That's quite impossible. As a matter of fact, the increase in prices has not been so fast as the increase in people's incomes for 90% of the population. So their actual purchasing power has not lowered."

On the Chinese economy overall:

"The Chinese economy is full of vitality. Industry and agriculture have been growing quite rapidly — more than 10% a year. Since the economy is so strong, I'm sure we can get the prices under control."

Taiwan still says it represents all of China

Chinese riddles: They're famous for their intricacies.

The Republic of China, known to most as Taiwan, is a good example. Its identity crisis is a half century old — and continues to elude resolution.

Two million Kuomintang members (Nationalists) who fled mainland communism in 1949 changed Taiwan from a province of China to the proclaimed government in exile.

Leaders still insist they represent not only Taiwan's 20 million citizens, but a billion mainlanders as well.

Few nations concur. The USA dropped diplomatic links with Taiwan in 1979 and established formal relations with Beijing. Some 140 nations maintain cultural ties, but only 22 exchange ambassadors with Taiwan.

However, the Taiwanese continue to prosper: Per capita income is $6,016 a year — among the highest in Asia. Taiwanese save 40% of their earnings — highest percentage in the world. Taiwan does $88 billion in foreign trade each year, 12th in the world. Trade with the USA: $31.2 billion. The literacy rate is 99%.

Democracy seems to be on the upswing, too. Martial law was lifted in July 1987 after 38 years, and a 40-year ban on Taiwan-mainland travel was relaxed in November 1987. To date, more than 80,000 members of separated families have made the trip.

DRILL TEAM: Dancers practice for a high school commencement in front of the Chiang Kai-shek memorial in Taipei.

'People here appreciate free, democratic society'

On the reunification of China:

"Reunification is the aspiration of the Chinese people on both sides of the Taiwan Strait. If the people experience in a long period of peace the two completely different political and economic systems, they will choose from between them a way that is suited to all Chinese people. The way they choose will for certain be one that guarantees freedom, democracy, prosperity and equitable distribution of wealth."

On Republic of China-U.S. relations:

"Relations between us in commerce, trade and culture are closer than before the break in formal diplomatic relations. Although we have had some differences on the issue of trade imbalance, I am confident R.O.C.-U.S. relations will continue to develop smoothly."

On trade with the USA:

"Our trade relationship should be complementary and not confrontational. For those items we don't grow, we will do our best to buy those products from the United States."

On how visits to the mainland affect the people of the Republic of China:

"They now appreciate the sharp contrast between the two sides of the Taiwan Strait. They appreciate the free and democratic society here."

Lee Teng-hui, 65, has been president of the Republic of China since the death in January 1988 of President Chiang Ching-kuo, 77, son of Chiang Kai-shek, founder of the republic. Lee met with the JetCapade news team in his heavily guarded presidential palace decorated with large Oriental paintings and antique furniture.

On whether Hong Kong will remain the same after Communist China assumes control in 1997:

"The Chinese communists want to use Hong Kong to demonstrate their 'two-systems, one-country' plan. How can communism and democracy co-exist? The scheme looks good, but it won't work."

OUTSIDE JOB: Run-Hwang Kou, 40, gardener at the Performing Arts Center in Taipei, cuts flowers and grass.

RECREATION: A couple plays badminton in a downtown park in Taipei.

PARK OF ROCKS: Tourists cross a bridge at Yeh-liu Park in northern Taiwan. The park is known for odd rock formations shaped by erosion.

COSTA RICA

Featured in USA TODAY: Feb. 11, 26

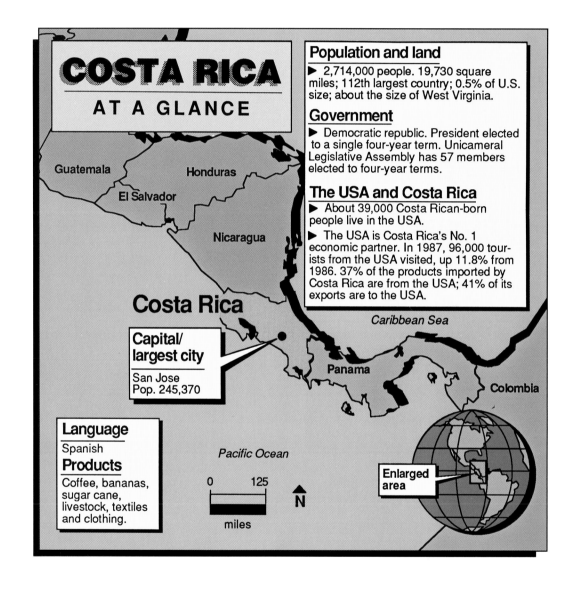

COSTA RICA
AT A GLANCE

Population and land
▶ 2,714,000 people. 19,730 square miles; 112th largest country; 0.5% of U.S. size; about the size of West Virginia.

Government
▶ Democratic republic. President elected to a single four-year term. Unicameral Legislative Assembly has 57 members elected to four-year terms.

The USA and Costa Rica
▶ About 39,000 Costa Rican-born people live in the USA.

▶ The USA is Costa Rica's No. 1 economic partner. In 1987, 96,000 tourists from the USA visited, up 11.8% from 1986. 37% of the products imported by Costa Rica are from the USA; 41% of its exports are to the USA.

Guatemala

Honduras

El Salvador

Nicaragua

Costa Rica

Capital/ largest city
San Jose
Pop. 245,370

Caribbean Sea

Panama

Colombia

Language
Spanish
Products
Coffee, bananas, sugar cane, livestock, textiles and clothing.

Pacific Ocean

0   125

N

miles

Enlarged area

A peaceful pearl prospers in troubled waters

It has no army. Yet, it's squeezed between countries with gun-toting ruffians and rebels. A treasure of tranquility in a troubled area.

Costa Rica — means "rich coast" in Spanish.

Rich it is, by Central American standards, in:

▶ Brainpower. Nearly 20% of the budget goes for education. Literacy 93%, highest in Central America.

▶ Democratic pride. 100th anniversary as a democracy will be celebrated next year. Over 80% of adults vote in presidential elections. In the USA: 53%.

▶ The work ethic. Unemployment 6%. About the same as the USA. Per capita annual income $1,400. Only 10% of that in the USA, but high for Central America.

Many older Ticos, as natives call themselves, still make their living off the land. Over $1 billion in farm products exported last year. Bananas and coffee lead the list.

Guillermo Emilio Montero Sanchez, 58, is the foreman at Hacienda Barrial, near Santa Rosa (pop. 3,874). "Coffee farming has been my whole life. It provides my food and shelter. But I don't drink it," Montero admits.

For younger Costa Ricans, the professions, politics, sports have replaced farming. Many venture into the world, but often return home.

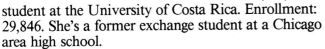

MONTERO: Grows coffee beans, but doesn't drink coffee.

Delia Maria Amolia, 30, is a law student at the University of Costa Rica. Enrollment: 29,846. She's a former exchange student at a Chicago area high school.

"Students in Costa Rica are well-versed about other parts of the world. We can discuss anything and any place. Most students in the United States don't know anything about other countries," says Delia.

Sylvia Poll, 17, is a national heroine for winning eight medals in swimming, three of them gold, at the 1987 Pan American Games in Indianapolis. Her near-term goal: a medal in the summer Olympics in Seoul.

But, after that, Sylvia's sights are set on education at home. "I want to study international diplomacy in Costa Rica."

The country is about the size of West Virginia. Population about that of Chicago. But its purposefulness and pride match that of Switzerland, without the banks.

Some 20,000 citizens of the USA share that peaceful and peace-loving purpose as permanent residents.

Fred Pitts, 60, a former neurosurgeon in Madison, Wis., and his wife, **Lavilla**, 43, own and run a 150-acre sheep farm on a mountainside outside San Jose.

"I was burned out from long days in the operating room. We are at peace in this country," says Pitts.

Peace of mind and

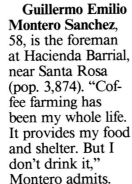

POLL'S GOAL: Olympic medal, then diplomacy.

warlessness is what Costa Rica is all about. It has been since it dismantled its army in 1948. But it took **President Oscar Arias Sanchez**, elected in 1986, to put this tiny country on the world map. Arias, 46, has:

▶ Won the Nobel Peace Prize (1987).

▶ Addressed the U.N. General Assembly twice.

▶ Addressed a joint session of the U.S. Congress (1987).

His "give peace a chance" call before Congress clearly impacted a vote to reject further aid to the Nicaraguan Contras, despite President Reagan's plea to the contrary.

U.S. RETIREES: Lavilla and Fred Pitts at peace on their Costa Rica sheep farm.

I asked Arias, "Does that mean that you were a better salesman with our congress than was President Reagan?"

"My product was a better product," Arias quipped and smiled.

That's Plain Talk from Costa Rica.

PUPPY AND PAL: Andrea Alvarez, 4, keeps a tight grip on her puppy outside a house in Cartago.

CART ART: Fernando Alpisar Chaverri, 48, paints the wheel of an ox cart at the Chaverri Ox Cart Factory in Sarchi.

ROADSIDE MONUMENT: A statue of Christ stands guard over Pacagas, near the Irazu volcano.

PICKED TO PERK: Plantation worker Florentino Marin, 56, of Santa Rosa sorts coffee beans.

Ricardo Lankester, 43
Lawyer
San Jose

"Costa Ricans are more laid back than people in other countries. They don't want to hurt others in their quest to be the best. Nobody wants a bigger piece of the pie. Everyone wants to make sure the pie is evenly distributed."

Franklin Chang-Diaz, 37
Space shuttle astronaut
Born in San Jose

"Costa Rica has a high emphasis on education, which allowed me to compete with U.S. students. . . . I knew I carried into space all the dreams and aspirations of all Costa Ricans. It's a tremendous source of pride."

Roxana Teran-Victory, 27
Teacher
San Antonio

"We're not as neurotic or aggressive as other Central American countries. A member of the lower class feels the same way as a member of the upper class — and he demands to be treated the same way."

Francisco Torres, 43
Cab driver
San Jose

"In Costa Rica, we are free to say anything we wish about any candidate or political leader without being afraid. We are a free country and you can't say the same about the other Central American nations."

We chose bread, schools, not rifles

On how the USA sees Costa Rica:

"We would have to admit that U.S. citizens are not the most knowledgeable people in geography. Until a few months ago no one knew where Costa Rica was located in the Western Hemisphere. We were always confused with Puerto Rico. Fortunately for us, after the success of the Guatemala Accord, I was able to persuade my colleagues to reach an agreement against all odds. Then on the 10th of December, I was awarded the Nobel Peace Prize. Now I suppose most people know who we are, what are our main values and why Costa Rica is different from many other Latin American nations."

On his hopes for peace as a result of the U.S. Congress rejecting military aid for the Contras:

"The House of Representatives has given the peace plan a chance. I think we have a much better chance now to advance in a quicker way. I think now we have to get the Cubans and the Soviets and all those countries from the socialist bloc that are supporting the guerrillas in El Salvador to stop that support."

On why Costa Rica has a reputation as the Switzerland of Latin America:

"First of all, our ancestors decided 120 years ago to introduce compulsory and free education. That's why we have an illiteracy rate of 6½%. We have many, many universities, about 75,000 university students. Per capita-wise I think we have more university students than any other Latin American country. We built a welfare state more than 40 years ago. Today, we have a national security system that covers the whole population. The poorest Costa Rican can get the best, the most sophisticated surgery in one of our hospitals and not have to pay a penny. Life expectancy here is 75 years, the same as the U.S. Nevertheless, we have an income per capita that is one-tenth of the U.S."

On the fact that Costa Rica has not had a standing army since 1948 and whether there is any pressure to change that:

"No one would dare change that. No one would like to be remembered in Costa Rican history as the person responsible for establishing the army. Spending money on arms is incompatible with economic and social growth. We had to choose between rifles and bread, machine guns, tanks, helicopters, airplanes, and schools, hospitals, and secondary roads."

On solving Central America's $14 billion debt problem — especially Costa Rica's debt, which is the highest per capita debt in the region:

"That is changing very rapidly. I am determined to make Costa Rica the most developed country in Latin America. For that, we need to introduce some impor-

Oscar Arias Sanchez, 46, is the 38th president of Costa Rica. The son of a wealthy landowner, he was educated in Costa Rica and at the London School of Economics. He was elected president in 1986 to a single four-year term. In 1987, Arias won the Nobel Peace Prize for his Guatemala Accord — a plan for bringing a settlement to the Nicaraguan conflict. He plans to use $350,000 in money from the Nobel prize to set up a foundation for the poor. Arias met with the JetCapade news team in his large, one-story residence in San Jose's most fashionable neighborhood. Dressed in slacks and an open-collar sports shirt, he spoke for more than an hour in his antique-filled drawing room.

tant economic changes, some structural changes. Here the extent of debt plays an important role. We cannot grow as fast as we want if we have to pay our external debt as it was arranged or scheduled. So we are in the process of rescheduling our debt. We don't want any fresh money from private banks but want better conditions to pay."

On what he'll do when his term as president is up:

"I've been offered many new jobs — to teach in a few well-known universities. I was recently offered the Simon Bolivar chair at Cambridge University. I come from academic life, and I would like to return to academic life for a while, but one never knows."

CUBA

Featured in USA TODAY: Feb. 22, March 3, 4, 18

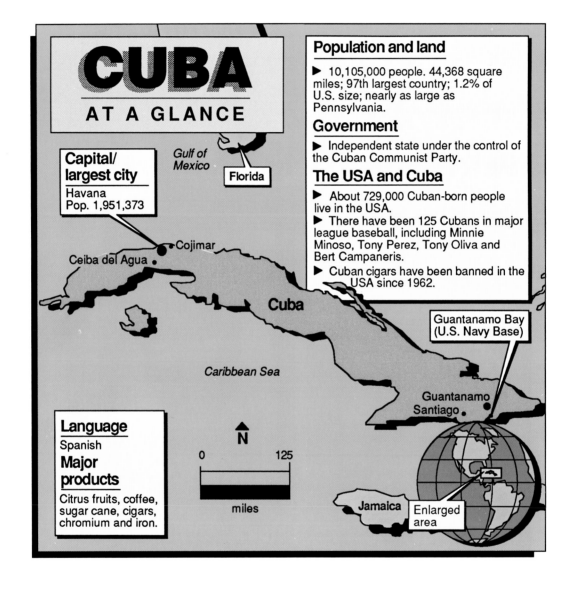

CUBA
AT A GLANCE

Capital/largest city
Havana
Pop. 1,951,373

Gulf of Mexico

Florida

Cojimar

Ceiba del Agua

Cuba

Caribbean Sea

Language
Spanish
Major products
Citrus fruits, coffee, sugar cane, cigars, chromium and iron.

N
0   125
miles

Population and land
▶ 10,105,000 people. 44,368 square miles; 97th largest country; 1.2% of U.S. size; nearly as large as Pennsylvania.

Government
▶ Independent state under the control of the Cuban Communist Party.

The USA and Cuba
▶ About 729,000 Cuban-born people live in the USA.
▶ There have been 125 Cubans in major league baseball, including Minnie Minoso, Tony Perez, Tony Oliva and Bert Campaneris.
▶ Cuban cigars have been banned in the USA since 1962.

Guantanamo Bay (U.S. Navy Base)

Guantanamo
Santiago

Jamaica

Enlarged area

30 years under Fidel: How Cuba has changed

First, you have to remember that Cuba is communist. Second, that **Fidel Castro** is hard-core. If you keep that in mind, you might understand Cuba today.

I last visited Havana early in 1958. Final year of the Batista regime. Some facts, some impressions on the return trip. And, some comments from some inside Cuba:

▶ Wealth: Then, many business and professional people were wealthy or well-to-do. The masses were extremely poor. Now, what wealth there is belongs to the state. It owns everything. Sets wages and salaries. Average workers make 150-200 pesos per month (about $170 U.S.). Managers can make up to 400 pesos ($340 U.S.). But, the price of necessities is low. Government housing costs only 10% of the pay of the head of the household.

▶ Health: About 3,000 of Cuba's 6,000 doctors fled to Florida when Castro took over. "Some of them were good doctors but they were not the best citizens," says Fidel. So, he established 20 new medical schools, one in each province. Now, there are about 17,400 doctors. All medical care is free. Then, the infant mortality rate was 60 per 1,000 births. Now, it's 13.

▶ Education: Then, the illiteracy rate was 22%. Now, it's under 2%. Then, there were 24,273 students in the university system. Now, there are 295,000.

▶ Religion: Then, there were 362 Catholic and Protestant churches. Castro says he hasn't closed any. But very few people attend. Then, about 15% of the Catholics attended Mass regularly. Now, about 1%. Then, there were 333 parochial schools. Now, there are none.

Impressions: Most elderly seem content.

FUENTES, AGE 99: Former Hemingway friend is happy with memories.

Some middle-aged uneasy. Young hooked on Castro. Three examples:

Gregorio Fuentes, 99, a retired ship captain, enjoys three square meals and two cigars a day in the small coastal village of Cojimar (pop. 3,000). Reminisces about fishing and sailing with **Ernest Hemingway**.

Fuentes says Hemingway approved of the revolution. "He told me he was going to come back to Cuba for good. If he had lived, I know he would be here."

Monsignor Carlos Manuel de Cespedes, 51, Havana (pop. 1,951,373), is thoughtfully outspoken: "I am not a communist. I do not approve of everything that is happening. At the same time, I agree with a lot of things.

"In education, health, housing, the situation is better now than before. I criticize the government not in the field of social human rights, but individual human rights. It's time to grant liberty of expression."

Among the young, there seems little question of philosophy or loyalty.

At Che Guevara High School, in Ceiba

FATHER DE CESPEDES, 51: Uneasy, but realistic.

del Agua (pop. 1,806), student body president **Rose Marie Ruiz**, 16 (she was elected in a democratic vote), enthuses:

"The revolution has given us everything."

We mixed and talked with large numbers of the students. They spoke of ambitions to be doctors, engineers, computer programmers.

"Do any of you want to be president when you grow up?" we asked.

A gasp in unison. A chorus of "No!" We asked, "Why not?"

"Fidel. Fidel Forever!" was the chant.

That's Plain Talk from Cuba.

STUDENT LEADER ROSE MARIE RUIZ, 16: Teen-age theme cry, "Fidel Forever!"

CITY LIFE: Havana, Cuba's capital and commercial center, is a mixture of contemporary buildings and traditional tile-roof houses.

SENIOR SESSION: Mariana Calzada, 73, exercises as part of a fitness class in Havana.

PROBING THE PAST: Irma Perez Bravo, 12, student at Che Guevara High School in Ceiba del Agua, describes murals about the revolution at the Museum of Che.

CUBA: PEOPLE AND PLACES

ARTIST AND ART: Raul Martinez, 60, poses with one of his paintings.

TRACK STAR: Alberto Juantorena, 38, gold medalist in the 1976 Olympics, is a sports hero in Cuba.

Adria Santana, 39
TV actress
Havana

"I will be the first to admit that Cuba does have its problems. But I also know that you can't fix our problems from Miami or anywhere else. I am staying here so that I can help improve this country. I want to work from the inside, not the outside. I like the way our country has changed since the revolution."

Felix Savon, 20
Boxing champion
Guantanamo

"I think I could beat Mike Tyson. Well, at least I would try. We have a saying in Cuba: 'Give fire to the gun until it loses its bottom.' Why shouldn't I win? At least I have two hands and maybe I'm taller than he is."

Donna Corbett, 34
Tourist in Havana
Hamilton, Ontario

"You feel restricted here. You feel confined. It's a lot cleaner than I expected. I expected slums. You feel your tour guide has been told what to say. You have to ask yourself, 'Are the Cubans really thrilled with all of this, or are they just saying so because they have to?' "

Jose Fernandez, 65
Minister of education
Havana

"Human rights are not just free speech. Parents here have the human right for their children not to be in drugs, prostitution and crime."

Fidel to the USA: You're not No. 1

Many Cuban Americans, particularly in the Miami area, are hostile toward your government. How do you feel about them?

"You cannot talk to the people here about the ones who go to Miami. The ones in Miami cannot speak about the ones who are here. You have every kind of person there among the Cubans who went to America. You have people who committed crimes . . . people who did not like discipline. We had 6,000 doctors and 3,000 of them left — some good doctors. But they were not the best citizens. The best citizens remained in the country with lower salaries. I do believe that future generations in the United States will have a better opinion of the Cubans who are here and a worse opinion of the Cubans in Miami."

At the time of the revolution, you did not proclaim the socialist nature of your administration. Did you deceive your people?

"No. We were not the ones who created a socialist consciousness. The revolutionary laws created the revolutionary awareness. The people realized that, for the first time, there was a government that was not a servant of the wealthy, the oligarchy, the criminal interests. The people had wanted that for a long time."

What would happen if the people of Cuba decided your government was no longer serving their interests?

"When the revolution was victorious here, the people were armed. The people have weapons here. If the people wanted to remove the revolution, they wouldn't have to wait for the CIA to send weapons. They could do that in three days because they have the weapons. The people have the power. They are the force from which the revolution emanates. How long would other governments last if they gave the power to the people?"

Can someone with a deep faith in God play a prominent role in the party?

"No. Not yet. But it is not a matter of dogma. We have raised the need for Christians and Marxists to join forces as a prerequisite for social change. I say we can agree on the matters of this earth and let everyone interpret the creation of the earth and the universe in his own way. Latin America is a Christian continent. Many priests are against injustices, against corruption."

You follow the U.S. presidential primaries closely. Why do they hold such interest for you?

"What happens in the United States affects the whole world in one way or another. The Third World suffers all the worst consequences, even though we can't cast a vote in those elections. You call that democracy?"

What are your perceptions of the USA's system of elections?

Fidel Castro, 61, president of Cuba, has been in power since 1959 when his revolution overthrew the dictatorship of Fulgencio Batista.

"Your elections become a carnival. Whoever is funnier, nicer or has a better voice can win. It's not always the best man."

If elections were held in Cuba, how much of the vote would you get?

"It depends on who is my opponent. If it is Ronald Reagan, I'd get 110%. Here in Cuba, our elections are different. We vote for the party rank and file. The candidate submits a biography and the people vote."

How would you compare life in the USA and Cuba?

"We're getting closer to you in sports, medicine, and from a social point of view, we're ahead of you. We don't have people sleeping in the streets, begging. We don't have drugs or alcoholism. Economically, there are others ahead of you. You have been left behind in the chemical, steel, automotive and electronic industries. You are no longer No. 1."

Does Cuba consider itself an enemy of the USA?

"I don't think I'm an enemy, but I've always thought that the USA was an enemy of ours."

Today Cuba is viewed with suspicion by many in the USA. Yet in the beginning, your revolution seemed to captivate the imagination of our country.

"We were like the Robin Hoods in the mountains. Everyone has sympathy for someone fighting someone larger. We started from scratch. We believed in our people, we received help from no one."

Were you indeed Robin Hood?

"We were not Robin Hoods. He was a romantic. We were revolutionaries."

What is your recollection of President Kennedy and the Bay of Pigs invasion 25 years ago?

"Kennedy was a man with scruples. He did not like direct intervention. If he had sent in U.S. troops, the war would have lasted until today, because we had hundreds of thousands armed and willing to fight. We have to be grateful to Kennedy that he did not make that mistake. Later he made other mistakes by accepting plans for assassination via the CIA and the mafia."

How do you think Kennedy handled the missile crisis?

"He avoided humiliation at the end of the missile crisis, with great national and international authority . . . he capitalized on the Soviet mistakes."

Whose idea was it to have missiles in Cuba — yours or Khrushchev's?

"I'm saving that for my memoirs."

Can we assume that you agreed with the decision to withdraw the missiles?

"I agreed with the settlement, but I tell you frankly we were prepared for battle. A better settlement could have been found. By and large, there was a demand that the missiles be taken out of Cuba, but what about the ones at the U.S. military base at Guantanamo? And what about economic benefits? And what about the assassination plots?"

What are your feelings about Guantanamo now?

"No country would feel comfortable with having a naval base in its territory. That base is of no strategic value. It is an instrument of humiliation. But we do not want the base to be a motive of conflict between Cuba and the USA."

Any other memories concerning Kennedy?

"Kennedy sent an emissary — a French journalist — to talk to me. The very day I was talking to that envoy, Kennedy was assassinated. The devil must have been involved in that. I think a great opportunity was lost. Perhaps detente would have arrived sooner."

What do you think about Soviet leader Mikhail Gorbachev and why is he so popular?

"He's a communicator. He's nice. He has a direct style. He's honestly analyzed problems in the Soviet Union. Some even believe he'll turn to capitalism. Of course, he won't do that. He knows the Western mind."

Is Cuba dependent on the Soviet Union politically or economically?

"Politically, no. Economically, we all depend on others. The United States depends on the Persian Gulf. The United States depends on the Middle East. No country is more economically dependent on others than the United States. We've never had as good a relationship with the Soviet Union as Reagan has with Gorbachev. You are going to Mars together."

Did you ever dream your revolution would be so successful, that it would last 30 years?

"Of course. If I didn't think the revolution would last for more than 30 years, I would never have bothered."

Working the late shift with candid Castro

The call came at 9:50 p.m. at La Habana Libre, formerly a Hilton, in the heart of Havana.

"The president has granted your request for an interview. Be downstairs in five minutes."

We had been on hold since our arrival the previous day. Castro may see you, we were told, but there would be no definite appointment in advance.

Minutes after the call, we careened through the streets at high speeds in state cars driven by state drivers.

The ride was fast-paced, but the interview — held in Castro's office in the Council of State Building — was not.

Castro, wearing his familiar military fatigues, settled in for almost six hours of often animated conversation. Throughout the interview, he would frequently jump to his feet to make a point or pace the floor. He answered questions and asked some.

CASTRO: Animated talker in the early morning.

"What is your newspaper's circulation? What is the price per copy?" he asked.

Told that USA TODAY lost money during its first four years and was subsidized by other profitable Gannett operations, Castro laughed and said, "So your company and my country are both socialistic!"

The personal Fidel: Quit smoking his classic cigars in 1985, to set an example. He is now as strongly anti-smoking as he is anti-gambling and anti-drugs.

He's a non-stop night person, who often sleeps until mid-morning. The interview ended over Cuban rum and coffee at 3:55 a.m. "Perhaps if we had started earlier, we could have covered more," Castro said.

Castro, the former ballplayer once scouted by the Washington Senators, autographed Cuban baseballs for each of us.

As he walked us to the elevator, Castro told us he was going home to swim. "I prefer to play basketball," he said, "but my friends are not fond of being called at 4 a.m. for a game."

HEADED FOR OPEN SEAS: A tank-landing ship, the USS La Moure County, leaves Naval base docks in Guantanamo Bay.

At Cuba's doorstep, 7,000 U.S. military

Through a high-powered telescope atop a post, a U.S. Marine keeps an eye on Cuban soldiers at similar lookouts on the communist side.

That's the situation, 24 hours a day, at the U.S. Naval Station at Guantanamo Bay in Cuba. Both sides are well-armed. But it is an easy truce.

"People need to realize that just because we're the only base on communist soil doesn't mean we're on the verge of being attacked," says John McCary, 23, a Navy journalist from Lexington, Ky. "You almost have to live down here to recognize how peaceful things are."

"We realize that we're it," says Capt. John R. Condon, the 50-year-old base commander. "We're 7,000 free people living on communist soil. Transport aircraft come in twice a week, taking people in and out. Besides taking a ship, that's the only way for people to come and go."

Gitmo — the base's nickname — is separated from Cuba by ideology and the fence. But it also is cut off from the world by the Caribbean Sea. That means

- ▶ **HISTORY:** The Guantanamo Bay U.S. Naval Station was established as a fuel stop for U.S. ships in 1903, shortly after Cuba defeated Spain in the Spanish-American war.
- ▶ **RENT:** Under a treaty entered into before Fidel Castro took power, the U.S. pays Cuba an annual fee of $4,085 for use of the land. Since 1959, Castro has cashed only one of the checks.
- ▶ **POPULATION:** About 7,000 military personnel and support workers.
- ▶ **PERIMETER:** 17.4 miles.

GATEWAY: Cuban commuters leave Guantanamo Bay.

businesses, goods and services normally found outside other U.S. military bases are located on this base. Or they are imported.

"Home is what you make it," says Noel Jackson, 55, a Cuban exile who has lived here since 1964. "What do you find here that you find in a city? Everything."

Within the boundaries are a McDonald's, a Baskin-Robbins, cable television, an elementary and high school, a fire department, a library, a beauty salon, a barbershop and a single stoplight in the sleepy downtown area.

"It's like a small town, even smaller than where I'm from," says Navy photographer Billy Sexton, 25, from Mandeville, La. "We have three stoplights at home."

But there are major differences. Just ask Yvette Rivera, a 24-year-old Navy wife from Jamaica, N.Y.:

"Sometimes there's live fire at night. You can hear the planes flying over head at night, practicing shooting at targets. Pictures shake on the wall. The kids hold onto my legs."

EGYPT

Featured in USA TODAY: March 7, April 8

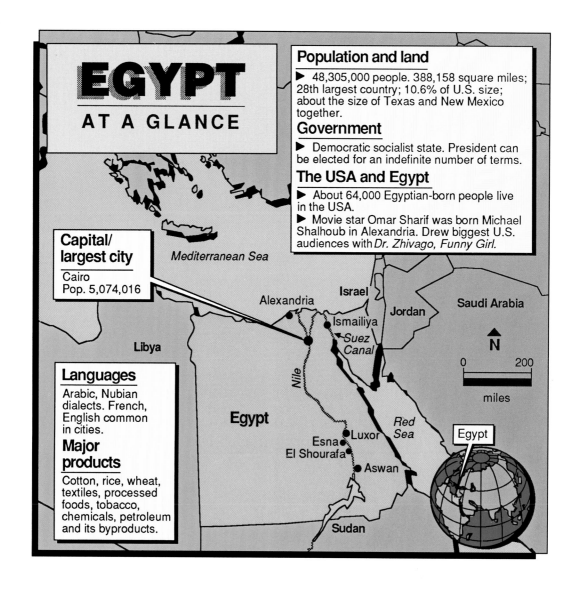

EGYPT
AT A GLANCE

Population and land

▶ 48,305,000 people. 388,158 square miles; 28th largest country; 10.6% of U.S. size; about the size of Texas and New Mexico together.

Government

▶ Democratic socialist state. President can be elected for an indefinite number of terms.

The USA and Egypt

▶ About 64,000 Egyptian-born people live in the USA.

▶ Movie star Omar Sharif was born Michael Shalhoub in Alexandria. Drew biggest U.S. audiences with *Dr. Zhivago, Funny Girl.*

Capital/ largest city

Cairo
Pop. 5,074,016

Languages

Arabic, Nubian dialects. French, English common in cities.

Major products

Cotton, rice, wheat, textiles, processed foods, tobacco, chemicals, petroleum and its byproducts.

Mediterranean Sea

Alexandria
Israel
Ismailiya
Suez Canal
Jordan
Saudi Arabia

Libya

Nile

Egypt

N
0   200
miles

Red Sea

Esna Luxor
El Shourafa
Aswan

Egypt

Sudan

Egypt is everlasting: Age-old, up-to-date

The USA and the world have been intrigued or awe-inspired for hundreds of years by this seat of ancient civilization.

▶ Pyramids and the Sphinx.

▶ Limitless Saharan deserts and the lush Nile Valley.

▶ Camels and turban-wrapped peddlers and workers.

All those pennants of the past are still here. But when you scratch beneath the age-old symbols, modern Egypt is an up-to-date place with problems and potential to match.

Tourists from the USA, Japan, Europe, the Mideast sat with us in silence under the floodlights during the nightly hour-long historic ceremony at the foot of the Sphinx and the pyramids.

The scene resembled that on any summer night at

SPHINX: Eroding, but still on guard after 4,500 years.

Mt. Rushmore in South Dakota's Black Hills. There, we revere the stone faces of four former presidents. Here, the somewhat eroded shrine has the face of a man and the body of a lion.

The historic site is less than an hour from mid-Cairo, capital and largest city (pop. 5,074,016). Cairo and its surroundings offer the oldest and the newest, the best and the worst:

▶ A new subway system that is alleviating traffic problems slightly; a new sewerage system that has eliminated downtown stench.

▶ A 100,000-seat sports center. A new Opera House was to open in 1988.

▶ About 1 million new babies a year. Overpopulation means much housing here is substandard — like some in New York or Detroit or other major U.S. cities.

Cairo's university campuses are where old and new meet. Education is free. And a "social contract" guarantees every university graduate a job.

Alia Foda, 22, is studying graphic arts at the University of Helwan in Cairo (enrollment 91,000).

"I lived in California, but I wouldn't leave Egypt to return there. Here I can express my feelings and emotions. In the U.S., you have to hold everything back," says this worldly woman with Western wear and Egyptian views.

Foda eyes the future of Egypt. **Mervat Gamal**, 30, a saleswoman in a boutique in Alexandria (pop. 2,317,705) clings to the past. A devout Moslem, wrapped in traditional attire, only her face exposed, she says:

"Tourists come into the shop wearing tiny bathing suits. It's no good. It should be forbidden."

More than half of Egyptian workers still make their living off the land, in agriculture, forestry, fishing. The rich valley of the Nile, which runs from the Mediterranean Sea to the Sudan border, produces sugar, rice, cotton, vegetables.

President Hosni Mubarak, while proud of progress in the cities, also

FODA, 22: Modern woman in modern Cairo likes Egypt's ways.

points out 50% of the Nile area from Cairo to Alexandria is now planted in greenery.

Abd al Rahman, 32, farms the west bank of the Nile at the village of El Shourafa (pop. 2,500). Raises sugar cane, alfalfa and vegetables.

"I use my cow and a water wheel to pump water to my fields. I love my land and I love this village. My two brothers and two sisters live in Cairo, but I'm staying here," says al Rahman.

Mahmoud Rehab, 22, is working in the fields to prepare for a different future. He harvests sugar cane near Esna (pop. 32,158). Earns 6 pounds ($2.65) a day. Saves some to buy books to study toolmaking.

"I won't be a farmer

AL RAHMAN: Loves the greenery along the Nile.

all my life. I want to work in a big factory. In the meantime, working in the fields makes me strong. My hands aren't soft, but I'm healthy."

That's Plain Talk from Egypt.

MASSIVE MAUSOLEUMS: Egyptian pharaohs were buried in these pyramids, built between 2650 B.C. and 2500 B.C. Nearly 2 million tourists a year visit the monuments, which were constructed without iron tools.

WOMEN'S FASHION: Shahira Mehrez, 43, owner of four handcraft shops in Cairo, displays a galabia, a full-length traditional garment.

SUGAR CANE FARMING: Moaud Mohammed Moaud, 45, of Esna, carries harvested sugar cane. Moaud charges 15 pounds ($6.64) per day for the use of his only camel.

URBAN LANDSCAPE: Egypt's capital, Cairo, crowds the east bank of the Nile, about 14 miles from the head of the Delta.

EGYPT: PEOPLE AND PLACES

OUT OF ROOM: A rooftop view shows Cairo's crowded housing. The shortage is so severe, 500,000 people live in mausoleums.

Nabila Darwish, 22
Law student
Cairo University

"The older generation of Egyptians is more traditional in habits and customs. The younger generation is more exposed to the outside world and wants to be more modern."

Salah Abd El Hamied, 46
Driver
Luxor

"In Nubia, farmers have a very simple life. Some say, 'Just give me a piece of land, some water and a lady with a nice face.' They don't need Cadillacs or air-conditioning."

Chahira Sirry, 47
Boutique owner
Cairo

"(Even) if we are very modern here, there are limits. You never wear shorts in the street. You never go strapless. I am astonished when I go to Luxor and see how the tourists are dressed."

Hesham Kattan, 36
Hotel manager
Aswan

"Everyone has a memory about the Cataract Hotel. Many famous people stay here. Omar Sharif was here recently. 1987 was the best year for Egyptian tourism for a long time."

EGYPT **55**

My niche in history: Mideast peacemaking

On his role as peacemaker:

"This is my niche. I like people to be on good terms with one another. I would try to bring (U.S. Secretary of State George) Shultz and the Palestinians together. I have good relations with practically all the Arabs. I am trying hard with the Sudanese and the Ethiopians, and there are problems with other neighbors and Sudan. We have good contacts with nearly all the African countries. Africa has looked to Egypt as one of the most important countries in this area."

On the U.S. peace efforts in the Mideast:

"It's very important to keep trying. There should be progress in the peace process — in the West Bank and Gaza. As I told Secretary of State Shultz, his effort is the big step. I told him, 'Don't neglect it.' I told him they could just put down the uprising in the occupied territories by using force, but there will be explosions outside of the area — everywhere. Everybody is relying on the United States as a main element to push the peace process. That's why I told Shultz, 'Please, this uprising will not wait until the elections in the United States or Israel.' This is not something you can turn on or off. It's very, very dangerous. This uprising is just an alarm."

On the Soviet Union's role in the peace process:

"I think they are very important. They have their own interests also in this area. The United States has an important role with the Israelis, but without the Soviet Union, I don't think the peace process will prosper. They are not going to make it easy because they want to be participators. The Soviets have Syria in the process, so we have to please them."

On the many public works projects in Egypt:

"The infrastructure in this country had been neglected for 60 or 70 years. We had to start from scratch. We kept to the previous five-year plan and achieved a lot. Then we started another five-year plan, with another one planned after that. The economy had to suffer because we spent a lot on the infrastructure. That is the base of everything. If you don't have a sewerage system you can't have water. If you don't have electricity, private industry can't start producing things. Without telephones, there can be no contacts. Investors would come here but couldn't contact Europe, Japan or the USA by just asking for a line."

On communication and transportation before the latest improvements:

"Here in Cairo, communication was almost nil. It was the most difficult thing to ring any house or shop nearby. It was much easier to get in your car and go there instead of using the telephone. To try an international call, you would wait hours to maybe days or weeks. How could we let that happen? So we had to

*An energetic **President Hosni Mubarak**, 60, met the JetCapade news team amid extremely heavy security in the Presidential Palace at Heliopolis in suburban Cairo. In a lavish meeting room with blue rugs and tapestries, Mubarak emotionally explained his involvement with the peace process, often sitting on the edge of his chair and gesturing with both hands. Mubarak became president in 1981 and was elected to a second six-year term in 1987. Mubarak spoke at length about intensive efforts under way by the USA to start peace talks among Israel, the Arab states and the Palestinians. He exhorted Israeli Prime Minister Yitzhak Shamir to agree to an international conference. On a more personal note, Mubarak described his own role fostering a peaceful settlement in the Middle East and his aspirations to improve conditions in Egypt.*

start with electricity, water supplies, telephones, railways to meet transportation needs. You can't build a 30-story building without a solid foundation."

On Egypt's efforts to regain self-sufficiency in food, 50% of which is now imported:

"This depends on agriculture, which you can't change overnight. If you go from here to Alexandria, you find a desert road and a green road. Now more than 50% of the 220 kilometers have been planted. We have no problems with some vegetables and fruits. We were running short a few years ago and now they are available in any quantity you ask for. We stopped importing rice and now we are exporting it. We were importing beans, and now we are not. Still, I can tell you we are not going to regain (self-sufficiency) in a very short period."

FRANCE

Featured in USA TODAY: June 7, July 1

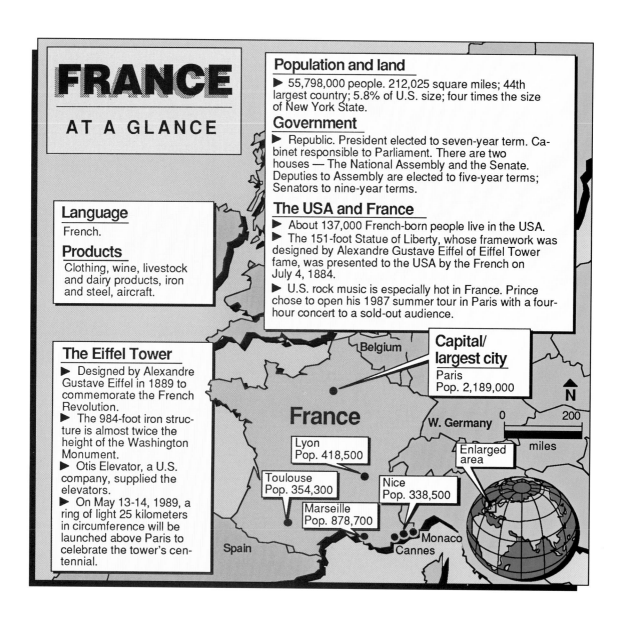

FRANCE

AT A GLANCE

Language
French.

Products
Clothing, wine, livestock and dairy products, iron and steel, aircraft.

The Eiffel Tower
▶ Designed by Alexandre Gustave Eiffel in 1889 to commemorate the French Revolution.
▶ The 984-foot iron structure is almost twice the height of the Washington Monument.
▶ Otis Elevator, a U.S. company, supplied the elevators.
▶ On May 13-14, 1989, a ring of light 25 kilometers in circumference will be launched above Paris to celebrate the tower's centennial.

Population and land
▶ 55,798,000 people. 212,025 square miles; 44th largest country; 5.8% of U.S. size; four times the size of New York State.

Government
▶ Republic. President elected to seven-year term. Cabinet responsible to Parliament. There are two houses — The National Assembly and the Senate. Deputies to Assembly are elected to five-year terms; Senators to nine-year terms.

The USA and France
▶ About 137,000 French-born people live in the USA.
▶ The 151-foot Statue of Liberty, whose framework was designed by Alexandre Gustave Eiffel of Eiffel Tower fame, was presented to the USA by the French on July 4, 1884.
▶ U.S. rock music is especially hot in France. Prince chose to open his 1987 summer tour in Paris with a four-hour concert to a sold-out audience.

Belgium

Capital/ largest city
Paris
Pop. 2,189,000

N

France

W. Germany

0   200

miles

Enlarged area

Lyon
Pop. 418,500

Toulouse
Pop. 354,300

Nice
Pop. 338,500

Marseille
Pop. 878,700

Monaco
Cannes

Spain

Wine, women, song: Oui, and new self-esteem

Paris is still for lovers. France still means fine food, fashions.

But there's a new seriousness and sense of purpose here. Self-confidence has replaced the self-chastisement that lingered long after France was overrun and occupied by Hitler's armies in World War II.

"It's a more pragmatic, less emotional way of looking at the world," says **U.S. Ambassador Joe M. Rodgers**, 55.

French President Francois Mitterrand, 71, gets much of the credit. He's completed one seven-year term, just been re-elected to another in May 1988.

A socialist, Mitterrand initially gave the communists a bear hug. Since, he has almost squeezed them offstage. They got only 11.3% of the vote in the June 1988 parliamentary election, down from a postwar high of 28%.

Mitterrand milestones:

▶ Terrorism has virtually disappeared. Major crime has dropped 8% in the past two years.

▶ Inflation is down from 14% to 3%.

▶ Military preparedness has high priority. France has its own nuclear-weapon warehouses.

▶ Sophistication and citification continue to climb. Only 7% of the French now are farmers. Just after WWII it was 35%.

On the Riviera, the cities of Cannes, Marseille, Nice, St. Tropez have their devotees. But Paris is the pinnacle.

It's firmly on my list of the world's five most fascinating cities. Alphabetically: Buenos Aires, Montreal, New York, Paris, San Francisco.

But, back to the basics of the good life here — wine, women, song, sex.

In daytime, dusk and darkness, love is in the air every-

FOIN, GAELA: Lovers under Eiffel Tower.

where. Hand-holding, hugging and even R-rated scenes on the city's benches, bridges, parks. Bois de Boulogne, 2,224 acres of greenery in the heart of Paris, is an asylum for the amorous.

Alexandre Foin, 19, university electronics student, and **Tanguy Gaela**, 16, junior college science student, prefer the Alexander III bridge in the shadow of the Eiffel Tower.

"The poetry of Paris is written around the bridges. They're full each night with lovers who hope to live out that poetry," says Gaela.

Adds **Nadege Amand**, 17, a junior college science student, "French women don't have to be flirtatious. French men are skirt chasers."

Romantics don't vanish with age. The Left Bank of the Seine is home to many. One such is **Leslie Caron**, one of the best known French show business figures in the USA.

Older USA movie goers remember her in *Gigi*. Younger ones have seen her on reruns of *An American In Paris*.

Now 57 and a grandmother, she does TV shows. Her

LESLIE CARON: Fan mail from USA continues for movie star.

popularity continues. "I'm surprised that I still receive a lot of fan mail from the U.S. I feel more famous now than I was then," says the attractive daughter of a French father and U.S. mother.

Food and fashion are big with all ages here. Some who provide them last forever, some come and go.

Christian Lacroix, 36, is one of the currently up-and-coming haute couture designers. "I design for women who are not looking for the little black number that goes everywhere. For French women, fashion means freedom."

Andre Perrier, 39, is a former butcher who purveys pate in the village of Vielmont, sells it worldwide.

In a dig at the USA's fast food, he says, "You could call what we make 'slow food,' because it is meant to be eaten with great awareness and appreciation."

The winemakers of this world wine capital display awareness, appreciation, maybe a little arrogance.

The **Senard** family has been making wine on their 30-acre vineyard in Aloxe-Corton for 116 years. Now run by **Daniel**, 75, and son, **Philippe**, 39. Workers still stamp the grapes with their feet, standing on a board to push the skins down into the juice.

Says Daniel: "There's a deep link between a human being and wine. After all, Christ chose wine as the symbol of his blood."

That's Plain Talk from France.

DESECRATED SHRINE: A granite bust of Jim Morrison was stolen from his tombstone in Paris' largest cemetery, Pere Lachaise. Morrison, lead singer of the 1960s rock group The Doors, died of a heart attack in 1971 at age 27.

A FRENCH CHEF: Christian Guillut, 33, chief chef of the Ecole de Gastronomie Francaise Ritz-Escoffier, conducts cooking school for would-be chefs.

NIGHT LIGHTS: Paris takes on romantic reflections when the 7,000-ton Eiffel Tower casts a bright glow. Coin-slot telescopes on the observation decks offer 55 miles of visibility on clear days. Best view: about an hour before sunset.

PARIS AT DUSK: A graffiti-covered statue on Notre Dame Cathedral seems to be inviting a closer look at the Seine River as sunlight fades in the City of Light. The cathedral is on the Ile de la Cite, a small island in the Seine River.

SNIFF TEST: Edouard Flechier, 39, a *parfumeur* or perfume creator, uses a paper stick to sniff a perfume at Roure Perfume in Argenteuil. Flechier created Poison perfume by Christian Dior.

Jean Amic, 51
Perfume executive
Argenteuil

"A French label can be a plus, if it's on a good product. The French were put to sleep by the fact that a French label was enough. They overlooked the growing U.S. market supply."

Andrea Chouknoun, 25
Tea shop owner
Paris

"I'm out to make my tea shop famous, turn it into a legend like some others on the Left Bank. I want there to be famous painters and writers coming in and out all the time."

Robert Grattepanche, 38
Maitre d'
Paris

"Wine, eating and drinking are traditions in France. Serving food is something that you do because you love it. If not, you cannot be the best."

Guilano Mancini, 42
Sculptor
Villeneuve-Loubet

"The Riviera is a magic place. All you have to do is look at the flowers in bloom, the rolling green hills and you will know why Chagall, Picasso and Matisse loved to paint here."

Soldierly, stately salute to USA, Allies

On D-Day 1944, Francois Mitterrand was in Paris with the French Resistance. He had been wounded and captured by the Germans in June 1940. Escaped from prison on his third try in December 1941.

He remembers war, wants peace, knows the price:

▶ Approves of the Reagan-Gorbachev summits. "The necessary balance of forces between the major powers must be constantly maintained."

▶ But emphasizes peace is not dependent on just the two superpowers. "Europe is the key. We must use the might Europe will derive from its independence and unity — The European Community — in 1992. Many think the Community is just an economic union. It goes much further. It will enable Europe to speak out with a single voice on world affairs."

▶ Favors reducing "over-armament" but opposes "disarmament." Reaffirms his belief in "watchfulness, because the lust for power and the spirit of intolerance could rise again."

▶ Under Mitterrand, France has the world's sixth largest defense expenditures and an estimated 300 nuclear warheads. (USA: 13,873. U.S.S.R.: 11,044).

▶ Called the Battle of Normandy Museum, which he dedicated on D-Day 1988, "a memorial of peace and vigilance." Accent on vigilance. Keep your guard up.

During his hour tour of the museum, which is reached through a Dwight D. Eisenhower Esplanade, Mitterrand studied the French, U.S., British, German displays. The museum is patterned after the Jimmy Carter Center in Atlanta. Continuous video and voices bring scenes alive.

The president paused at a plaque honoring Etienne Achavanne, a French peasant who sabotaged the German Wermacht's telephone lines near Revin June 20, 1940. He was killed by the Nazis on July 4, 1940.

Mitterrand walked slowly through the U.S. room. Among the mementos were three of our old war-used vehicles. Jeep, No. 21916062. Tank, No. 6320. Armored car, No. 18475, still in full camouflage.

After the museum, Mitterrand strolled by and waved at the cheering crowd of 10,000. Mostly French, but 150 from the USA were led by Ambassador Joe M. Rodgers and his wife, Honey, of Nashville.

Among them was Sgt. Ted Liska, 70, Chicago. Landed with D Company, 12th Regiment, 44th Infantry Division on D-Day: "I still get tears in my eyes and a lump in my throat when I see the graves of my friends."

Mitterrand reminisced about the "immense undertaking" of the Normandy invasion and liberation by the Allies. "It was one of the longest, harshest, fiercest battles in history.

"The monument commemorates the suffering of war. It shows the rebirth of freedom. It will teach future gen-

Francois Mitterrand has been president of France since May 1981. While all of our other interviews routinely were in office settings with mahogany desks, couches, easy chairs, flags — all very proper, predictable, productive — in typical flair, the French had a different idea.

The message: "The president invites you to fly with him in his helicopter from Paris to Normandy and back for D-Day ceremonies. You can have a conversation with him aloft." We did. On June 6, D-Day 1988 — 44 years later. The presidential helicopter took 50 minutes from Paris to Caen in Normandy.

In the rear compartment: six assistants, a toilet, mini-refreshment-bar. (The president drank only Evian, French Alps natural springwater.)

In the forward compartment, three old soldiers and a younger one:

▶ *President Mitterrand, 71. Enlisted at age 27 and fought with the French infantry when World War II started.*

▶ *Foreign Minister Roland Dumas, 65. Twice imprisoned by the Nazis for French Resistance activities as a teen-ager.*

▶ *Al Neuharth, U.S. Ex-G.I., 64. Was a 20- to 21-year-old sergeant in the 86th Infantry Division in the German campaign.*

▶ *French Air Force General d'Aemes Aerienne Fluery, 54. Mitterrand's military chief of staff, a 10-year-old Brittany farmboy on D-Day.*

Mitterrand is every inch the old soldier. Stately. Stern. Only 5-foot-9 but has a bearing, even in civilian clothes.

erations about the tribulations of people born to live together."

When we landed in Paris, his car, a small Fiat, was waiting. So was Japan's Prime Minister Noboru Takeshita. He and Mitterrand were preparing for the then-upcoming Toronto summit.

Mitterrand: Smart, always stately. Takeshita: Smart, always smiling.

Each had seen his country suffer humiliating defeats in World War II. Now, one leads the newly self-confident biggest nation in Western Europe. The other heads the No. 1 power of the Pacific.

What a difference 44 years has made.

GREECE

Featured in USA TODAY: July 22

GREECE

AT A GLANCE

Greek Olympics

▶ The ancient Olympics were held in Olympia from 776 B.C. to 395 A.D. Women had separate games called Heraia.
▶ The first modern Olympic Games were held in Athens in 1896 with 13 nations participating.
▶ Athens has bid to host the 1996 Olympics to celebrate the games' centennial.

Population and land

▶ 10,015,000 people. 51,141 square miles; 88th largest country; 14% of U.S. size; about the size of Alabama.

Government

▶ Parliamentary republic. President, elected to five-year term by two-thirds majority in Parliament, appoints prime minister and can dissolve unicameral Parliament. Members of Parliament are directly elected to four-year terms.

The USA and Greece

▶ About 234,000 Greek-born people live in the USA.
▶ 13 U.S. towns are named Athens; Boston is nicknamed "The Athens of America" because of the number of colleges and universities there.
▶ U.S. Nike running shoes hold first place for running shoe sales in Greece. Nike was the winged goddess of victory in Greek mythology, thus the winged logo on Nike products.

Language

Greek

Major Products

Tobacco, cotton, wheat, raisins, petroleum, iron, steel, fruit, olives.

Yugoslavia

Thessaloniki
Pop. 410,000

Albania

Kastoria

Capital/ largest city

Athens
Pop. 885,000

Aegean Sea

Lesbos

Chios

N

0 — 100
miles

Turkey

Olympia

Greece

Piraeus
Pop. 200,000

Crete

Enlarged area

Cyprus

Their Dukakis dream: 'Flowers, not weeds'

It's the birthplace of democracy. European civilization started here over 2,000 years ago.

"Yes, democracy is a Greek word. But don't forget, so is dictatorship. Tyranny. And irony," says Athens **Mayor Miltiades Evert**, 49.

All Greece is a huge stage. Debate and drama play the street corners as they do the historic theaters.

Right now politics is center stage. The irony of the two stars of '88:

▶ **Prime Minister Andreas George Papandreou**, 69. Former U.S. citizen. U.S.-born wife. His personal and political styles have Greeks divided.

▶ **U.S. Democratic presidential candidate Michael Dukakis**, 54. His father, **Panos**, left the island of Lesbos in 1912 to seek fame and fortune in the New World. Now son Michael has Greeks united and excited.

They were excited once before about U.S. politics — when Greek-American **Spiro Agnew** was elected Nixon's vice president in 1968. And crushed when Agnew resigned in disgrace in 1973.

Political debaters here examine the pros and cons of every issue. **Tegogiannie Theodoros**, 52, retired civil servant, wants Dukakis to understand the difference between Greek dreams and nightmares. Says Theodoros:

"In every garden there are pretty flowers and there are weeds. Spiro Agnew was our weed. We hope **Michael Dukakis** will be our pretty flower."

SPIRO AGNEW: Prompts old nightmare for Greeks.

MICHAEL DUKAKIS: Represents a new dream to Greeks.

Actors, artists, writers are as vocally involved in politics as are street corner debaters. **Melina Mercouri**, 62, is Papandreou's Minister of Culture and Science. In the USA she's remembered as the soft-hearted hooker in the movie *Never on Sunday*. Got an Oscar nomination in 1960.

Now married to U.S. filmmaker **Jules Dassin**, Mercouri has been in parliament since 1977. A strong supporter of Papandreou, she says, "Greeks have something special . . . it's a sense of survival."

Vassilis Vassilikos, 54, author of the 1966 book *Z*, which became a political movie thriller, served as deputy director of the government-run television network from 1982-84. Now divides his time between Paris and Athens.

"The socialists in Greece are not radicals, they are social democrats. Socialism was a necessity in 1981 (when Papandreou became prime minister), but now we must turn toward the right," says Vassilikos.

MERCOURI: Actress takes on active political role.

VASSILIKOS: Author speaks out about politics.

While Greece is considered a crucial ally of the USA, official relations have been strained:

▶ **President Reagan** issued an advisory warning against travel to Greece after the 1985 and '86 hijacking and terrorist attacks here on TWA planes. U.S. tourists dropped from 400,000 a year to under 200,000.

▶ Papandreou countered by threatening to throw our military out when agreements on our bases here expire in 1989.

Despite the official coolness, most Greeks greet people from the USA warmly. Tourism is picking up and — barring new incidents — expected to be back to normal by 1989.

Its location as the crossroads of the Middle East, Asia and Europe makes this a troublemaker's target. But we saw nothing to make us uneasy.

Outside Athens, especially on the more than 1,400 Greek islands, the pace is peaceful. Hard-working peasants or villagers welcome tourists, talk warmly about their friends or relatives in the USA.

While some are concerned that the presence of tourists encourages terrorists, such as the July cruise ship attack near the island of Aegina, most welcome visitors.

Says **Eleni Chrysicou**, 85, of Athens:

"Some people want the tourists to stay home. But I say let them come, even more than before. They bring their money here after all. Then it becomes our money. That's fair."

That's Plain Talk from Greece.

FISHERMAN AND HIS CATCH: Stylianos Karayiannakis, 76, shows off a squid he caught while fishing near the village of Rethymnon in Crete. "I'm retired, but I still fish when I want to. The movement of the boat and the sea keeps me healthy," he says.

ISLAND INCOME: Erene Skoulas, 58, who sells hand-woven, embroidered goods, is one of several merchants plying the streets in the village of Anogia on Crete. Her income of $74 a month, she says, is only a supplement to the money her husband earns as a shepherd.

TOURIST TREAT: The Old Town Square of Navplion, lined with tiny shops and restaurants, attracts many tourists. It's a favorite port for cruise ships.

APPEALING ATHENS: Its sunny climate, natural beauty and historic ruins make Greece a magnet for vacationers. U.S citizens usually spend a few days enjoying Athens before leaving its crowded streets to board cruise ships headed for the islands.

PILLARS OF STRENGTH: Caryatids support a portion of the Erechtheion temple on the Acropolis in Athens. Built 421-405 B.C., the temple is the most important monument of the Ionic style.

Maria Kolomvou, 78
Farmer
Chios

"Almost every family here has relatives who left to go to the U.S. But go myself? I wouldn't dream of it. These fields would be fallow. There would be only tourists here."

Manos Hadzidakis, 62
Composer
Athens

"We can't say American culture is flooding Greece. I don't consider Michael Jackson American culture. Greeks don't know Dos Passos or Aaron Copland. But they know Madonna."

Eleni Lycaki, 35
Bakery store owner
Athens

"These days, most women in big cities work. Many people think women should be talking about rights at work, but in Greece the battlefront has now moved to the home."

Manolis Vardakas, 59
Fisherman
Chios

"I have to know the bottom of the sea like the top. And when the other boats follow me because I know where the fish are, I have to make a hard decision. That's the time I take a day off."

'Greece for Greeks,' says ex-U.S citizen

Despite the fact that Andreas Papandreou spent 20 years in the USA and became a model success story for Greek immigrants, he is now one of the USA's harshest critics. In office since 1981, he has:

▶ Pledged to throw the U.S. military out of Greece.

▶ Accused the U.S. government of manipulating the press to exaggerate the terrorist threat in Greece, thereby pressuring him to keep the U.S. bases.

The JetCapade news team interviewed people on the street in Greece who were concerned about the friction between the USA and Greece. Eva Siorvanes, 35, a lawyer, was one:

"Greeks are prejudiced against Americans because of what we read in the Greek newspapers. They say we don't need America or NATO. Papandreou is spreading this. But the young people are more open-minded."

After arriving in New York in 1939 as a political exile because of his leftist beliefs, Papandreou earned a Ph.D. in economics at Harvard University, became a U.S. citizen and served in the U.S. Navy in World War II.

In the next 15 years, he found elite status as an economist at the University of Minnesota, Northwestern University and the University of California at Berkeley.

But when he returned to Greece in 1959 at the urging of his father, a liberal premier, Papandreou organized a leftist political movement, dropped his U.S. citizenship and became a U.S. critic.

Friends and former colleagues were puzzled.

While Papandreou was at Harvard, he showed little interest in Greek politics, says former colleague Roy Macridis of Brandeis University. "Suddenly he became a socialist and very anti-American."

Papandreou describes his style of governing as walking a tightrope. His strategy regarding the U.S. bases is a good example, observers say. If he seems to give in to the USA, he loses support on the left. If he fails to come to terms, he endangers a crucial alliance in a precarious region.

Another example: He often has favored anti-U.S., pro-Soviet policies. That has kept him from being invited to Washington, and ex-Defense Secretary Caspar Weinberger blamed Papandreou's policies for terrorist flare-ups in Greece.

Part of Papandreou's determined, independent character no doubt was forged just before he left Greece the first time, when government agents interrogated him because of his leftist views and broke his jaw. The impact of that experience was reinforced in 1967 when he was kept in solitary confinement for eight months.

As for his anti-U.S. feelings, Papandreou says they were born when he returned to Greece in 1959 and saw

*Two words from the Greek language best describe **Andreas Papandreou's** political career — paradox and, most recently, scandal. Prime Minister Papandreou, 69, married with four children, openly cavorted with Dimitra Liani, 33, former Olympic Airways flight attendant who was also married.*

The Papandreou-Liani liaison apparently would not have created such a stir in Greek political circles had it not been for one development: Papandreou canceled plans in August 1987 to attend ceremonies marking the anniversary of an earthquake in Kalamata because of his "workload." But later it was reported that he actually was on an Aegean cruise with his girlfriend Liani. Pictures were published of the two together.

The conservative daily Kathimerini charged that Papandreou had "abandoned his wife after 36 years and abandoned earthquake-stricken Kalamata for the sake of a cruise and private pleasure."

The story broke in the fall of 1987. As of July 1988, Papandreou's Panhellenic Socialist Movement government was still secure. If anything, his political successes in smoothing Greece's historic differences with Turkey had taken the limelight.

The paradox in Papandreou's political career is less titillating but no less headline-grabbing.

(Papandreou refused to meet with the JetCapade news team.)

the dominance of the USA. Not surprisingly, one of his favorite campaign slogans is:

"Greece for Greeks!"

HONG KONG

SINGAPORE

Featured in USA TODAY: May 13

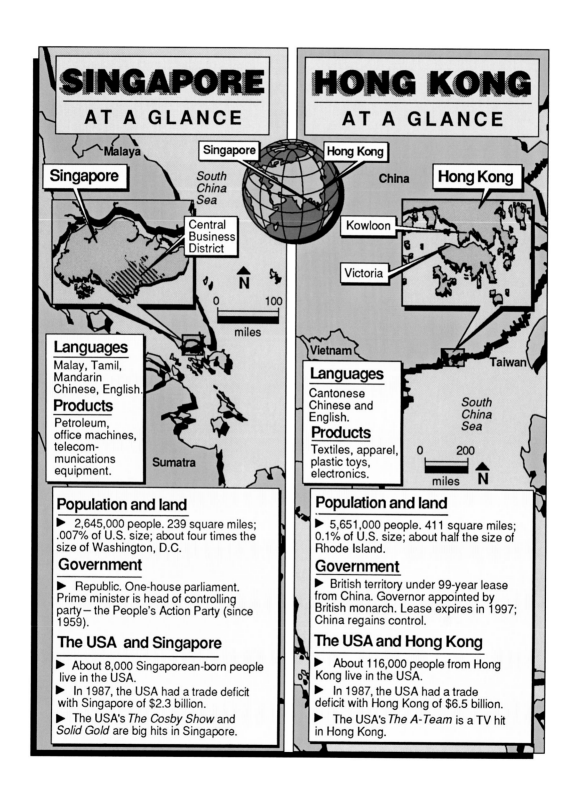

SINGAPORE
AT A GLANCE

Malaya

Singapore

Singapore

South China Sea

Central Business District

N

0 — 100

miles

Languages
Malay, Tamil, Mandarin Chinese, English.

Products
Petroleum, office machines, telecommunications equipment.

Sumatra

Population and land
▶ 2,645,000 people. 239 square miles; .007% of U.S. size; about four times the size of Washington, D.C.

Government
▶ Republic. One-house parliament. Prime minister is head of controlling party — the People's Action Party (since 1959).

The USA and Singapore
▶ About 8,000 Singaporean-born people live in the USA.
▶ In 1987, the USA had a trade deficit with Singapore of $2.3 billion.
▶ The USA's *The Cosby Show* and *Solid Gold* are big hits in Singapore.

HONG KONG
AT A GLANCE

Hong Kong

China

Hong Kong

Kowloon

Victoria

Vietnam

Taiwan

South China Sea

0 — 200

miles

N

Languages
Cantonese Chinese and English.

Products
Textiles, apparel, plastic toys, electronics.

Population and land
▶ 5,651,000 people. 411 square miles; 0.1% of U.S. size; about half the size of Rhode Island.

Government
▶ British territory under 99-year lease from China. Governor appointed by British monarch. Lease expires in 1997; China regains control.

The USA and Hong Kong
▶ About 116,000 people from Hong Kong live in the USA.
▶ In 1987, the USA had a trade deficit with Hong Kong of $6.5 billion.
▶ The USA's *The A-Team* is a TV hit in Hong Kong.

Two Asian mighty mites: Pragmatic, prosperous

They have only a few million people. Very little land. Virtually no natural resources. Yet they are two of the richest business and banking centers in the world.

▶ **HONG KONG.** British colony since 1841. 5.7 million people, 99% Chinese or Asian. Control reverts to Communist China in 1997.

▶ **SINGAPORE.** Independent from British rule since 1965. Trade titan of the Malaysian Peninsula. Only 2.6 million people.

Pragmatism and pursuit of profit prevail in both places. High per capita income, especially for this part of the world. In U.S. dollars: Singapore: $7,410. Hong Kong: $6,720. By comparison, Philippines: $570. South Korea: $2,370. China: $300.

SINGAPORE: MODERN MIRACLE

It was not always thus. **Prime Minister Lee Kuan Yew**, 64, took office when Singapore gained independence. Re-elected six times. Most credit him with Singapore's surge.

"We were almost a hopeless case in the '60s. This was a dirty, filthy place going down the drain. But I said we will 'clean and green' Singapore. It worked because we have a hard-working people. Very few sit under a coconut tree playing tiddlywinks."

Newcomers agree. **Alan Steelman**, 45, former U.S. congressman from Dallas, came in 1984 to set up Asian headquarters for Florida's Alexander Proudfoot consulting firm.

CLEAN, GREEN: Or else $1,000 fine.

STEELMAN: System works.

CHOO: Careers before kids.

"Things work here. The government means what it says. They are strict, but you don't have an oppressed feeling," says Steelman. One of 6,700 from the USA living here, he shrugs off complaints about censorship from U.S. publications such as *The Asian Wall Street Journal* and *Time* magazine. "Anything we give up is more than made up for by what we gain."

Higher education for women and strong birth control policies were pushed by the government in the 1970s. Lee thinks they may have gone too far too fast and now urges larger families.

Karen Choo, 28, sales supervisor for five China Silk House stores, is a product of that policy. She's married but childless by choice.

"My career comes first. If you work you have more freedom and more friends. Our living standard is high and money is important."

Californians here call Singapore the Silicon Valley of Asia. But its cleanliness is more like Salt Lake City, its trees and greenery like the Duke University campus in Durham, N.C.

HONG KONG: CONTINUITY OR CHANGE?

Hong Kong, where money also means much, is more like Manhattan, with a little of Hollywood thrown in.

The upcoming change of control from Britain to China dominates all talk. Many here now fled China or Vietnam to escape communism.

Says Britain's **Governor David Wilson**: "The agreement gives assurance of the continuity of the way of life ... the economic, capitalistic and legal systems."

Ji Shaoxiang, foreign affairs director of China's Xinhua News Agency, who is in Hong Kong as one of the ranking transition directors, says: "For the average person, only the flag at the governor's office will change."

Not all "average persons" agree.

Nancy Hsu-Anderson, 41, imports and sells fortune cookies: "Things will change. All but two of my best friends have left for Canada or the U.S. Younger, middle-class professionals don't want to stay here and take a chance."

Stephen K.C. Cheong, 47, managing director of Lee Wah Weaving factory, disagrees:

HSU-ANDERSON: Concerned as friends leave for West.

CHEONG: China will stoke economic engine.

"Hong Kong will continue to be a thriving place and China will become the economic engine of the world by sheer populace."

That's Plain Talk from Singapore and Hong Kong.

FINANCIAL CROSSROADS: International trade thrives in Hong Kong's Kowloon Shopping District. Both Hong Kong and Singapore are known as hubs of activity for businesses and financial institutions.

Ahmad Aljunied, 33
Store manager
Singapore

"I travel a lot, and I find Singapore easier to do business in because it's flexible. It's a totally free market. We can import what we like and export what we like."

Sam C. Seet, 50
Taxi driver
Singapore

"Fifty years ago, this place was a jungle. I've seen this place change to an international city. The villages are gone. They were replaced by skyscrapers, international trade and jobs."

Rohini Davis, 27
Marketing director
Hong Kong

"I love Hong Kong. It's one of the world's best cities to do business in. There's a wonderful work ethic here, a very can-do mentality."

Ricky Liu, 39
Jade salesman
Hong Kong

"Here in Hong Kong, doing business is very important. If Hong Kong goes down, China goes down too. China would also lose money. China will never let that happen."

CROWDED CRUISING: Junks and sampans make their way through the crowded port of Aberdeen — Hong Kong's largest fishing community. The port shelters Hong Kong from typhoons and hosts ships that harvest a bounty of eel and sardines.

SMALL-FRY FISHERMAN: While the family steers the boat into a crowded dock at Aberdeen, a child waits atop the boat where laundry is drying.

NIGHT LIGHT: The bright neon signs of the Kowloon Shopping District form a rainbow of color reflections on wet pavement.

SERVIN' SLINGS: Ngiam Fook Heng, 56, head bartender at Raffles Hotel, serves a tray of Singapore Slings. He sells about 700 of them daily at $4.50 each. The famous fruity concoction was invented here by his uncle Ngiam Tong Boon in 1920.

VEGETABLE VENDOR: Ahpoh Hu, 80, takes a break from selling to smoke a hand-rolled cigarette. She and son Ahwah Hu, 47, run a stand in Chinatown on Kangaroo Street.

SINGAPORE SHORES: This view from a cable car to Mount Faber shows the city side of the port of Singapore. Beyond the highrise buildings is one of the busiest shipping ports in the world.

'We serve as China's gateway to the world'

On Hong Kong's ties to China:

"People are re-establishing contacts with the mainland that have been broken for years. Hong Kong is the largest external investor in the mainland of China. So, an economic nexus is being created between Hong Kong and the mainland."

On emigration from Hong Kong:

"There has been an increase in the percentage of people going from the middle management class — people who are looking for some insurance policy for the future. A significant number of those people get whatever they need, a green card or other passport, and then come back. It is a problem but not a crisis."

On Hong Kong's importance to China:

"It fulfills a role as a gateway between China and the rest of the world, as a source of knowledge on Western managerial skill, technological skill and their source of foreign exchange."

On Hong Kong's reaction to internal political disputes in China:

"If there were ever a return to political confusion in Peking, then it would worry people in Hong Kong. (But) the way in which politics are developing there is encouraging to people in Hong Kong."

Gov. David Wilson, 53, heads the British territorial government in Hong Kong that ends with the transition to Chinese rule in 1997.

On Hong Kong's strength of character:

"People in Hong Kong are very realistic. It is why Hong Kong has been able to survive and prosper — that realism, that practicality."

On the economy's reaction to the transition:

"It is booming in terms of investments, increase in exports, and in terms of American imports into Hong Kong. Per head of population, we buy nearly four times as much as Japan does per capita — over four times as much as the European Economic Community does."

'People will have same lifestyles after 1997'

On China's future role in Hong Kong:

"The democrats here worry the central government may interfere. This is not true. China will not be foolish. If we make sweeping changes, this is no good. If Hong Kong people don't have confidence, how could it work? We have promised that they will have as many rights and democracy as they have now."

On how Hong Kong will change after 1997:

"The average person won't see any big changes. Only the flag will change at the governor's office. There will be some other changes, though. Foreign affairs will be handled by the Chinese government. Defense will be handled by the People's Liberation Army. (But) people will keep their existing lifestyles. Local law will remain the same. The central government will not levy any taxes here, and most civil servants will stay. The one big question is the Executive Council of Hong Kong. Will that change? We don't know. That is being discussed."

On people leaving Hong Kong:

"Lots of people are leaving Hong Kong. Especially the middle class, the educated people, like the technicians, the teachers. But the emigration is a longtime phenomenon. It started before any (transition) agreement was discussed. The number has increased. When the agreement was published in 1984, it was warmly received.

Ji Shaoxiang, 49, foreign affairs director of China's Xinhua News Agency, represents Beijing in Hong Kong during the transition to Chinese rule. Ji says the Hong Kong bureau is the "peacemaker" between the two governments.

Later, with the dispute in power in China, there was lots of worry. These worries aren't justified. The two governments will come to an agreement. The new leadership will implement the changes truthfully."

On why China is so interested in securing Hong Kong:

"Hong Kong's strongest asset is its geographic location. Hong Kong will play the role as a bridge to the outside world."

Media: 'Don't judge us by your standards'

On what Singapore represents:

"What I'd like to have thought of Singapore is that there is hope in the world. There is no reason for poverty, misery, anger, frustration, quarrels and war. There is enough in this world to feed, clothe and satisfy everybody if we are prepared to make adjustments for each other, and if conditions are such that you have capital coming across to help underdeveloped people to borrow not just the machines, but the expertise, the personnel — and maybe also get access to markets."

On the key to Singapore's success:

"We maximized our assets. We had a hard-working population because we are immigrants or their descendants. The desire to achieve is higher than average."

On the impact of Western influences:

"Universal education for boys and girls and equal job opportunities had unexpected repercussions. We did not understand; we can put new knowledge into people, new views of life, but their patterns of behavior, their values are very deeply entrenched. It's been passed on from mother's milk. Maybe the wife is of strong personality and advises the husband what to do, but he must be seen as the master. As a result of some women going to the university and into jobs, men don't marry them. They marry down. Men have left the highly educated women stranded."

On his advice to the USA's media:

"This is a plea. Don't believe that what has worked in America must work elsewhere. Yes, we are all human beings, but we are different kinds of human beings, different histories, different mind-sets, different ambitions, different ideas of what makes for fulfilling lives. The more you try to judge others by your standard, the more you put their backs up because you show total disregard for their own circumstances."

On Singapore's economy:

"We expect to slow down in the second half of 1988 from our 11% first-quarter gain. A lot depends on what happens to the economy in the USA and Japan because they are two major markets. If growth is fast, the financial markets will get nervous. Interest rates will be pushed up. We take a conservative view."

On competition with Hong Kong:

"There's a popular notion that what Hong Kong loses, we gain. That is a fallacy. This is not a zero-sum game. We never believed that. The more they grow the more we have a player in Southeast China to play with. We buy from them. They buy from us. They do certain things which they can do better than us and we do certain things better than they can. 1997 has already acted on their economy. People are already making arrange-

Prime Minister Lee Kuan Yew, 64, has been in office since self-rule began 29 years ago. He played a key role as Singapore made the transition from self-rule to full independence from Great Britain in 1965. Lee, who plans to retire in 1989, is known as a powerful leader. He has imposed his sense of propriety with campaigns to ban smoking and long hair, break dancing and video games. He also has a high profile in the international arena. For example, the U.S. government has expressed "concern" about restrictions on newspaper distribution in Singapore and about reports of detention without trial. Lee is extremely articulate. He pauses deliberately, contemplates, then speaks, then contemplates some more. He was interviewed by the JetCapade news team at his private residence, which is set off in greenery.

ments just in case things are not as good as they are made out. We would far rather have them strive and prosper because that means there is more for us."

On his concerns about Singapore's neighbor, the Philippines:

"Something must be done before Mrs. Aquino's term of office ends. She's something like a Joan of Arc, above the level of an ordinary politician. If you don't spend $1 now on a mini-Marshall Plan, you will spend $10 with a successor."

INDIA

Featured in USA TODAY: April 29

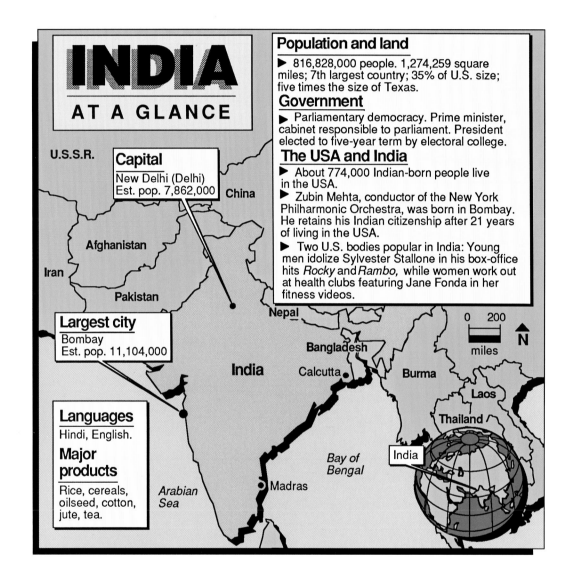

INDIA
AT A GLANCE

Population and land
▶ 816,828,000 people. 1,274,259 square miles; 7th largest country; 35% of U.S. size; five times the size of Texas.

Government
▶ Parliamentary democracy. Prime minister, cabinet responsible to parliament. President elected to five-year term by electoral college.

The USA and India
▶ About 774,000 Indian-born people live in the USA.

▶ Zubin Mehta, conductor of the New York Philharmonic Orchestra, was born in Bombay. He retains his Indian citizenship after 21 years of living in the USA.

▶ Two U.S. bodies popular in India: Young men idolize Sylvester Stallone in his box-office hits *Rocky* and *Rambo,* while women work out at health clubs featuring Jane Fonda in her fitness videos.

U.S.S.R.

Capital
New Delhi (Delhi)
Est. pop. 7,862,000

China

Afghanistan

Iran

Pakistan

Largest city
Bombay
Est. pop. 11,104,000

Nepal

Bangladesh

India

Calcutta

Burma

Laos

Thailand

India

Languages
Hindi, English.

Major products
Rice, cereals, oilseed, cotton, jute, tea.

Arabian Sea

Madras

Bay of Bengal

0   200
miles
N

Poverty with dignity; continuity amid change

Three times the population of the USA. Nearly twice that of all of Africa. Every shade of race. Five major religions.

Progressive young democracy. Tradition-bound old bureaucracy. The most poverty-stricken place on earth. India, motherland of mystique.

▶ Freedoms abound. **Mahatma Gandhi**, father of the country, spawned them with his non-violent protests of the '30s and '40s, which led to independence from Britain in 1947. The constitution guarantees them. Politicians and the press practice them vociferously.

▶ World's fourth largest military force, behind U.S.S.R., China, USA. Over 1 million under arms. **Prime Minister Rajiv Gandhi** maintains strong ties with the USA, a warm friendship with the U.S.S.R.

▶ One-third of the world's poor subsist here. 37% of the people, nearly 300 million, live below the poverty level. Per capita income last year $239. Egypt $600. Saudi Arabia $8,000. USA: $14,461.

While 80% of the population is in the villages, the cities are where the mix of fascination and frustration comes together. Cows and goats vie for the right-of-way with vehicles of all sizes and shapes. Looks like a zoo, but animals and people survive. Some people thrive.

STREET SMARTS: Cows challenge cars, buses, bikes.

Omparkash Yadav, 32, was a poor farm boy with only a fifth-grade education when he came to the capital city of New Delhi (pop. est. 7,862,000) in 1972. Washed taxis for half a rupee (3½ cents). Now he owns three cabs, makes $230 a month.

"Soon we'll move into a four-room flat. I have a tutor for my children. They will get a very good education," says this entrepreneur.

But most Indians don't make out as well. **D.F. Channa**, 76, served 44 years in the army and air force. His pension is $31.50 a month.

Channa, his wife, **Amina**, 53, and daughters **Rosalina**, 20, and **Rebecca**, 12, live in a small wood and mud hut.

No water. No toilet.

But, like many villagers, theirs is a poverty with dignity. Clothes are clean and colorful. Manners majestic.

"A man must be tough. We do what we can. We don't cry about what we can't do. If you are happy, the world is happy," philosophizes Channa.

India's conflict between continuity and change is most openly apparent in the attitude of young and old on the matter of marriages. Arranged weddings are a big business. In the *Sunday Times* of India, nearly two pages of classified ads were headed "Grooms Wanted" and "Brides Wanted."

POOR WITH DIGNITY: The Channa family in a wood and mud hut.

Dowries were outlawed in 1962, but fathers of prospective brides are expected to deliver purity, pageantry and pay the groom's family handsomely.

Anil and **Manju Hinduja** were married amid pomp and pageantry in Bombay (pop. est. 11,104,000) last month. 500 attended the reception. Anil, a financial controller at International Hospital, emphasizes theirs was "a love match. We fell in love, then our families got together on the financial arrangements."

Two young law students in New Delhi, **Suresh Kait**, 25, and **Saroj Bala**, 24, are engaged. But their parents won't stage the wedding until 1990. In the meantime, romance is taboo. But the young lovers find a way.

Says Saroj, striking in her red costume: "Today I said I was going to see

AN 'ARRANGED' BRIDE: Manju, bejeweled beauty.

a friend who had an accident. Instead I came here to the park to meet Suresh. We can talk and kiss here. It's exciting to do it this way."

That's Plain Talk from India.

MARKET BOUND: An Indian girl in New Delhi carries her wares in a large basket.

MAJESTIC MEMORIAL: The Taj Mahal was built as a tribute by Emperor Shah Jahan to his wife, Arjumand, better known as Mumtaz Mahal, "ornament of the palace." The famous mausoleum at Agra is one of the most photographed structures in the world.

BOMBAY JAM: A hectic evening rush hour gets into full swing as thousands of workers start their way home. This crowd is heading for Churchgate Train Station.

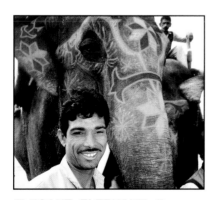

ELEGANT ELEPHANT: Ramprasad leads Chanchan the elephant down a New Delhi street. The decorated animals are rented for weddings and other occasions.

SEA OF COLOR: Bhupindeo Sarne, 19, turns dyed, orange thread to help it dry. Sarne works at the government's Weavers Service Center in New Delhi.

FOCUS ON FAMILY: Children of the Chanayakapuri Colony in New Delhi gather around Pushpa, 40, holding her 18-month-old daughter, Meera.

Shrichand Yadav, 60
Farmer
Haryana

"Much is changing. Now everything is coming in modern. We used to use the bull. We used to use a bucket and chain for water. Now roads, buses and trains are coming in. It's better."

Suman Karayi, 24
Boutique manager
New Delhi

"Our tradition dictates that unmarried women are much more protected than in other countries. (But) we have freedom when we want it and protection when we need it."

A.H. Tapia, 60
Chicken farmer
Bombay

"To get a job in India is easy. To get a house is very different. We have a saying here about that: 'You can get bread to eat, but you can't get a house to eat it in.'"

Krishna Kapoor, 50
Beauty salon manager
New Delhi

"Our children used to say that our country was backward. Things are changing, even in those areas like computers. We are going forward very fast. But we have kept the best of our traditions."

'We're non-aligned to end power blocs'

On India's image in the USA:

"We'd like Americans to see India as a popular democracy. That really means that we're both working for similar values. If you look at our constitution and your Constitution, there are a lot of similarities. . . . We would like India to be seen as a country that gives the most freedom to its people, comparable to any country, especially to the press."

On India's often noisy parliament:

"Oh, every now and then they let off a lot of steam, but that is part of democracy. When I first came to parliament, it used to embarrass me terribly when they started doing those rowdy things. Especially every now and then when we would have a delegation visiting parliament and there would be chaos going on in the house. I would sheepishly make excuses to the delegation and they said, 'No, this is what shows that you have a real democracy. If it's too calm or too controlled it means that people are not really free to speak their mind.'"

On relations with the USA:

"When I went to the U.S. in 1985 and I spoke with President Reagan, we decided we must build a foundation on trust. We've been doing that. In the past three years, we've had very substantial high-tech exchanges with the U.S. We are very worried about U.S. arms aid to Pakistan. What it means is that we have to spend a lot of our money on defense, which is totally contrary to our economic development. We've been told by the U.S. that Pakistan has not been able to enrich uranium beyond 3%. I don't want to reveal my source, but we have very hard information that they have enriched uranium capable of building a nuclear weapon."

On defining India's non-alignment policy:

"We feel the world needs to break down the artificial barriers it has built up. Capitalism versus communism. North versus south. If the world is to progress, then these barriers must be removed. The concept of power blocs must also end. The only way to end power blocs is to be non-aligned."

On India's economic and social development:

"What we're looking for are two things: Economic development, because that is a must. A lot has to be done to bring the poor people up. The second is: We don't want development if it means losing our spirituality, the sense of moral values. The caste problem is almost gone. It was taken care of in the constitution, but it takes time for society to change. When you look at a country like India with 800 million people, and look at the percentage below the poverty line, which is about 37%, one sees a country which is very poor. But if you

The latest leader of India to bear the magical Gandhi name is 43-year-old **Rajiv Gandhi**, prime minister since 1984. In that year, his mother, Indira, also prime minister, was assassinated by her own guards. Rajiv is no relation to the famous Mahatma Gandhi, the father of modern India, but his grandfather, Jawaharlal Nehru, was a close collaborator of the Mahatma's. Later, Nehru became India's first prime minister upon its independence from Great Britain in 1947. Gandhi met with the Jet-Capade news team in his private New Delhi home, surrounded by gardens and guards.

translate the percentage into numbers, then we have over 100 million people who are part of the middle class."

On helping India's poverty-stricken:

"I've targeted the end of the century for ending poverty. We feel India is ready now to move ahead rapidly. We have good technological manpower. We are good in many areas of science and technology. Our people are good at getting things done. But initiative is not there. If we can break out of this, and we can, I don't see any problems."

On India's space program:

"Ours is a modest program with meager financing. It's a peaceful program. We have a number of things we do on our own. For example, the IRS (satellite) is a completely Indian satellite. All this work used to be done by the government. Now we're contracting out to private industry."

On internal problems, including violence in the Punjab region:

"I think the internal situation is exaggerated, especially outside India, because people don't know India. We have our problems, but we also have our strengths. In Punjab, we've had this terrorist activity going on now for six or seven years. The terrorists want to make a division between Hindus, Muslims and Sikhs, the three major communities. The fact is that the people of Punjab are just not splitting."

IRELAND

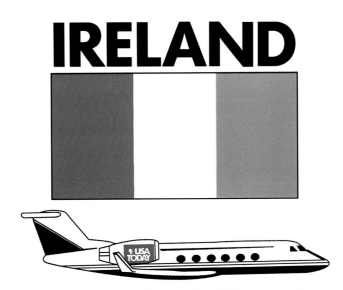

Featured in USA TODAY: Aug. 19

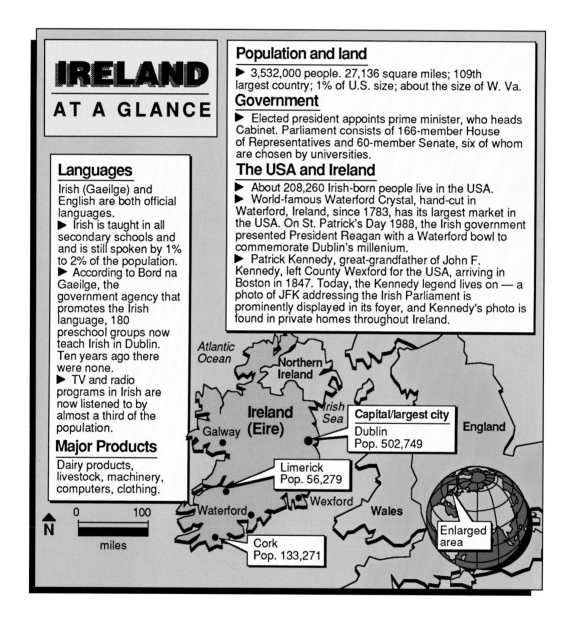

IRELAND
AT A GLANCE

Languages
Irish (Gaeilge) and English are both official languages.
▶ Irish is taught in all secondary schools and and is still spoken by 1% to 2% of the population.
▶ According to Bord na Gaeilge, the government agency that promotes the Irish language, 180 preschool groups now teach Irish in Dublin. Ten years ago there were none.
▶ TV and radio programs in Irish are now listened to by almost a third of the population.

Major Products
Dairy products, livestock, machinery, computers, clothing.

Population and land
▶ 3,532,000 people. 27,136 square miles; 109th largest country; 1% of U.S. size; about the size of W. Va.

Government
▶ Elected president appoints prime minister, who heads Cabinet. Parliament consists of 166-member House of Representatives and 60-member Senate, six of whom are chosen by universities.

The USA and Ireland
▶ About 208,260 Irish-born people live in the USA.
▶ World-famous Waterford Crystal, hand-cut in Waterford, Ireland, since 1783, has its largest market in the USA. On St. Patrick's Day 1988, the Irish government presented President Reagan with a Waterford bowl to commemorate Dublin's millenium.
▶ Patrick Kennedy, great-grandfather of John F. Kennedy, left County Wexford for the USA, arriving in Boston in 1847. Today, the Kennedy legend lives on — a photo of JFK addressing the Irish Parliament is prominently displayed in its foyer, and Kennedy's photo is found in private homes throughout Ireland.

Atlantic Ocean

Northern Ireland

Ireland (Eire)

Irish Sea

Galway

Capital/largest city
Dublin
Pop. 502,749

England

Limerick
Pop. 56,279

Waterford

Wexford

Wales

Cork
Pop. 133,271

Enlarged area

0   100
N
miles

Their Irish is up and that's no blarney

More Irish eyes are smiling and this Emerald Isle is looking greener again.

Austerity has replaced the borrow-and-spend approach of the early '80s that put the Hibernians deeply in hock. And most Irish seem happy about the belt-tightening.

The new pragmatism is aimed at lessening these lingering problems that have plagued the Irish for most of this decade:

▶ $38 billion national debt, highest proportionally in Western Europe.

▶ High income taxes. 58% for single persons earning $14,000 per year, for couples making more than $29,200. (U.S. top rate is 28% and kicks in at $17,850 for singles, $29,750 for couples.)

▶ High unemployment, 19%. (USA: 5.4%.)

Because unemployment remains the biggest problem, many young people want out.

SHANNON: No way to make it.

KEOGH: Green Card the goal.

"There is no way for a guy or girl to make enough money to settle down here. They have to leave the country to make a decent living," says **Pauline Shannon**, 22, clerk-typist.

"All people talk about here is the Green Card, the paper that allows them to stay and work in America," adds **Ann Keogh**, 58, homemaker.

But there are hopeful signs and most Irish think that their luck is changing:

▶ Inflation is down to an annual rate of 1.8%, from 20% just seven years ago. (USA: 4.2%.)

▶ Government spending was cut 3% in 1987, will be down another 4.5% in 1988.

In a country famous for soothing brogue and braggadocious blarney, a single sports event this summer did more than anything else to get the Irish pride back up.

Ireland's soccer team scored an astounding 1-0 win over England in the European Soccer Championship matches — first major victory ever over England.

That made this the No. 1 hit on Ireland's charts:
We're the Boys in Green,
the best you've ever seen . . .

Pub celebrations continue. Some compare it to winning their independence all over again, something that happened 66 years ago after a bloody struggle and hundreds of years of British rule.

"The Brits are always slugging the Irish," says **Tom McGuire**, 25, a motorcycle courier. "It's great to be Irish after our lads beat those blokes."

For many of the Irish, there's still an unsettled matter with the Brits: Northern Ireland. It stayed British when the rest of Ireland gained independence in 1922. Some still dream of reunification. Others, like **Victor Griffin**, 64, dean of St. Patrick's Cathedral in Dublin, say, "It won't be solved, not in our lifetime."

A gift of gab is considered part of the Irish heritage. One who makes a living promoting that is **"Big John" Dineen**, 39, who helps and holds some of the 150,000 visitors a year as they stop to kiss the "Blarney stone" at Blarney Castle in County Cork.

The legendary stone is inlaid in the castle 83 feet above the ground. To kiss it, visitors are held upside down by Dineen.

"All Irishmen have the gift of gab. Blarney is talk meant to deceive but not offend. They kiss the stone to make sure they don't lose the gift," says Big John.

During this political season in the USA, the Irish in Dublin talk much about

BLARNEY STONE: Big John with Mickey O'Brien of Ohio.

the many successful Irish politicians in the USA. Among them:

▶ **President Ronald Reagan.**

▶ The late **President John F. Kennedy**, for whom a 480-acre park has been dedicated in New Ross.

Maurice Manning, 45, professor of politics at the University College of Dublin, explains it:

"The Irish who went to the States took along a very good knowledge of how the political machine works. They tend to have a peculiar imagination, a facility with words, a capacity to inspire that the colder WASPish Anglo-Saxons tend not to have."

That's Plain Talk from Ireland.

READY TO RUN: Horses are led around the track in preparation for a race at Naas Race Track outside Dublin. A haven for horse lovers, the Emerald Isle is dotted with 78 racecourses.

STABLE WORK: Joe Ryle, 58, hangs up the harnesses used by the horses he cares for at Slatterly Travel Agency in Tralee. The horses are rented out for caravans.

BLARNEY CASTLE HOUSE: Two hundred yards from Blarney Castle, home of the famous Blarney "kissing" stone, are the Blarney Castle House and formal gardens. Sir Colthurst owns the castle and the recently restored mansion near Cork.

CARAVAN VACATION: Roy Hunt, 52, and his wife, Pat, 51, of Chester, England, tour the Dingle Peninsula near Tralee in a caravan. The horse-drawn wagons usually travel about four hours each day.

KENNEDY ROOTS: Visitors can tour the ancestral Kennedy home at the small dairy farm owned by Jim and Patrick Grennings in County Wexford in southeastern Ireland. Patrick Kennedy, great-grandfather of President John F. Kennedy, was born there in 1822 or 1823 (Sources differ on the year).

Dorothy Tubridy, 58
Corporate executive
Dublin

"We are famous for writers, poets, musicians and good horses. But most of all, we're famous for our people — people who go all over the world and make good contributions to every country."

Pat Busher, 34
Cab driver
Wexford

"St. Patrick's Day is something we celebrate, but I don't think it's such a big deal. Some people wear a shamrock and get drunk. But we don't go around wearing something green."

Kathleen Flanagan, 22
Clerk-typist
Dublin

"Pubs here are the center of the social scene. People of all ages start their evenings there. When you say you're going out, you're usually headed for a pub."

Bairbre Fhloinn, 32
Archivist
Dublin

"Leprechauns and fairies are part of Irish folklore. I've encountered belief in fairies among older people. They say that fairies died out because no one believed in them anymore."

'We have emotional ties to the USA'

On U.S.-Irish relations:

Haughey: "Our two countries share a deep commitment and respect for the democractic way of life. Our constitution, like yours, enshrines those basic concepts of freedom and justice."

Lenihan: "We have strong emotional ties. We do have times when there is a lack of understanding, such as immigration quotas. I'm visiting Washington next month (September 1988) to seek a guarantee on quotas. We're asking for 14,000 to 15,000 visas for a country whose people can offer skills to the U.S. We're concerned that Irish people are going there illegally." (Throughout the 1980s, Ireland has tried to get U.S. immigration rules eased to permit more people from Ireland to enter or stay legally.)

Briscoe: "You would find it very difficult to find an Irish person who doesn't have a relation in the U.S. That's why we're anxious for immigration laws to be eased."

On the economy:

Haughey: "When my government was elected last year (1987), we accepted that the revitalization of the Irish economy was our first priority. We have achieved a great deal in the last 18 months. We agreed on a program for national recovery with employers, trade unions and farmers. We have restored business confidence and created the right economic environment for growth."

Briscoe: "Our future is bright. We're going to attract more multinationals. There's a new air of confidence."

On the Irish people:

Lenihan: "We're good at seeing things in perspective. Our mocking sense of humor gets us in and out of any situation."

Briscoe: "The friendliness and warmth of the Irish is known throughout the world. It's genuine."

On Northern Ireland:

Lenihan: "I do believe reunification is possible, but I have no timetable. Our firm policy is to move toward a reunification of minds, which will lead to political reunification."

Briscoe: "Britain created the problem and only Britain can solve it, by telling the unionists that they have to sit down with their counterparts and discuss what kind of Ireland they want."

On keeping skilled, educated, young people in Ireland:

Lenihan: "We have very good education and culture here. What's needed is to match that with a substantial increase in investment."

Briscoe: "We can and will turn that around by providing jobs. The Irish have always been an immigrating

Prime Minister Charles J. Haughey

Deputy Prime Minister Brian Lenihan

Lord Mayor of Dublin Ben Briscoe

Prime Minister Charles J. Haughey's nickname — "The Great Survivor" — could easily apply to all of Ireland. Despite the Republic of Ireland's recent economic problems and the seemingly endless violence linked to predominantly Protestant, British-ruled Northern Ireland, the Irish survive. In fact, they're beginning to thrive. In 1987, when Haughey, 63, ran for this third term, his slogan was, "There must be a better way" to salvage Ireland's economy. He has since announced the biggest cuts in government spending in 30 years. That, and no doubt the luck of the Irish, seem to be turning things around. Since 1987, national income has grown, interest rates have dropped and inflation has slowed. Some people are even calling Ireland the "Silicon Valley" of Europe. Haughey, Deputy Prime Minister Brian Lenihan, 57, and Lord Mayor of Dublin Ben Briscoe, 54, shared their views of the Emerald Isle with the JetCapade news team.

people. Even if we had 100% employment, people like to visit elsewhere for a couple of years."

On the Irish reputation for drinking:

Lenihan: "The Irish don't drink any more than other people, but the ability to get along with people, well, that is usually done in a pub. The Irish like to stop and have a drink. We have time for people, more so than any other race."

ISRAEL

Featured in USA TODAY: March 7, 25

ISRAEL
AT A GLANCE

Mediterranean Sea

Lebanon

Syria

**Capital/
largest city**
Jerusalem
Pop. 428,668

West Bank

Tel-Aviv
Ariel

Bethlehem

Gaza Strip

Dead
Sea

Most countries
have their
embassies here.

Saudi
Arabia

N

Languages
Hebrew, Arabic,
English.
**Major
products**
Citrus fruit, wheat,
diamonds, grains,
food processing,
textiles, electronics,
vegetables.

Israel

Jordan

Egypt

0   miles   100

Enlarged
area

Population and land
▶ 4,085,000 people. 8,031 square miles;
131st largest country; 0.2% of U.S. size;
slightly smaller than New Hampshire.
Government
▶ Republic with parliamentary government based on a multiparty system. No
elections in occupied territories: West
Bank and Gaza Strip.
The USA and Israel
▶ About 91,000 Israeli/Palestinian-born
people live in the USA.
▶ Formal U.S. diplomatic recognition of
Jerusalem as Israel's capital is subject
to future negotiations. Two out of 39
countries have embassies in Jerusalem.
▶ Israel receives the most U.S. foreign
aid — $3 billion in 1988.

How to settle score in 'world's stress lab'

Peace on Earth. Good will toward men.

There isn't much of either in this age-old Holy Land as young Israel observes the 40th anniversary of its independence.

For you to understand the turmoil in the Mideast today, this 40-year perspective is essential:

▶ 1948: British occupation of Palestine ended. A U.N. plan created two new states, one Jewish (about 56% of the land), one Arab. Arabs in and outside Palestine rebelled, tried to crush the new Israel militarily. But a 1949 cease-fire gave Israel 75% of Palestine. Score one for Israel.

▶ 1967: Egypt blocked the Israeli port of Eilat. In a blitzkrieg retaliation, Israel won the Six-Day War, took over the West Bank from Jordan, all of Jerusalem, the Sinai Peninsula, Golan Heights, Gaza Strip. Score another for Israel.

Ever since, the Arabs have been trying to even the score. The United Nations and the USA have been trying to referee.

What about the people inside this "World Stress Laboratory," as Haifa University psychology **Professor Ray D. Wolfe** calls Israel.

One of the hottest of many hot seats is that of Jerusalem's Viennese-born **Mayor Teddy Kollek**, 76. Keeps a huge aspirin tablet, a foot in diameter, on his desk as a symbol of his headaches.

Jerusalem's population includes 381,000 Jews, 127,000 Arabs. No Arabs serve on the city council, but about 20% of them vote in local elections.

After 23 years in office, Kollek will run again this fall. "For hundreds of years, people have lived here in absolute separation. Sometimes relations are good. Sometimes bad. But the city is still working," Kollek says.

Elsewhere in Israel:

▶ Population 4 million-plus, about 85% Jewish.

▶ In 1948, the population was 1.6 million, only about 40% Jewish.

MAYOR KOLLEK: Huge headaches, huge aspirin.

CAPT. KRAMER: From tanks to kids with stones.

CPL. SABBAG: Younger soldiers don't say "Hey, Honey."

Because it is surrounded by enemies — Lebanon and Syria in the north, Jordan to the east, an uneasy "peace" with Egypt to the southwest — military security is tight.

Armed men and women dot the landscape. Uprisings in the Gaza and West Bank have diverted combat units there.

Capt. Moti Kramer, 30, forward base commander of the "Iron Treads" armored brigade, describes the difference in duty:

"Before, we were on the Golan Heights, facing armed Syrians with tanks. Now we have to deal with children throwing stones."

Cpl. Bat-Chen Sabbag, 19, typifies military women. "The older soldiers say 'Hey, Honey, can I have your phone number?' The younger ones accept me as their superior," she says, patting the sub-machine gun slung over her shoulder.

Prime Minister Yitzhak Shamir's tough policy regarding the Palestinian uprisings has the country politically divided.

Arabs are outspoken. **Ahmad R. Abdin**, 37, manager of a Palestinian plastics manufacturing company in occupied Bethlehem (pop. 20,000) says philosophically:

"Our plant is shut down for a while. Now, I'm playing cards more. And, we Arabs are making love more. If this keeps up, we'll have more children, which won't be good for the Israelis. Soon, there will be more of us than them."

That's Plain Talk from Israel.

PALESTINIAN ABDIN: Soon, more of us than them.

JEWISH TRADITION: Yehiel Cohen, 32, an electrician in Jerusalem, says, "Thank God there is a place for Jews. This is our place. There is no other."

ARAB MERCHANT: Abd al-Karim al Qimari, 36, an Arab Muslim Palestinian, sits outside the Damascus wall in Old Jerusalem selling zibda — cream made of sheep's milk.

MOSLEM MOSQUE: The Dome of the Rock in Jerusalem — a holy shrine for Muslims — covers the spot from which Muhammad is believed to have risen to heaven. Jews believe ancient Hebrew leader Abraham prepared to sacrifice his son here.

CHERISHED SHRINE: The Wailing Wall on Mt. Moriah in Jerusalem — a symbol of faith and unity — is all that remains of the ancient temple of King Solomon. The temple was destroyed by Roman soldiers in A.D. 70. According to legend, the wall itself weeps because of the destruction. Lyrics in the Israeli folk song *Hakotel* refer to the wall: "There are some men with hearts of stone and there are some stones with human hearts."

Yael Dayan Sion, 49
Author, politician
Tel Aviv

"I think the country misses a Moshe Dayan (her father) today. I get phone calls from people I don't know who say this is exactly when we need someone like him."

David Zayyad, 29
Jewelry maker
East Jerusalem

"I wish I were married and had children. I would send them into the streets to throw stones. We Palestinians don't want much. What we want is to live in peace and feel we are living."

Eveline Kluger-Kadish, 25
Israeli soldier
Kfar Saba

"I don't think other countries need to have men and women in uniform like Israel. Men and women fought together when Israel became a state. It is service, not a job."

Moshe Berka, 74
Lawyer
Jerusalem

"We have a turbulent past, but we've always been secure because God has been with us. This time it's no different. The world has always had a bad image of Israel. People don't like us unless we're in trouble."

'For us, U.S. is only honest peace broker'

On prospects for a permanent peace between Israelis and Arabs:

"One of our main slogans (in upcoming elections) will be to make peace. And I am sure we will get it. We will succeed. The Arabs are upset to understand that they are going to live together with us in this area. There is no other way but to live together. They have to take into account our interests and our presence and our aspirations for the future. I think we have to make peace in the framework of the (1979) Camp David Agreements. The framework of the Camp David Agreements is the most realistic solution and the most appropriate for the situation of the Palestinian population in the territories of Gaza and other places."

On the USA's role in peace negotiations:

"I am convinced that the United States is the only power in the world that could be useful in such an effort to bring peace to the area because of the simple fact that the United States is the only power that has friendly and close relations with Israel and, at the same time, with Arab countries."

On the Soviet Union's role in peace negotiations:

"With us, the Soviet Union doesn't have normal relations and, therefore, we don't have talks. For us, the United States is the only honest broker."

On the United Nations' involvement in the Mideast:

"We don't like very much the involvement of the United Nations in the peacemaking process. They don't have a record for achievement in this regard. In the United Nations, we always have an automatic majority against us."

On the Palestinian refugee camps:

"I don't know if you know the terrible conditions of these camps, which exist from 1948. They exist because the Arab countries have decided to maintain these camps for political reasons — to show the international community that the Palestinians are suffering because of the establishment of the State of Israel."

On what to do about the camps:

"It would be very easy to solve this problem, to give decent conditions of life to these people, especially housing. We need the help of the international community. It's a question now, I would say, of $2 billion. It could be done in a period of 10 years if only the rich countries of the world would contribute — and we are ready to do so also."

On the immigration to Israel of Jews from the Soviet Union:

"We have to keep fighting to bring them here. We need them. They have so many qualifications. Many are

*Israel's **Prime Minister Yitzhak Shamir**, 72, is a short man, with a coiled physique. He smiled often during the interview with the JetCapade news team, but his eyes had a steely look that recalled his turbulent past in political terrorism and espionage. Shamir was born in Poland and immigrated to Palestine in 1935, leaving his family behind. They were killed by the Nazis during World War II. In 1942, he became one of the three leaders of the so-called Stern Gang, the most violent underground organization seeking the ouster of the British occupiers of Palestine. The group was accused of several assassinations and assassination attempts. After the State of Israel came into being, Shamir joined the Israeli secret service, becoming chief of European espionage operations. Today, he heads Israel's conservative Likud Bloc, which opposes giving back the territory Israel won from Arab states in the 1967 war. His party shares power with the more moderate Labor Alignment of Foreign Minister Shimon Peres.*

professionals. We are very interested in working with the United States in their relations with the Soviet Union, so that the Soviets can be convinced to permit many of the Soviet Jews who want to get out to let them do so and come here."

On improving Israel's economy:

"We have to strengthen our economy by going more in the direction of privatization. There has been a tradition of Israeli governments in the past to be inclined more toward socialistic methods. Now it's clear for the great majority of people that the only way to improve our economy is the way of privatization, of giving priority to the business sector."

ITALY

Featured in USA TODAY: July 29

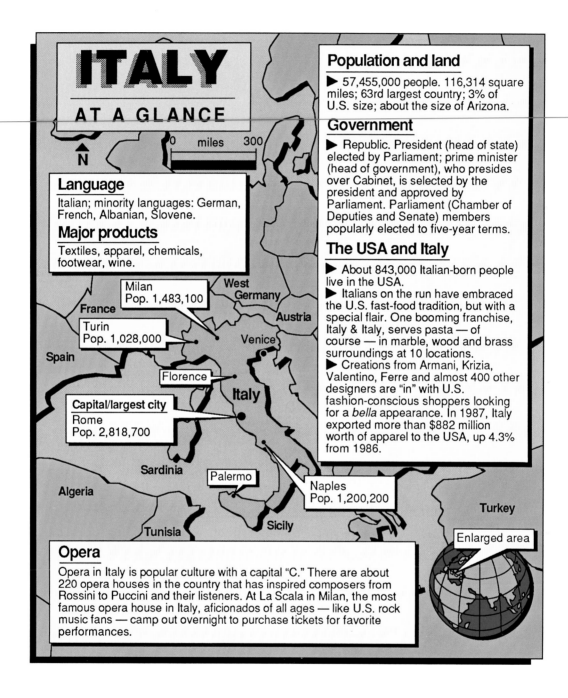

ITALY
AT A GLANCE

N

0 miles 300

Language
Italian; minority languages: German, French, Albanian, Slovene.

Major products
Textiles, apparel, chemicals, footwear, wine.

West Germany

Milan
Pop. 1,483,100

Turin
Pop. 1,028,000

France

Austria

Venice

Spain

Florence

Italy

Capital/largest city
Rome
Pop. 2,818,700

Sardinia

Algeria

Palermo

Naples
Pop. 1,200,200

Turkey

Tunisia

Sicily

Enlarged area

Population and land
▶ 57,455,000 people. 116,314 square miles; 63rd largest country; 3% of U.S. size; about the size of Arizona.

Government
▶ Republic. President (head of state) elected by Parliament; prime minister (head of government), who presides over Cabinet, is selected by the president and approved by Parliament. Parliament (Chamber of Deputies and Senate) members popularly elected to five-year terms.

The USA and Italy
▶ About 843,000 Italian-born people live in the USA.
▶ Italians on the run have embraced the U.S. fast-food tradition, but with a special flair. One booming franchise, Italy & Italy, serves pasta — of course — in marble, wood and brass surroundings at 10 locations.
▶ Creations from Armani, Krizia, Valentino, Ferre and almost 400 other designers are "in" with U.S. fashion-conscious shoppers looking for a *bella* appearance. In 1987, Italy exported more than $882 million worth of apparel to the USA, up 4.3% from 1986.

Opera
Opera in Italy is popular culture with a capital "C." There are about 220 opera houses in the country that has inspired composers from Rossini to Puccini and their listeners. At La Scala in Milan, the most famous opera house in Italy, aficionados of all ages — like U.S. rock music fans — camp out overnight to purchase tickets for favorite performances.

The pope and pasta, plus an awesome past

They come to see the pope and savor the pasta. They leave awestruck after looking through this window on the past. "They" are:

▶ About 50 million visitors annually from around the world.

▶ 1.8 million last year from the USA. Italy is our second most popular destination — just behind the United Kingdom and ahead of France and Germany.

We asked **Prime Minister Ciriaco De Mita**, 60, why this cowboy boot that sticks out from under the belly of Europe attracts visitors in such numbers.

"If you really want to see how the world developed through time, you have to come here," the prime minister said.

The Eternal City of Rome ruled the world for about 500 years. Its historic avenues of awe wind past such remarkable ruins as the Colosseum. Built by hand in eight years. Completed in 80 A.D. Held 50,000 spectators. Now, draws thousands daily to marvel at what's still standing.

But the biggest attraction is walled off from the rest of Rome. A state within a state, Vatican City:

▶ Spiritual center for 845 million Catholics worldwide.

▶ A 108-acre autocracy overlooking the Tiber River. Houses only 1,000 residents within its walls. Home of the Sistine Chapel, with Michelangelo's famed ceiling fresco. A controversial restoration to brighten colors is near completion.

Here the longest-playing spectacle on earth draws a full house every Wednesday: the papal audience.

When we were here, 13,000 jammed Paul VI Hall. Mostly Catholic, but also large numbers of Protestants and Jews. Began lining up at dawn for a ceremony that started at 10:15 a.m., ended at 12:25 p.m. When the audience is held outside in St. Peter's Square, the crowd is even larger. Admission: Free.

This non-Catholic's account of the most moving moments:

Unannounced, 15 minutes after the scheduled time, **Pope John Paul II** enters from the left. Walks slowly to his chair at center — smiling, waving, exuding warmth. The crowd responds with cheering, clapping, crying, laughing, singing.

This is not just a religious ritual. Touches of the theater, political pep rallies, sports spectaculars.

The pope's prepared message is scriptural and pragmatic. Delivered in Italian, with some ad-libbing in Polish. Then he reads summaries in English, French, Spanish, German, Portuguese.

On this day, he welcomes a delegation from the NATO Defense College: "Your presence expresses your appreciation of moral and spiritual truths. One of the primary aims of NATO is to protect and promote freedom. In those efforts, remember the words of Jesus

Christ: 'the truth shall make you free.'" (John 8:32)

The really personal touch of this Polish pope comes when the preaching ends.

He walks slowly past front rows, up and down the aisles. For 30 minutes. Kisses a child. Wipes tears from the cheeks of an emotional elderly woman gently with his fingers. Hugs a crippled man in a wheelchair.

The pope never grants official newspaper interviews. But after the ceremony, he chatted amiably with USA TODAY's International President **David Mazzarella** and me.

We reminisced about his visit of September 1987 to the USA. He thanked us for that morning's international edition of USA TODAY printed via satellite in nearby Lucerne, Switzerland.

Before leaving the Hall, he paused for picture-taking with the Assumption Church Choir from Cincinnati. Earlier that group had responded to his introduction of them by singing the last verse of *America The Beautiful* to the applause of the entire audience.

Said chorister **Mary Prisant**, 36, a homemaker back in Cincinnati:

"I never dreamed it would be this beautiful. The memories of him reaching out to people and me touching him — it's a miracle. Every Catholic should experience this. It would bring them closer to God."

That's Plain Talk from Italy.

THE POPE AND NEUHARTH: The pontiff's personal touch includes firm handshake, blessing.

CITY OF DOMES: Rome's skyline is dominated by nearly 500 churches. The church in the foreground is St. Carlo Al Corso. In the background is the dome of St. Peter's Cathedral, the world's highest brick dome.

BALLOON PROTEST: Marchers concerned about ozone depletion use sky-blue balloons to attract attention in front of Rome's parliamentary building.

GONDOLIER: Umberto Pavan, 60, steers a gondola.

THE BEAUTY OF THE BASILICA: Visitors to St. Peter's Cathedral at the Vatican are awestruck by the detailed frescoes.

VIEW FROM A BALCONY: Shoppers crowd the Via del Condotti in one of Rome's most fashionable districts.

Gabriella Caporicci, 45
Restaurant manager
Rome

"The people in the North, in Milan, think they are the motor engine of Italy. We think otherwise. They live to work. In Rome, we think work is a means of living the good life — the Italian way."

Cinzia de Carolis, 32
Vendor
Rome

"I'm Roman and wouldn't want to live anywhere else. I have traveled through Europe and have seen beautiful cities and places but they don't have what we have in Rome: the people, the atmosphere, the streets, the climate."

Piero Vivoli, 56
Gelato maker
Florence

"The passion that Michelangelo had for art, we have for ice cream. The work reflects part of me. The secret of good gelato: passion, good sense, great ingredients, and a feel for it in yourself."

Diana Stefani, 52
Perfume maker
Florence

"In Florence, anything that's later than the 16th century is considered modern. There are a few baroque churches, but nobody likes them. They think they're too new and too pompous."

'U.S. isolationism must be prevented'

On his first visit to the USA as prime minister early in the summer of 1988:

"The visit to the United States took place at a singular point in history because President Reagan had just returned from the summit in Moscow, where he confirmed the possibility of some very important initiatives for all the world. My visit enabled me to form a personal analysis of the international political situation. I saw an element of change, of innovation, in East-West relations."

On isolationist tendencies in the USA:

"What did strike me in discussions I had in the States with all levels of the administration and members of Congress, was a very evident concern about the possibility of a pro-isolationist movement in the States. This isolationist thrust is linked to economic concerns in the United States at this time. It is identified as a strong threat — a negative possibility — and in the interest of solidarity with Europe, everything possible should be done to offset such a trend."

On the prospects for a unified Europe after 1992 when customs barriers are removed for Common Market countries:

"Economic unity is raising the problem of how to foster the same type of political unity. We now see the need for a common currency among countries in the single market. For this you need a central bank. Discussions are now under way as to the time, ways and means for establishing such a bank. This is not only a technical problem, but very much a political problem in that any decision would lead to reduced sovereignty of the nations involved."

On relations between Italy and the USA:

"The solidarity between Italy and the United States has been constant since the Second World War. One factor is the presence of a very large Italian community in the United States. Also, after fascism, we learned a lesson. It was that our own development could only take place together with the free and democratic countries of the world, and so this also lies behind our solidarity with the United States."

On Italy accepting U.S. fighter planes forced to leave Spain as part of negotiations regarding U.S. bases in Spain:

"Our decision to accept the transferral of the F-16 fighter aircraft was looked upon by the United States as a guarantee of stability and way of ensuring the protection of the military balance of the southern flank of the NATO area. The United States also looked upon it as an act of friendship."

Prime Minister Ciriaco De Mita, 60, has held office since April 1988. If his government lasts the average of previous Italian governments since World War II, De Mita will be in office six more months.

Even though Italy has had 48 postwar governments, its ruling structure is among the most stable in the world. That's because De Mita's Christian Democratic Party has remained the largest in Italy. The party needs coalitions with other leftist or centrist parties to govern, and realignments of power within these alliances cause the governments to change. But the Christian Democrats have provided a core of stability.

De Mita was born in a small town in Southern Italy. He turned to politics in 1963 and rose to become leader of the Christian Democrats.

The prime minister met the JetCapade news team under the vaulted, frescoed ceilings of a drawing room of his centuries-old Chigi Palace in the heart of old Rome.

On Italy's appeal to U.S. travelers:

"Italy has been enriched down through history, so everything goes back in time. Wherever you look, you find something that has a story. And this perhaps sets us apart from other countries. The history that has unfolded in Italy affects all of us. It can be seen in so many ways — in theater, in music, in literature. You can look at the churches and see the history of architecture, of construction. Look at the city squares. Look at the gardens. When you visit Italy, you relive history."

JAPAN

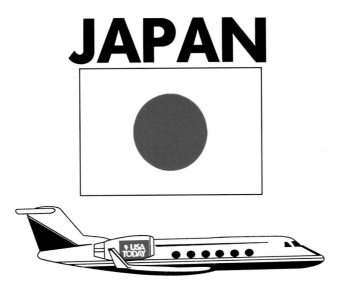

Featured in USA TODAY: May 27

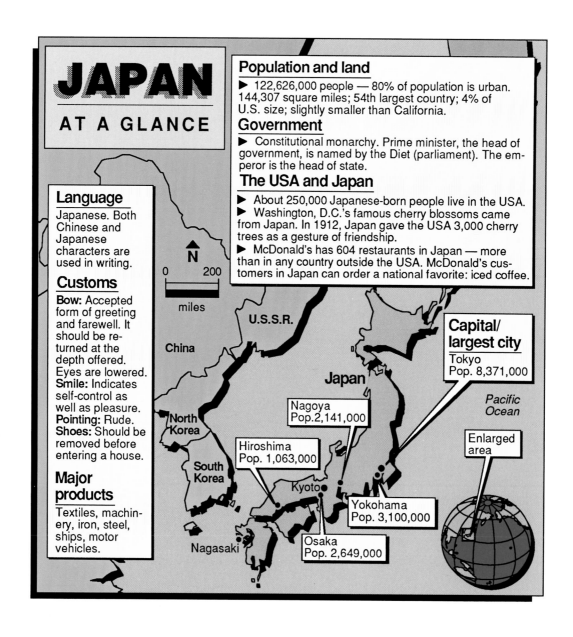

JAPAN
AT A GLANCE

Language
Japanese. Both Chinese and Japanese characters are used in writing.

Customs
Bow: Accepted form of greeting and farewell. It should be returned at the depth offered. Eyes are lowered. **Smile:** Indicates self-control as well as pleasure. **Pointing:** Rude. **Shoes:** Should be removed before entering a house.

Major products
Textiles, machinery, iron, steel, ships, motor vehicles.

Population and land
▶ 122,626,000 people — 80% of population is urban. 144,307 square miles; 54th largest country; 4% of U.S. size; slightly smaller than California.

Government
▶ Constitutional monarchy. Prime minister, the head of government, is named by the Diet (parliament). The emperor is the head of state.

The USA and Japan
▶ About 250,000 Japanese-born people live in the USA.
▶ Washington, D.C.'s famous cherry blossoms came from Japan. In 1912, Japan gave the USA 3,000 cherry trees as a gesture of friendship.
▶ McDonald's has 604 restaurants in Japan — more than in any country outside the USA. McDonald's customers in Japan can order a national favorite: iced coffee.

N
0   200
miles

U.S.S.R.

China

Japan

North Korea

South Korea

Hiroshima
Pop. 1,063,000

Nagoya
Pop.2,141,000

Kyoto

Yokohama
Pop. 3,100,000

Nagasaki

Osaka
Pop. 2,649,000

Capital/ largest city
Tokyo
Pop. 8,371,000

Pacific Ocean

Enlarged area

Unconditional surrender, unparalleled prosperity

Defeated in war. Victorious in peace. From a shamed loser to a proud leader in less than half a century. That's the irony of Japan.

▶ Dec. 7, 1941. Pearl Harbor day. "A date which will live in infamy," **President Franklin Delano Roosevelt**.

▶ Sept. 2, 1945, V-J Day. "It is my earnest hope . . . that from this solemn occasion a better world shall emerge," the conquering **General Douglas MacArthur**.

What they're saying now:

▶ You are the pillar of our foreign policy, **Japan Prime Minister Noboru Takeshita**.

▶ "Bilateral relations between the U.S. and Japan are the most important in the world," **U.S. Ambassador Mike Mansfield**.

▶ "I have a very high feeling about being stationed here. It's one of the best things that's happened to me," **U.S. Air Force Maj. Ronnie Stokes**, 40, Fort Worth, one of 57,485 USA military still stationed in Japan.

Japanese talk freely about World War II, only they call it the "Pacific War." Old and young vow "never again." Their "peace constitution," drafted at MacArthur's behest, says never again will this country go to war.

Memories are sharp and sad. Especially at Hiroshima, where the first atomic bomb was dropped from our B-29 "Enola Gay" at 8:15 a.m. Aug. 6, 1945. 260,000 died then or later; 160,000 wounded, 92% of the city destroyed.

Graphic reminders everywhere. Peace cathedrals, halls, flames, foundations, museums. One is the Children's Peace Monument in Peace Memorial Park. Designed by junior high school students, its base is covered with colorful pieces of paper folded in the shape of cranes.

Like the rest of Japan, Hiroshima has recovered remarkably. A bustling port city of 1 million. Mazda headquarters.

HIROSHIMA: Children's Peace Monument.

Automobiles are the best example of Japan's perseverance to prosperity. Studied how we did it. Now:

▶ No. 2 car producer in the world. More than 13 million vehicles produced last year. USA about 16 million.

▶ Japan's No. 1 industry. 764,501 employed by auto or auto-related firms.

Hisashi Kaneko, 52, assembly line supervisor at Gunma-Ken, near Tokyo, explains why he thinks their products are superior:

"Every morning the section chief calls the workers into a corner and they examine the defects they made yesterday. And he tells them not to repeat those mistakes. On major defects, we have bells and whistles on the assembly line that signal when a worker forgets something."

Other exports to the USA and the world: TV and radio equipment, optical instruments, heavy machinery, textiles. The economic strength means:

KANEKO: Why Japan's cars are better.

▶ Per capita annual income $12,850, among the highest in the world. USA $15,340.

▶ Unemployment 2.6%. USA 5.4%.

While Japanese work hard, they also are learning how to play, the Western way. Japan's Disneyland, patterned after California's Disneyland and Florida's Disney World, is one of the most popular places. Opened five years ago. Averages 10 million visitors a year.

DISNEYLAND ASIA: Japanese love Mickey, Goofy.

Keisuke Fujii, 35, Tokyo banker, his wife **Kyoko**, 31, and daughter, **Ayako**, 3, enjoyed it while we were there.

Says Kyoko: "My daughter walks around the house singing the Mickey Mouse song in English. She's got us doing it, too. I can tell you almost anything you ever wanted to know about Goofy."

That's Plain Talk from Japan.

MONEY MADNESS: Traders at the Tokyo Stock Exchange rush to place orders during a day's last 30 minutes of trading. Daily, 114 members trade as much as $2.8 billion in stocks at the world's largest stock exchange.

PLAY BALL: Baseball is a national craze in Japan, especially among young fans like Masahiko Sunam, 11, of Tokyo.

GRAPPLING GAMESMEN: Sumo wrestling, one of Japan's most popular spectator sports, dates back 2,000 years. Six 15-day tournaments are held every year in Tokyo and other large cities.

PACIFIC METROPOLIS: Tokyo is a mixture of East and West, old and new. Concrete and steel skyscrapers in crowded commercial districts reflect a booming modern economy that supports 8.4 million people.

GEISHA SHOW: Entertainers clad in traditional silks portray geisha girls in a nightly show in Tokyo. Geishas are well-bred Japanese girls trained in singing, dancing, the art of conversation and to serve as hired companions to men.

Seikou Komatsu, 52
Peace Foundation
Hiroshima

"I want to tell the younger generation about my experiences as an A-bomb victim and to tell them that if a nuclear war takes place, there will be no winners or losers."

Kaori Sumi, 27
Professional emcee
Tokyo

"It's uncommon to be an independent businesswoman in Japan. When I tell women office workers what I do, they envy me because I can control my own time."

Yuzo Iseki, 61
Director, International
House, Osaka

"This region has turned out more venture business than any other place in Japan. Merchants still greet each other with, 'Have you made any money today?'"

Hidehiko Yamada, 28
Salesman
Yokohama

"In Tokyo, the cost of living is very high. That's why I stayed in my hometown, even though it takes me one hour and 50 minutes each way on the train."

USA: You are pillar of our policy

The television cameramen were lined up outside Japanese Prime Minister Noboru Takeshita's offices in Tokyo.

The news: State Minister Seisuke Okuno's repeated statements that Japan was not the aggressor in World War II — a comment that spurred serious international and political repercussions.

The day was filled with calls for the state minister's dismissal. Okuno submitted his resignation that evening.

If the controversy was of paramount concern to Takeshita, he didn't show it. He was at ease and cordial, even playful in his responses.

A member of the Japanese press corps had cautioned us that Takeshita could be ill at ease with journalists — especially foreign journalists. Two indications:

▶ His staff asked that any comments made by Takeshita in our conversation not be directly quoted. They said we could share with our readers anything that Takeshita said, but they asked that his words be paraphrased.

Such a request is sometimes a sign of a public figure who finds himself less than eloquent, but Takeshita never seemed at a loss for words.

▶ The prime minister sat stiffly during the photo session just prior to the meeting with the JetCateers. He sat perfectly straight and stared at the cameras, smiling only occasionally. After only a few moments, he asked JetCapade photographer Callie Shell and members of the Japanese press corps to stop shooting.

Takeshita had just returned from an eight-day tour of Western Europe, including stops at Vatican City, Italy, Great Britain and West Germany.

He told us that the trip was important because it gave him an opportunity to explain Japan's trade policy to the world. He said visiting other countries is especially important since many leaders consider Japan to be a closed country.

Despite trade tensions, Takeshita said his country's warm relationship with the USA overrides economic concerns. He said the goodwill between the two nations cannot be expressed in trade or money. He said the USA is the pillar of Japan's foreign policy.

When told of the JetCateers' visit to the Yokota Air Force Base, Takeshita was quick to note that although there are sometimes tensions with the military bases, the Japanese have great affection for the people of the U.S. military and their families.

Takeshita clearly had been briefed on his visitors. He observed that Neuharth and he were both born in 1924.

Noboru Takeshita, 64, a member of Japan's ruling Liberal Democratic Party, took office as prime minister Oct. 30, 1987. Despite a pressure-packed day that included the resignation of a state minister, Takeshita walked in only seven minutes after our scheduled appointment and immediately apologized for being late. He met with the JetCapade news team in a large meeting room decorated simply with tan chairs and brown square tables.

He smiled and predicted that both would live well into the 21st century.

Takeshita also had very warm words for U.S. Ambassador Mike Mansfield. He said that the senior members of parliament hold Mansfield in particularly high regard and wished him well during his recent hospitalization.

Takeshita picked up a copy of USA TODAY during the meeting and said he was surprised that the newspaper published its readership figures on the front page. He said he doesn't think it's a good idea to provoke the competition.

"Provoking the competition" is something Takeshita and Japan are clearly concerned about. Trade tensions worldwide seem to be directed at the very prosperous Japan, and Takeshita and President Reagan were expected to discuss bilateral trade issues at a meeting in London in June 1988.

The hottest issue: The USA's efforts to have Japan end restrictions on citrus and beef imports.

A plan released by Takeshita's Economic Policy Council also promised to be a key topic in London. It outlined Japan's shift from an export-dependent economy to one that centers on domestic expansion.

AIRMEN AT YOKOTA: Capt. Kenneth E. Hosterman, 35, of Fayetteville, N.C., and Staff Sgt. Steven J. Metheny, 27, of Washington, Ind., are on the maintenance team for C-5s.

GIs: Weaker dollar makes living harder

Forget the military uniforms and that they're stationed in the middle of a foreign culture. What's really on the minds of U.S. military personnel in Japan?

Finances. Child care. Housing. Coping.

USA TODAY went to Japan and polled 400 GIs, conducted dozens of interviews and held a town meeting at Yokota Air Base to find out what life is like for GIs and their families overseas.

Their answers:

▶ Never mind the cost of living allowances — pay us better.

▶ Give us better day care for our kids.

▶ Worst thing about living here? Prices. Best: experiencing another culture.

The plummeting dollar is a culprit.

"You can't afford anything out there," says Air Force Master Sgt. Clarence Robinson, 39, of Kansas City, Mo. " ... $10 to get to downtown Tokyo on the train — give me a break."

Yokota's population of 13,651 includes 4,362 military personnel and their 5,672 family members. The rest: Japanese workers, Department of Defense teachers and other civilians.

Almost 70% of the military community are married; 75% live in barracks and apartments on base and 25% live in six Japanese towns bordering the base.

Cheri Lopez, 21, of Rockport, Ind., lives off base near

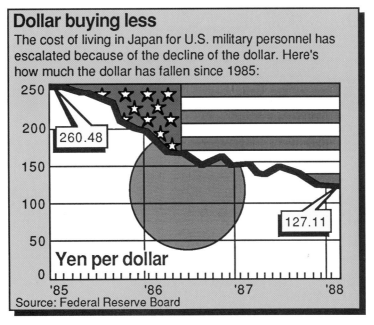

Dollar buying less
The cost of living in Japan for U.S. military personnel has escalated because of the decline of the dollar. Here's how much the dollar has fallen since 1985:

260.48

127.11

Yen per dollar

'85   '86   '87   '88
Source: Federal Reserve Board

Yokota with her husband and pays dearly for it: $900 a month for rent, $450 for utilities. Even with rent subsidies from the military, our rent and our bills take "almost one of our salaries," she says.

And living on base doesn't mean you're home free. Baby-sitting bills run as high as $600 to $800 a month for three children,

In grocery stores in Fussa, a city outside the base, four small oranges sell for $3.30; three asparagus spears, 83 cents; two monster carrots, $2.30; a flawless cantaloupe, $37.

"Last week I was able to afford one leaf of lettuce," said Staff Sgt. Mark Schore, 23, of Hopkins, Minn.

Military families find creative ways around the yen-dollar dilemma. Sally Spires, 36, an Air Force wife from Terre Haute, Ind., buys "anything I can get my hands on" in South Korea at bargain-basement prices.

Military spouses have trouble finding jobs comparable to those at home because the number of jobs available on the base is limited.

Some turn to modeling — many advertising agencies in Japan are looking for the blond, blue-eyed look.

Wendell Chestnut, 57, a native of DeKalb, Ill., who has been in Japan for 24 years and is a civilian employee at Yokota, has been modeling for years: "They think I look British."

USA AND JAPAN: In the morning, Mt. Fujiyama rises through the clouds as the first plane of the day leaves Yokota Air Base in the foothills of the Okutama Mountains. Cargo planes such as the C-130, above, C-141 and the giant C-5 bring supplies from the USA to be distributed to 40 U.S. bases across the Pacific.

Bobby Williams, 43
Air Force master sgt.
Brooklyn, N.Y.

"Basic pay is the issue. We're way behind the private sector in basic pay."

Donna Christ, 34
Navy wife
Virginia Beach, Va.

"(Spouses) are like a nonentity. I wish the military would give us a little recognition."

Ken Spires, 38,
Air Force captain
Warner Robins, Ga.

"My family is just as committed to (defense) as I am."

Sharon Luster, 26
Petty officer 3rd class
Bronx, N.Y.

"I went into labor at 2:30 a.m. My husband tried to get (a store clerk) to call a cab and he just looked and said, 'Coke?'"

KENYA

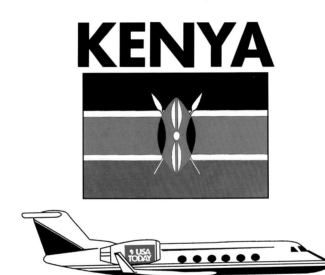

Featured in USA TODAY: Feb. 29, April 15

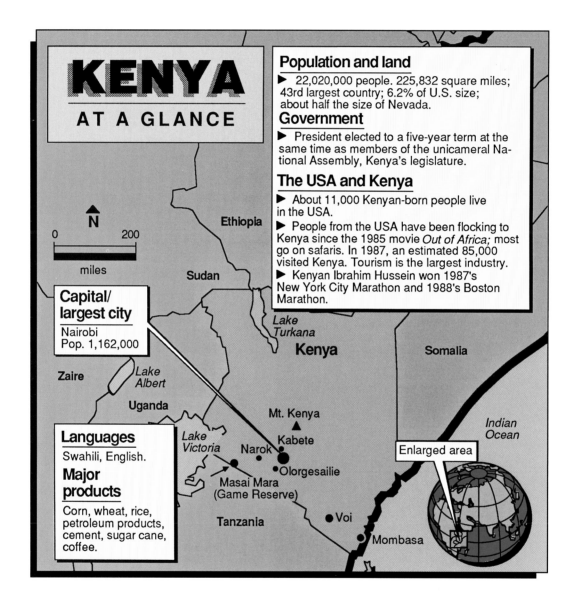

KENYA
AT A GLANCE

Population and land
► 22,020,000 people. 225,832 square miles; 43rd largest country; 6.2% of U.S. size; about half the size of Nevada.

Government
► President elected to a five-year term at the same time as members of the unicameral National Assembly, Kenya's legislature.

The USA and Kenya
► About 11,000 Kenyan-born people live in the USA.

► People from the USA have been flocking to Kenya since the 1985 movie *Out of Africa;* most go on safaris. In 1987, an estimated 85,000 visited Kenya. Tourism is the largest industry.

► Kenyan Ibrahim Hussein won 1987's New York City Marathon and 1988's Boston Marathon.

Capital/ largest city
Nairobi
Pop. 1,162,000

Languages
Swahili, English.

Major products
Corn, wheat, rice, petroleum products, cement, sugar cane, coffee.

Ethiopia

Sudan

Lake Turkana

Kenya

Somalia

Zaire

Lake Albert

Uganda

Mt. Kenya
Kabete

Lake Victoria
Narok
Olorgesailie

Masai Mara
(Game Reserve)

Tanzania

Voi

Mombasa

Indian Ocean

Enlarged area

Can Mother Nature survive 'progress'?

This is Mother Nature still mostly unvarnished. Vast plains. Verdant plateaus. Home to the buffalo, elephant, giraffe, leopard, lion, monkey, rhino.

It is also, according to many believers in Darwin's theory of evolution, birthplace of the human race. Anthropologist **Richard Leakey** (of TV's *The Making of Mankind*) claims to have found human remains here 2.7 million years old.

Will man or nature prevail? Or can both survive and thrive?

Key questions facing this nation of 22 million that celebrates its 25th anniversary of independence this year:

▶ Can the ways and wealth of the Western World be assimilated without losing the colorful tribal customs and culture?

▶ Can this democracy continue to fend off troublesome leftist and rightist neighbors?

LOIBONI, 65: Clings to past.

LEOYIE, 20: Future beckons.

▶ Can the more than 50 species of wild animals be protected from professional poachers, seeking high prices for horns and hides?

President Daniel arap Moi, 64, re-elected to a third five-year term this year, promises an era of "peace, love and unity."

Here's how some others see it:

Most Kenyans live out in the country. Dozens of different tribal units have their own distinct traditions. But some are slipping.

The Masai tribe, traditional warriors, seems to have surrendered the most. No longer are the men allowed to kill a lion to prove their manliness. Their spears are gone. Red-ochred locks are shaven.

Noomatasian Loiboni, 65, in the tiny Masai village of Olorgesailie (pop. 50), clings to the past and is fearful of the future.

"This is where our children should stay," says the colorfully clad Loiboni, who lives in a grass hut. "But I fear most will move to Nairobi."

Her grandson-in-law, **Mula Leoyie**, 20, in tribal costume, still seems content to herd sheep and cattle. But his brother-in-law, **Charles Loiboni**, 20, wears Western clothing and runs a roadside refreshment stand for tourists.

Nairobi, capital and largest city (pop. 1,162,000) is where the past and future come together. Tourists, from the USA, U.K. and elsewhere, make a big impact here. **Bill Eve**, 44, manager of the Nairobi Safari Club, says the movie *Out of Africa* spurred the tourist trade.

"Most of them come here expecting to see lions or giraffes walking down the streets. Some are disappointed at what a modern city this is," Eve says.

While big game animals aren't on the loose, in Nairobi's city park,

EVE IN MODERN NAIROBI: No lions loose on the street.

tame and playful monkeys by the hundreds mix with humans.

At Nairobi National Park, one of 34 national parks and game preserves, visitors can peek at, if not pet, giraffes and other big game.

In cities and in the country, traditionally large families exacerbate the problems of housing, food, employment. More than 50% of Kenyans are under 15 years of age.

Francis Gitiu, 58, his wife, **Lucy**, 48, and their 15 children live in a three-room farmhouse outside Kabete (pop. approx. 500).

GITIU FAMILY: 17 live in 3 rooms.

A carpenter, Gitiu earns 3,000 shillings ($150) each month. The family raises potatoes, beans and coffee and sells some for extra income.

Gitiu approves of the government's campaign for birth control. He says: "I'm telling my kids not to have any more than two. Remember, God only had one son."

That's Plain Talk from Kenya.

RHINO KEEPER: Enos Okode, 41, is keeper for Amboselli, an orphaned female black rhino, an endangered species. Okode works and lives at the Nairobi National Park.

TRADITION LIVES: Women from a Masai village near Nairobi, in traditional dress, take pride in their centuries-old culture.

NAIROBI SKYLINE: This noisy, bustling town of Mercedes' and Land Rovers is home to 1.16 million people.

COTTAGE INDUSTRY: Ann Muthanie (at sewing machine) works five days a week at a seamstress business she has run for two years. Pauline Nkirote (knitting) works with her in the one-room flat in Nairobi that is also Muthanie's home.

Grace Gitia, 40
Secretary
Nairobi

"*Kenyans are friendly people. We are proud to be Africans. But we want to remain indigenous. We don't like cultures that interfere with ours.*"

Chhaganlal Shah, 70
Boutique owner
Nairobi

"*We make all our own safari clothing. For 2,500 shillings ($125) — for pants, shirt, socks and hat — I can make you look like Robert Redford.*"

Roger Marsh, 60
Game park tourist
Milwaukee, Wis.

"*It's amazing how we yelled when we saw the first elephant. Now we look at them like they're another McDonald's along the road.*"

**Simon S.B.
Ole Makallah, 40**
Game warden, Narok

"*What worries me is the increase in tourism, which is not parallel with development. We can't forbid off-road driving when there are no roads.*"

'We're USA's only true friend in Africa'

On Kenya's relations with the USA:

"As any anthropologist knows, attitudes differ from society to society. We want Kenyans to be understood in our business and our government. We want you to know we value friendship, and it must be supported in every way. If countries like the United States can assist Kenyans in a big way, we'll appreciate it. We want Kenyans to prosper, to have population growth reduced, and above all, security should be on the priority list. Every country in Africa is shaken by forces that don't bode well for them. Kenya is the only (African) country that is truly friends with the U.S."

On allegations that Kenya persecutes dissidents:

"Foreign journalists sometimes write about our human rights, but they base it on hearsay, and people think that Kenya has gone wrong. We stand firm on human rights. Democracy must have freedom of speech. It is not the purpose of government to undermine human rights. If an officer of Kenya does something bad, the law is there to punish him. What he does is not the policy of the government."

On Kenya's one-party government:

"Within government, you've got liberal, conservative, whatever. African societies differ from European societies whose traditions go back to the 1500s. Here, each tribe was a nation. During colonialism, they were kept divided so the colonialists could rule them. A multiparty system looks good in the U.S. Here, it would lead to tribal alliances. You would create chaos."

On what he hopes to achieve in the next five years:

"Nine years ago when I took office there were 16 million people. The population is now 22 million and growing. Without backing from the U.S., Great Britain and others, we can't achieve our goals. We want to provide water. That is priority No. 1. We want to protect the environment, to improve our education — elementary, secondary and university level — to provide shelter. We don't want slums. We want each district to plan training centers so people can build their houses."

On population control:

"We want to educate families and feed them, and we are doing this at the districts. People see that this is true. This will reduce population and we're applying family planning rigorously. We're not pessimistic. I think Kenya is doing a lot in the right direction."

On Kenya standing out among African nations:

"Since our independence, we have shown a continuity of stability. There haven't been any disruptions, but if brilliant ideas aren't backed by money, you wind up with nothing. Money has been invested here, and people

President Daniel arap Moi, 64, received the Jet-Capade news team in his government palace on the outskirts of Nairobi. He was seated on a thronelike chair with the guests and government officials arranged in two parallel lines, giving the appearance of a court. Moi was dressed in a brown Western-style suit. He fingered a white cane, which is the traditional African chieftain's symbol of peace and authority. Two hours after the interview, Moi was proclaimed president for a third term by his ruling party at a tumultuous celebration in Nairobi's Uhuru Park.

got their money back. The gracious lady (U.S. Ambassador Elinor Constable) is doing what she can."

On the U.S. presidency:

"Let me tell you a weakness of democracy. A U.S. president holds office for eight years but in his eighth year, nobody does a thing, and that affects foreign policy. Somebody can do a nasty thing because they know the U.S. can't do a thing."

On U.S. leaders:

"Reagan and I can agree to disagree. We are friends. (Secretary of State George) Shultz is un-American in that he is not arrogant. (Former Secretary of Defense Caspar) Weinberger is a friend. These three are gentlemen."

MEXICO

Featured in USA TODAY: Feb. 12, 19

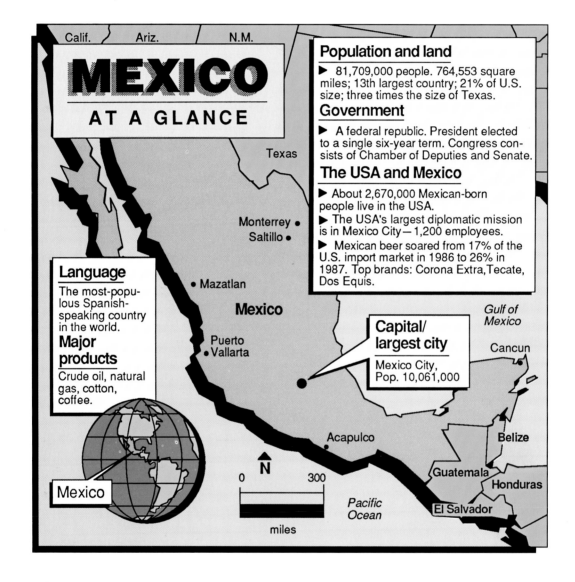

MEXICO
AT A GLANCE

Calif. Ariz. N.M.

Texas

Population and land
▶ 81,709,000 people. 764,553 square miles; 13th largest country; 21% of U.S. size; three times the size of Texas.

Government
▶ A federal republic. President elected to a single six-year term. Congress consists of Chamber of Deputies and Senate.

The USA and Mexico
▶ About 2,670,000 Mexican-born people live in the USA.
▶ The USA's largest diplomatic mission is in Mexico City—1,200 employees.
▶ Mexican beer soared from 17% of the U.S. import market in 1986 to 26% in 1987. Top brands: Corona Extra,Tecate, Dos Equis.

Monterrey ●
Saltillo ●

● Mazatlan

Mexico

Language
The most-populous Spanish-speaking country in the world.
Major products
Crude oil, natural gas, cotton, coffee.

Puerto
● Vallarta

Gulf of
Mexico

Capital/ largest city
Mexico City, Pop. 10,061,000

Cancun

Mexico

Acapulco

Belize

0   N   300

Guatemala
Honduras

Pacific
Ocean

El Salvador

miles

Our image of Mexico not quite the way it is

More than 11 million tourists from the USA visit Mexico annually. They come back with pictures and stories about:

▶ Bullfighting and cliffdiving.

▶ Margaritas and Mariachi and "Montezuma's Revenge."

▶ Street beggars and shack dwellers.

Playground for the rich and home for the poor. That's the perception most have of Mexico. The reality is different.

Our ambassador, **Charles Pilliod**, 69, from Cuyahoga Falls, Ohio, says, "The greatest misconception is that Mexico is an impoverished country. In truth, it's far better off than 90% of the world. Mexico only looks poor in comparison to the tremendously affluent USA."

What is our nearest Latin neighbor really like?

It's not hard to find Mexicans who can't find work, are fed up and want out. And it's very easy to find proud Mexicans who want to stay here and help make their country work. And the in-betweens:

Moises Hernandez, 26, farm worker from Michoacan (pop. 3.3 million), lined up with hundreds of others outside the American embassy to seek a work permit in the USA.

HERNANDEZ: "Our life is terrible here."

"Our life is terrible here. Inflation is eating everything we have. I wish **President de la Madrid** would think of the farm workers. We are Mexico," Hernandez said.

Lupita Ballesteros, 33, former airline stewardess, whose husband manages a domestic services company, is a native of Pachuca (pop. 102,000). She lived and studied four years in St. Louis, at Lindbergh High School and the Cor Jesu Academy. Eagerly came back home.

"I love my country, my customs, my people. I

BALLESTEROS: "I wouldn't live anywhere else."

would never live anywhere else," said Lupita.

Controversial and noted native novelist **Carlos Fuentes** puts down the capital as "Makesicko City" in his latest novel, *Cristobal Nonato* (Christopher Unborn). But while his novel despairs, his talk about the real world here is upbeat.

"Mexico is going through a tremendous crisis of development, of growth. Today it is mostly an urban country, to a great degree a literate country, with an intelligent middle class," Fuentes told the JetCateers.

Mexico ranks high worldwide by many measures:

▶ 11th nation in population, behind Nigeria.

▶ 13th in geographic size, ahead of Indonesia.

▶ 15th in industrial production.

Mexico City, the capital, has 20 million people in its greater metropolitan area, largest in the world. Over 10 million live within the city limits.

FUENTES: His make-believe "Makesicko City" isn't real Mexico.

This huge metropolis has its shiny skyscrapers and tin shacks. Sleek subway system and pollution-producing old cars. Block after block of solid concrete, surrounding Chapultepec (Grasshopper) Park — 1,655 acres of refreshing greenery in the heart of the city. That's twice the size of New York's Central Park.

When I jogged there at sunrise, pollution was less severe than it normally is in Los Angeles.

Mexicans have strong feelings about the USA:

▶ They resist and resent our political pressures.

▶ Embrace our economic models and management styles.

▶ Welcome dollar-spending U.S. tourists.

But some are miffed at our stories of "Montezuma's Revenge." Former **President Jimmy Carter** got in hot water over using the term when he suffered diarrhea and blamed it on their drinking water.

Restaurant owner **Andy Shaw**, 32, in the chic resort of

SHAW: Has own diagnosis for tourists' ills.

Acapulco (pop. 462,144), sees the problem this way:

"When tourists come here, their flight usually leaves at 4:30 a.m. They get here tired, drink a welcome cocktail at the hotel, then go out and have eight margaritas and dance all night. They sleep two hours, go lay in the hot sun. Who's not going to get sick from that? It's not the water."

Despite such assurances, most U.S. visitors keep their Kaopectate kits handy.

That's Plain Talk from Mexico.

THE WORKLOAD: Romalda Angel Sanches, 46, of Acapulco balances a bag of clothes. She does laundry for a living.

FROM BULL TO BEEF: Alejandro Gonzalez, 25, former bullfighter, works at a meat market in Santa Cruz.

LONG WAY DOWN: Divers demonstrate their skills at a cliff in Acapulco called La Quebrada or "Broken Rock."

MEXICAN SHRINE: Haze shrouds northern Mexico City. The shrine of Our Lady of Guadalupe is in the foreground.

Anabel Ortega, 21
Hotel cashier
Monterrey

"It used to be that women in Mexico didn't work. Everyone thought that women working outside the home was a real bad thing. Now, just like in the States, women go to work. Their salaries are needed."

Monico Ramirez, 30
Cliffdiver
Acapulco

"The thing is to learn how to control the fear. . . . When you're up there you think about a lot of things: 'How am I going to fall? Is it going to look good? Am I going to get hurt?'"

Lilia Gonzalez Boone, 41
High school teacher
Monterrey

"Motivating students is my biggest challenge. I try to convince them that it's in their best interest to learn. But some of them come from poor families where education is not as important as survival."

Guillermo Rodriguez, 26
Border policeman
Tijuana

"Thousands of people drive by here everyday, and I try to smile at each and every one of them. The American people get mad because of the traffic jams at the border, but I do my best. I want them to be happy."

We reject political, military intervention

On discussions with President Reagan regarding the Mexico-U.S. battle against drug trafficking:

"I recalled that Mexico has been developing an intensive and successful campaign to combat and eradicate the production of drugs and to limit the transit of drugs that arrive here from other countries destined for the United States. (We discussed) the importance of the United States beginning a determined fight against the links of the criminal chain, such as the local production, distribution, consumption and illegal financial operations that surround drug trade."

On whether Nicaragua poses a threat to Mexico:

"Mexico feels that it has sufficient strength to avoid any risk of that nature. Mexico is an eminently nationalistic country that accepts no foreign political models. Mexico has always rejected foreign intervention."

On his plan to curb inflation:

"As of March (1988), according to the Economic Solidarity Pact, we are going to set a realistic goal for inflation that will tend to decrease throughout the year. In accordance with this goal, the principal variables of the economy — wages, prices, interest rates, the exchange rate — will be adjusted."

On how Mexico incurred one of the highest foreign debts in Latin America:

"Mexico, as most developing countries and particularly those of Latin America, incurred an extremely great foreign debt growth during the 1970s when there were abundant loanable funds in the international banking system resulting from petrodollars. In the case of Mexico, the debt was not contracted to buy weapons, but basically for investment for growth in petroleum, in electricity, in steel, in fertilizers, and in highways — all investments of importance to the country."

On how the extensive debt throughout Latin America affects the rest of the world:

"It seems to me that it is not in the best interest of the world economy to have a stagnant Latin America, as this means less international trade. We Mexicans, for example, have had to greatly decrease our purchases in the United States, and this has affected the American economy. I believe this is what generally happens throughout the world."

On the USA's new immigration law designed to curb the number of illegal workers in the USA:

"Up to now we have not noticed any serious problems. The American authorities themselves have tempered the enforcement of these laws, especially in the case of farm workers. A few weeks after the new immigration law was passed, the American government also

Miguel de la Madrid Hurtado, 53, a Harvard-educated economic planner, is in his final year as president of Mexico. Elected in 1982, his term ends Nov. 30, 1988. De la Madrid has faced substantial challenges, including staggering debt and inflation that reached 130% in 1987. He met with the JetCapade news team in the ornate, but comfortable Presidential Palace. His staff carefully choreographed the logistics of the meeting. De la Madrid speaks fluent English, but insisted that the interview be done in Spanish. The president spoke quietly, calmly with measured words. Hand gestures were few.

approved a program to attract Mexican workers."

On "maquiladoras," the largely U.S.-owned plants where Mexican workers assemble products made of U.S. parts:

"The maquiladoras have had a positive effect in Mexico. They have given us a high level of employment, they have generated foreign exchange, and they are a means of transferring technology. To restrict the maquiladoras in Mexico would have serious effects on the Mexican economy, which would be reflected in a greater flow of Mexican migrants to the United States."

On relations between the USA and Mexico:

"I think that relations between the United States and Mexico are basically good, because the two governments and the two people want to have the best possible relationship. What happens is that our relations are extremely complex. The fact that we are neighbors, share a border of more than 3,000 kilometers, have intensive economic, trade and financial relations and communication between all the social groups in both countries makes this a very intense and complex relationship. That frequently gives rise to problems, differences of opinion, and also, differing interests. I feel, however, that the two governments have maintained the will to face these problems with complete candor and find a solution. I think that Americans and Mexicans do not always think alike, but we have grown used to respecting our differences and to trying to expand cooperation."

On his remaining time in office:

"I want to keep the country at peace, with freedom and democracy, and with an improved economy."

PHILIPPINES

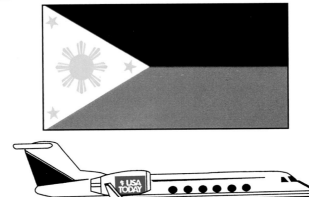

Featured in USA TODAY: May 10, 26, 31 and June 17

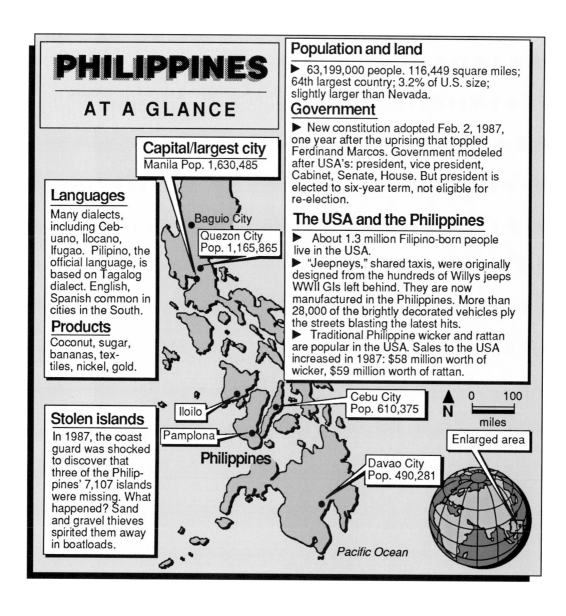

PHILIPPINES

AT A GLANCE

Population and land

▶ 63,199,000 people. 116,449 square miles; 64th largest country; 3.2% of U.S. size; slightly larger than Nevada.

Government

▶ New constitution adopted Feb. 2, 1987, one year after the uprising that toppled Ferdinand Marcos. Government modeled after USA's: president, vice president, Cabinet, Senate, House. But president is elected to six-year term, not eligible for re-election.

The USA and the Philippines

▶ About 1.3 million Filipino-born people live in the USA.

▶ "Jeepneys," shared taxis, were originally designed from the hundreds of Willys jeeps WWII GIs left behind. They are now manufactured in the Philippines. More than 28,000 of the brightly decorated vehicles ply the streets blasting the latest hits.

▶ Traditional Philippine wicker and rattan are popular in the USA. Sales to the USA increased in 1987: $58 million worth of wicker, $59 million worth of rattan.

Capital/largest city

Manila Pop. 1,630,485

Languages

Many dialects, including Cebuano, Ilocano, Ifugao. Pilipino, the official language, is based on Tagalog dialect. English, Spanish common in cities in the South.

Products

Coconut, sugar, bananas, textiles, nickel, gold.

Stolen islands

In 1987, the coast guard was shocked to discover that three of the Philippines' 7,107 islands were missing. What happened? Sand and gravel thieves spirited them away in boatloads.

Baguio City

Quezon City
Pop. 1,165,865

Iloilo

Pamplona

Philippines

Cebu City
Pop. 610,375

Davao City
Pop. 490,281

▲ N   0   100
         miles

Enlarged area

Pacific Ocean

Love, hate, jealousy: All here for the USA

These pearls of the Orient have run the full range of relations with the USA for 90 years:

▶ 1898: Ceded to us by Spain after the Spanish-American war.

▶ 1942: Conquered by Japan in World War II.

▶ 1945: Recaptured by U.S. forces led by **General Douglas MacArthur.**

▶ 1946: Granted independence, but with long-term leases for major U.S. military bases.

Now tensions are tightening as people and politicians debate whether to kick us out or renew leases to the bases, which expire in 1991.

"People talk about the love/hate relationship. I'd add jealousy. Americans have so much; Filipinos have so little," says **Johnny Green**, 42, Manila airline employee whose father is from the USA and mother is Filipino.

The love affair was strongest during and right after World War II. I was last here in September 1945 — V-J month — as a sergeant in the 86th Infantry Division.

Then, over a million U.S. Army, Navy, Marine and Air Force troops were here. Warmly hailed as heroes everywhere.

Now, there are 17,871 U.S. military here — mostly cooped up at Clark Air Base or Subic Bay Naval Base.

I walked among the white crosses at Manila's American Cemetery, our largest outside the USA. Gracefully green and clean. Every bit as imposing as Arlington National Cemetery.

17,206 are buried here, most identified by name, rank, hometown, serial number. But hundreds more lie unidentified, their crosses marked "Known but to God."

Nearby, rows of marbled walls carry the names of 36,280 U.S. missing-in-action — not unlike the Vietnam Wall in Washing-

U.S. WORLD WAR II VICTIMS: 17,206 are buried in Manila's American Cemetery.

ton, D.C. A guest registration book holds mostly names of visitors from the USA. 167,870 traveled here last year to honor dead friends or loved ones, re-live the past.

Filipinos themselves are preoccupied with present-day problems. That's where love, hate and jealousy clash.

Followers of Aquino, who still seem to be a very solid majority, love us for helping her get rid of 20-year ruler **Ferdinand Marcos.** But Marcos' loyalists, a bitterly determined minority, hate us for having abandoned him.

Both sides, and the in-betweens, are jealous or envious because, as Green said: "You have so much, we have so little."

Here's how little:

▶ Per capita annual income is $560, among the poorest in Asia. USA: $15,340. (The world's richest country — Switzerland, $17,680.)

▶ Unemployment is about 10%. "Underemployment" is estimated at 33%. That includes professional people as low-income street vendors, degree-carrying architects or engineers as waiters or laborers.

Secretary of Labor and Employment Franklin M. Drilon, 42, says the big problem is Filipinos having to leave the country to find work.

DRILON: "We are losing our best people."

"We are losing our best people. We are losing doctors, nurses. It is a very difficult problem to solve."

Government leaders are hopeful the proposed multinational $10 billion aid program planned by the Reagan administration will start a turnaround. But the average Filipino does not yet see much hope.

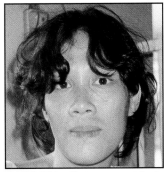

RABACAL: Future very bleak.

FUNTERA: Business down.

Violete Rabacal, 28, mother of four and pregnant again, says: "My husband works at the pier sometimes. But often there is no work. We have trouble getting enough money for our family. My son Joseph (age 6) is in the hospital with TB and malnutrition. The future does not look better."

Priscilla A. Funtera, 42, intelligent, refined president of Pristine Arts and Crafts Centrum in Manila, has seen her employee force shrink from 150 to 45 because of bad business.

She says: "Tourists are a trickle now. It's probably because of the bad publicity in newspapers in your country."

That's Plain Talk from the Philippines.

WEDDING CELEBRATION: Flower girls, festive in pink dresses, gather outside the Manila Cathedral.

MASS TRANSIT IN MANILA: Jeepneys — fashioned from discarded U.S. Jeeps after World War II — are big business. At least 17 companies make the little buses, the lifeblood of the Filipino transit system.

THE OLD WAY: Some Filipinos still use man-powered tri-carts as a means of transportation.

MAKING A LIVING: Young scavengers collect paper at "Smokey Mountain" garbage dump in Manila. More than 20,000 people live there, many earning 20 or 25 pesos ($.95 to $1.19) a day collecting paper, glass and metal.

ENTICING EXORBITANCE: More than 13,000 people a month tour Malacanang Palace in Manila, former home of ousted President Ferdinand Marcos. The Marcos family accumulated a breathtaking collection of artwork, jewels and clothing during his rule.

Douglas Diago, 45
Farm owner
Pamplona

"Marcos controlled everything. We had to take what we could get. Now, with the better prices I can earn 350,000 pesos ($17,500) a year. Sugar is sweet again."

Neal Cruz, 48
Journalist
Manila

"If there is a word that describes Filipinos, it is 'opinionated.' They have opinions about everything, but mostly about the country. Political rallies take the place of entertainment."

Marithel Uyanib, 21
Saleswoman
Cebu Island

"I voted for the first time in 1986. It was a very big occasion because it was important to select the best president the Philippines has ever had."

Jose Luis Yulo Jr., 40
Trade center director
Manila

"It is important for the government to keep an ambiance of stability. Peace and order should return; and we must work like hell — like we never worked before."

'It will not do to let Marcos come back'

Will the Philippines ever be able to recover the money that Ferdinand Marcos has been accused of taking?

"We have been able to recover some of the ill-gotten wealth surrendered to the government by his cronies."

What effect would a possible Marcos return have?

"I have said before — and that is the reason why I could not give in to the request for him to come home for his mother's funeral — that I have to think what is best for the national interest. At this moment, it will not do for us to allow him to come back because we have made enormous gains during the past two years, and I am afraid these gains may be negated. If, on the other hand, the Filipino courts decide otherwise, I will, of course, respect and bow to the will of the judiciary."

How has your image changed from "the average housewife" to the president of the Philippines?

"I don't consider myself the average housewife. It's true I did refer to myself as just a housewife. Maybe I should have elaborated then that I was a housewife but I was married to one of the leading political leaders in the Philippines. Having been married to someone of his stature, some of it must have rubbed off on me."

Are you pleased by the "mini-Marshall Plan," the $10.5 billion plan put together by U.S. Rep. Stephen Solarz, D-N.Y.?

"I am very grateful that such a plan is being talked about. I also appreciate the fact that many governments realize that if we are to preserve the democracy that we have restored in this country, it is also necessary for us to have support in our economic recovery."

How do you assess the strength of the communist insurgency? Is it weaker now than it was a year ago or two years ago?

"Definitely so. However, the presence of the insurgence, of course, has a great deal to do with the economic situation in our country. Where people do not have employment and where people suffer certain injustices, this is perhaps some of the reason why they turn against the government. It is the goal of the administration to seek a better life for the Filipino people. What I'm trying to do is attract foreign investors to this country so that we will be able to generate more employment."

Is this insurgency a threat to the country?

"No. The mere fact that we have been able to arrest some of the top leaders certainly has been a big plus, and also we have been able to gain many people on our side: people living in the countryside who in the past did not help the military in identifying the hideouts of the insurgents."

Are the communists receiving any support from outside the Philippines?

Corazon Aquino, 55, has been president of the Philippines since 1986. One minute, Aquino is laughing about her teen-age daughter's dislike for some foreign foods. "I constantly tell her, 'Chris, keep your mouth shut and eat it,' " says the bubbly 5-foot-2-inch mother of five. Another minute, she intensely explains her country's economic policies and stands firm on her refusal to allow ousted strongman Ferdinand Marcos to return. No smiles here. Since Marcos was ousted, Aquino, widow of slain Filipino leader Benigno Aquino, has been thrust into the presidential spotlight. She has been frank but friendly, firm but feminine, during her short term as president.

"There have been some reports about their receiving aid from foreign sources. When I visited China, I solicited a statement of support from Chairman Deng Xiaoping in the name of the Communist Party of China that they support the Aquino administration. So, definitely, the communist insurgents here are not getting any support in terms of weapons from China."

Are the Filipino people in favor of retaining the U.S. military bases right now?

"I really don't know how the Filipinos would vote on that matter. One thing that the Filipinos are most concerned about is an improvement in the economy."

Are you optimistic there will be an agreement between the U.S. and Philippines for an extension of the bases?

"Right now, there is a review of the bases agreement. The terms and conditions are being negotiated. Let us just wait until after that review is over and the recommendations will be forwarded to me."

Where does the Philippine military stand?

"I have the support of the great majority of the military ... that is evident by the fact that in spite of the five coup attempts, I am still here and continue to be the president."

Do you think that another attempt will occur?

"Attempts will always occur as in the case of Spain where they had restored democracy in 1976. Where my opposition comes — from the extreme right — are people who are no longer in power and would like to recover that power. There is always the threat, but I am confident that as long as the Filipino people support me, I need not worry."

'I hope to live to save the Philippines'

Do you think the Philippines is more troubled today than when you left?

"I left the country solid and now it's bankrupt. I left the country with $28 billion in the treasury. No one can account for it now. We had obtained the surrender of many communists. Now, the communists are in the city and are free to roam."

Do you think the communist strength will continue?

"It is continuing. The soldiers of the armed forces are not skilled in the use of power. When I left them, we had organized 68,000 with training of at least six months. The communists are coming down, ready to come down into the city, the streets."

How do you feel about the U.S. attitude about that?

"I have my own attitudes, but I don't want to talk about them right now."

Do you still have significant support in the Philippines?

"All I know is that the people who came out to meet the body of my mother when she was brought to the church shows a large group is supporting me. It's not a matter of emotions. I cannot tell you the number of people who come here and say they cannot understand it. Even if I do not return, there are enough willing to die to change the administration. My goal is to stay in my country and fight the danger."

What danger?

"Corazon Aquino represents one side of the danger but she is not the danger. The danger is communism. Anyway, let's take them all out. The danger is that the Communist Party will try to take over, whether I'm there or not. It will be more risky if I am not there."

Has the Soviet Union put a high priority on the expansion of communism in the Philippines?

"They deny supporting directly the communists. But why are there such sophisticated weapons there?"

Will the USA be able to work out an agreement with the Philippines on the military bases there, or will that relationship end in 1991?

"Those bases will terminate even before. Before then, the communists will take over."

Before 1991?

"Their secretary general has said that they have organized regional confidential governments, and that they are organizing a national communist government."

You don't feel Mrs. Aquino has the military strength to resist the communists for another three years?

"Several months is an estimate. But let's not talk about military strength. She does not ask the people for

Ferdinand Marcos, 70, was ousted as president of the Philippines in 1986. He had been president since 1965 and also was prime minister, 1973 to 1981. He was a lieutenant, and later captain, in the Philippines Army and in U.S. forces in the Far East during World War II. When Marcos' mother died in May 1988, he requested that he be allowed to return for the funeral. President Corazon Aquino denied the request because she felt Marcos' return was not in the "national interest." Marcos met the JetCapade news team in his lavishly decorated $5,000-per-month rented Honolulu home overlooking Diamond Head. The home was filled with pictures of the Marcos family, mementos of his presidential years, and a microphone and amplifier used by his wife, Imelda, for family sing-a-longs. A few hours after the interview, Marcos was hospitalized complaining of chest pains.

help. How can you be a leader when you're not fair to your people?"

Do you think you made a mistake by leaving when you did? Should you have stayed?

"Probably I should have, but I didn't want to shoot anybody."

What are your hopes now?

"My hope is to live long enough to save our country. My hope is to be able to recover from this ailment that I have. I am not healthy. I think I will live long enough to save my country. If I don't, it's God's calling."

Why has Mrs. Aquino's presidency lasted two years? Does she have the support of the people?

"No. She has the support of the American government and that's important. It didn't appear she would sit easy in her stolen presidency. There would be attempts to unseat her, and they could succeed. Violence begets violence. It will not help the economy and the fight against communism for the armed forces to be fighting Cory Aquino."

Would your return prevent a civil war?

"If I go back, I would be in a better position to prevent civil war. If I go back in a pine box, you will have some kind of civil war. Even her communist companions will not save her."

POLAND

Featured in USA TODAY: Aug. 1, 12

POLAND
AT A GLANCE

Language
Polish.

Major products
Machinery, coal, textiles, leather, food, chemical products.

0   200

miles
▲
N

Norway

Sweden

Baltic Sea

Solidarity
In 1987, the U.S. Congress appropriated $2 million for this trade union federation led by 1983 Nobel Prize winner Lech Walesa. When legal (1980-81), its membership was estimated at almost a third of Poland's population.

France

East Germany

Gdansk

Poland

Wroclaw Pop. 640,000

Katowice

Zabrze

Krakow Pop. 744,000

Wadowice

U.S.S.R.

Capital/largest city
Warsaw Pop. 1,664,700

Enlarged area

Population and land
▶ 37,958,000 people. 120,728 square miles; 62nd largest country; 3% of U.S. size; about the size of New Mexico.

Government
▶ Socialist republic. First secretary of the United Workers' (communist) Party holds effective political power. Head of government: prime minister. Head of state: president and Council of State, elected by 460-member Sejm (Parliament).

The USA and Poland
▶ About 468,700 Polish-born people live in the USA.

▶ Chicago is home to about 1 million people of Polish ancestry — more than any city in the world, except Warsaw.

▶ *CNN Headline News* broadcaster Bobbie Battista is a big celebrity in Poland. Since 1987, she has appeared nightly, dubbed in Polish, on Poland's government program *Panorama*. She toured Krakow in June 1988.

Best is yet to come, but when is tomorrow?

"**P**oland has always been a country with faith in the impossible," wrote Nobel Prize-winning Polish poet **Czeslaw Milosz**.

Maybe that explains the pride and perseverance of Polish people today. They seem to hover in a twilight zone between hope and despair. But still full of faith.

By Eastern European standards, Poles are not living too badly. But in the West, to which they like to compare themselves, the Polish picture pales.

In the area of human rights and freedoms, Poles seem to be progressing. But, again, by Eastern standards.

"The reforms which are currently under way in this country preceded what is happening in the Soviet Union," says **President and Communist Party Chairman Wojciech Jaruzelski**.

Even Jaruzelski's chief adversary, trade union activist **Lech Walesa**, agrees to a degree. The Solidarity spokesman, jailed for his union activities in 1981 and released in 1982, now is not only tolerated but allowed to speak freely.

"There are reforms, big reforms, going on in Poland. We want to achieve these revolutionary changes in an evolutionary way, a peaceful way," says a solemn but somewhat subdued Walesa, his walrus mustache now graying.

Neither Jaruzelski nor Walesa seems to have the power to move the Poles toward prosperity. The economic slide continues. The inflation rate is 60%.

Jaruzelski urges patience, assuring people the best is yet to come. "If we are to have a better tomorrow, today must be perhaps more difficult."

A typical response from **Barbara Surmacz**, 27, Warsaw dressmaker and model, "When is tomorrow?"

WALESA: Peaceful programs have replaced protests.

The faith that prevails despite the problems is deeply rooted in religion. Poland is 95% Catholic. Polish pride in one of their own having been selected pope feeds their faith.

Results of a recent government poll asking Poles their sympathy or support for world and local leaders:

▶ **Pope John Paul II**, 96%.
▶ Soviet leader **Mikhail Gorbachev**, 76%.
▶ Jaruzelski, 48%.
▶ **Fidel Castro**, 30%.
▶ **President Reagan**, 26%.
▶ Walesa, 23%.

But the Poles also have great faith in themselves. They've been through it all before and somehow survived.

Almost squarely in the middle of Europe, Poles have watched history's pendulum swing back and forth and have been hit hard by it. In World War II, 6,348,000 Poles died — 22% of the population — proportionately the heaviest loss by any nation.

Auschwitz, most notorious of the Nazi death camps, is in Poland, an hour's drive from Krakow.

THE POLISH POPE: Comes in first in popularity polls.

The gas chamber, furnaces and barbed wire fence have been kept intact, as a grim reminder of the 4 million who were murdered there. 1.2 million victims were Polish Jews; 1.4 million other Poles.

Stanislaw Maczka, himself a Nazi concentration camp survivor, now guides visitors through Auschwitz.

AUSCHWITZ: Grim reminder of World War II carnage.

"Why?" he asks. "Why were so many Poles victims of the Nazis?" His answer:

"The Poles never accepted German occupation. From the very first day of occupation, there were resistance organizations all over Poland. So the Nazis rounded people up and herded them into the death camps. Any charge would do. Simply being Polish was enough."

That's Plain Talk from Poland.

A ROSE AND A SMILE: Anna Pacurowa, 60, makes 4,000 to 5,000 zlotys (about $10) a day selling flowers in Krakow. "In Poland if you visit someone, you bring flowers," she says.

STREET MUSICIANS: Band members perform in traditional costumes in Mariacki Square, Krakow.

CHOPIN'S BIRTHPLACE: Visitors peer into rooms of period furniture and portraits at a museum in Zelazowa-Wola. The alcove where Frederic Francois Chopin was born is marked by a marble urn filled with flowers.

IN THE FIELDS: Marek Ciurzynski, 17, plows a potato field on his family's farm near Warsaw.

RIVER REFLECTIONS: Anglers fish in the Vistula River, which reflects a peaceful view of Warsaw's Old Town. The Vistula is an important waterway and Poland's longest river — flowing 675 miles from the Western Carpathian Mountains to the Baltic Sea.

Maximiljan Kamienski, 66
Retired teacher
Wadowice

"I knew the pope well. He was in high school two years ahead of me. He was very disciplined. It was an inner discipline. He could discuss any subject — soccer or serious subjects."

Teresa Stachowicz, 33
Salesclerk
Warsaw

"I try to avoid the private shops. I can find everything I'm looking for in the state shops. It depends on your demands and what you're looking for. I'm not too demanding."

Zeno Zegarski, 30
Writer
Wroclaw

"I've just written a book of fables. I like to describe countries in terms of colors. Poland is gray. The U.S. is blue, like infinity. The possibilities there are endless."

Dr. Jacek Moll, 39
Clinic physician
Zabrze

"We still lack materials we need for operations. Sometimes a person is on a list one or two years for an operation. Some people die because they are waiting."

'Poland is a virgin area for the U.S.'

How would you describe the USA's current relations with Poland?

"They are gradually undergoing improvement. But I feel the steps being made toward improvement are much too short. Even from time to time, the march forward is halted. Poland is a virgin area for the U.S."

How do you think U.S. residents regard your country?

"The Americans are a highly pragmatic people. I really do think that there should be much more pragmatism in the way the United States assesses Poland. In comparison to a couple of years ago, the trade both ways between Poland and the USA has dropped by 80%."

How will the U.S. presidential election affect Poland?

"I don't feel the election will result in some sudden and violent change in Polish-American relations. But each new administration automatically undertakes a re-evaluation and modifies its priorities."

What do you think led to the deterioration of relations during the 1980s?

"I would like to look upon the past as a closed chapter. Many of the issues that arose then were based on misunderstandings and lack of knowledge of the reality and problems. And to some extent on political calculations. A big power has got those kinds of calculations always in mind. Poland is one of the elements in the policy of East-West relations. To some extent, I was a victim of those bad relations. That's why we are delighted with the improvement in relations between the United States and the Soviet Union."

What impact have Soviet leader Mikhail Gorbachev's reform policies had on Poland?

"This is of enormous importance to Poland. We are doubly excited that the reforms which are currently under way in this country — and which, chronologically speaking, preceded what is happening in the Soviet Union — are moving in a very similar direction as those in the Soviet Union."

How do you assess Gorbachev's popularity?

"That is one of these phenomena which to some extent is rooted in his personality and in his policies. These policies express respect for our sovereignty and respect for our traditions. This acknowledgment and his pointing to certain events that have been part of Polish-Soviet history and his openness created quite a unique climate for his visit to Poland."

Are Poland's relations with the West likely to improve?

"Historically, the Poles have understood they should be close to the Soviet Union due to the guarantees such

The interview was **Wojciech Jaruzelski's** first with the U.S. press in a year. Political watchers had warned that the Polish president and Communist Party chairman would be aloof — but he wasted no time in speaking his mind. Jaruzelski, 65, who met with the JetCapade news team in the Council of Ministers building, rarely smiles or shows emotion. He sat nearly motionless during the hour-long interview, shuffling his legs only once — when asked about his recent slip in popularity. Jaruzelski's clothing was simple: a brown suit, dark glasses and brown suede shoes. The dark glasses — he's never seen in public without them — are the result of a chronic eye ailment. Some say his eyes were damaged by blinding snow glare while he and his family were exiled to Siberia in 1939. He also wears a corset because of a spinal injury.

an alliance gives us. This understanding remains the same. But now, the Polish heart is beginning to beat in both East and West directions and is large enough to accommodate both. The thing is that we should be real friends: not in words but in deeds and reality."

Based on your popularity, can we expect short-step or long-stride reforms to meet the needs of your people?

"Any economic improvement is a long-term process. What is important is the direction of such processes and the mechanisms which are guiding it. The direction is through far-reaching reforms which are to lead to an improvement in economic effectiveness using some of those instruments which are operative in the West. I have in mind competition and market mechanisms. In those cases when we try to undertake far-reaching, more exhausting decisions, we encounter social resistance."

What political reforms lie ahead for Poland?

"Democratic transformations have reached very deep and they will go even deeper. Relations with the Catholic Church in Poland have undergone normalization, and the church is a very meaningful power in this country. This process of democratization of public life is no short-term flash in the pan. It's something that's here to stay. We are not masochists, and we are not a bunch of fools. We have become convinced democratization in an oversimplified manner leads to catastrophe. The road that we have selected is the correct one."

SAUDI ARABIA

Featured in USA TODAY: April 1

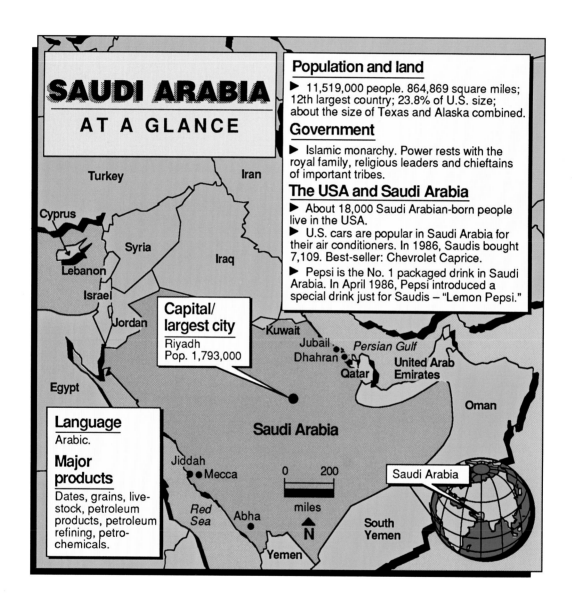

SAUDI ARABIA
AT A GLANCE

Population and land
▶ 11,519,000 people. 864,869 square miles; 12th largest country; 23.8% of U.S. size; about the size of Texas and Alaska combined.

Government
▶ Islamic monarchy. Power rests with the royal family, religious leaders and chieftains of important tribes.

The USA and Saudi Arabia
▶ About 18,000 Saudi Arabian-born people live in the USA.
▶ U.S. cars are popular in Saudi Arabia for their air conditioners. In 1986, Saudis bought 7,109. Best-seller: Chevrolet Caprice.
▶ Pepsi is the No. 1 packaged drink in Saudi Arabia. In April 1986, Pepsi introduced a special drink just for Saudis — "Lemon Pepsi."

Turkey

Iran

Cyprus

Syria

Iraq

Lebanon

Israel

Jordan

Capital/ largest city
Riyadh
Pop. 1,793,000

Kuwait

Jubail
Dhahran
Qatar

Persian Gulf

United Arab Emirates

Egypt

Oman

Language
Arabic.

Major products
Dates, grains, livestock, petroleum products, petroleum refining, petrochemicals.

Saudi Arabia

Jiddah
Mecca

0   200

miles

N

Red Sea

Abha

Yemen

South Yemen

Saudi Arabia

Written in oil: Saudis' rags-to-riches saga

This kingdom celebrated the 50th anniversary of the discovery of oil in 1988. A rags-to-riches golden era.

"We lived in the dark for 1,000 years. Now, we've done everything in a hurry," said **King Fahd**'s nephew, **Prince Abdullah Bin Faisal Bin Turki Al Abdullah Al Saud**, 37.

Big rush. Big money. Big results. Most of this true-to-life fairy tale has been acted out in the last 15-20 years:

PRINCE ABDULLAH BIN FAISAL: 1,000 years of darkness.

▶ Over $370 *billion* in petroleum products exported during the heyday of high oil prices, 1970-80. Despite much lower prices, last year's exports were $30 billion.

▶ Per capita income in 1987: $8,000. Twenty years ago: $1,500. (In the USA in 1987: $14,461.)

▶ Oil revenues have been pumped into a vast infrastructure of highways, airports, hospitals, housing, universities. Policy: Build everything bigger than needed, before it's needed.

Saudis shrug off critics of lavish government or personal spending. Reason for their surety: Saudi Arabia has 25% of the world's oil reserves. U.S.S.R.: 9%. USA: 3.6%.

Riyadh, capital city, had 300,000 people in 1970 when the boom and the planning began. Now: 1.8 million. "When we have 5 million, we will not have the problems of New York or Mexico City or Cairo," says **Deputy Minister of Planning Hussein Abdullah Sejini**.

Sparkling clean streets and highways are dotted — not crowded — with foreign cars. Some motorists complain about the "high" price of gas — 60 cents a gallon.

Despite the material progress, traditions and customs have changed little. Religion and Royalty see to that. The theme: Modernization without Westernization.

Saudi Arabia is the center of the Islamic religion, founded by the Prophet Mohammed in 610 A.D. Saudi Muslims:

▶ Pray five times a day.

▶ Ban consumption or sale of alcohol. "Saudi champagne" is apple juice and club soda, poured over an orange and mint leaves.

▶ Strictly segregate men and women outside the home. Women not allowed to drive cars. Separate entrances and separate dining rooms in public restaurants.

Virtue is in. Vice is out. Government censors screen published photos of females. Blackened out the legs and bustline of gymnast Kristie Phillips on the sports pages of hundreds of copies of USA TODAY's International Edition that arrived while we were here.

Saudis claim the lowest crime rate in the world. Justice is swift and harsh. Convicted thieves have their hands, arms, feet or legs cut off. Capital crimes are punished by public beheading ceremonies. The king must approve each. 51 reported in 1987; 11 in 1986; 44 in 1985.

Public behavior and appearance is straight-laced, especially for women. Most

CENSORED: Female gymnast's legs, bustline blacked out.

still wear a veil and a floor-length covering called an abayah outside the home. But Western wear and ways are appearing. 200,000 young Saudis, including many members of the royal family, have attended U.S. colleges and universities.

Iman Ibrahim Abou-Boutain, 32, went to George Washington University. Now is project manager of Al-Khailgia, a 20-female firm offering services in typing, word processing. She says:

"Five years ago there weren't many women in business. Now there are a lot. Our government and our society don't oppose that. People in the U.S. have a strange stereotype

ABOU-BOUTAIN: Favors modern Western ways.

about Saudi Arabia. They think our men have daggers in their mouths and our women are in a harem. It's not like that."

That's Plain Talk from Saudi Arabia.

ANCIENT VILLAGE: Ruins of the ancient Arab settlement of Diriyah. The nearby village is the site of the first home of the Saud royal dynasty. The Sauds first occupied the area in the 16th century.

ENERGIZED SCHOOL: King Fahd University of Petroleum and Minerals, Dhahran, is acknowledged in the Middle East as a leader in research in energy sciences. Founded in 1963, it is one of the smallest universities in the country with 4,418 students.

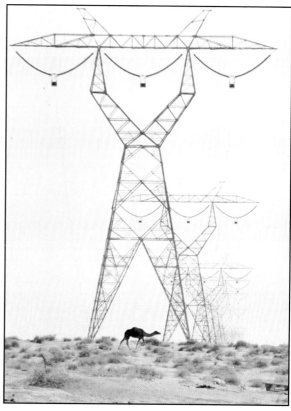

POWER TOWERS: A camel — representing ancient Saudi Arabian life — passes a tower representing the kingdom's economic future. Saudis plan to turn abundant natural gas into electricity to be used to make petrochemicals. The towers will carry power from gas fields to industrial locations.

PLANT SPECIALIST: Rashid Azad, 38, stands on an observation deck overlooking the rugged terrain of Asir National Park, Abha. Azad, a botanist from India with a doctorate in taxonomy, operates a laboratory at the park.

Awad Ali Mahboub, 37
Royal bodyguard
Abha

"It is an honor to serve (Prince Faisal) as a bodyguard. We carry a rifle and wear a revolver as well as the 'jambiah,' which is a dagger. It is a wonderful job."

Bakr A. Bakr, 50
University president
Riyadh

"We were able to develop economically and maintain our cultural values because we had the means to do it without aid. Most Third World countries always see Westerners on the giving end."

Donna Dillard, 40
U.S. Embassy officer
Riyadh

"We exist to help embassy families. When women come, they are mostly concerned with dressing, shopping, schools. In dressing, it's considered offensive if they call attention to themselves."

Ismail I. Nawwab, 55
Aramco manager
Dhahran

"We want to keep the Soviet Union out. Saudi Arabia has spent a lot of money aiding Third World countries, so communism doesn't spread there."

We invested in peace, people and prosperity

Saudi Arabia is a family-run country — literally.

No parties, no parliament, no constitution other than the holy laws of Islam. Just many brothers from two generations belonging to the House of Saud, the royal family.

The late Ibn Saud, father of the present King Fahd, 67, founded modern Saudi Arabia in 1932 after defeating other desert tribes in combat. Fahd's brothers, half-brothers, sons and nephews hold the important government posts.

They are among an estimated 5,000 persons belonging to the royal family. A few have gained notoriety abroad for lavish ways. Many, like the king's son, the up-and-coming Prince Mohammad Ibn Fahd, are educated, hard-working professionals.

KING FAHD: Free-spending monarch invests in quality.

The prince, only 38, is governor of the Eastern Province, home of most of Saudi Arabia's oil production.

Some of his views:

▶ **On Saudi Arabia's development:**

"People criticized us for spending so much in the 1970s, but look at what happened. If we didn't do it then, we couldn't have done it today, given the current oil prices. We feel we can't spend too much on defense or the welfare of our people. We've done in 15 years what it has taken others 50 or 100 years or more to do."

▶ **On relations with the USA:**

"We have probably better relations with the USA than any other Arab country does. Americans should know that we are not backward and are spending our money wisely to improve health care, education, housing."

King Fahd himself takes a hard-nosed, better-safe-than-sorry approach to spending that has caused consternation among his advisers.

When plans were being drawn for the imposing King Faisal Specialists' Hospital in Riyadh, King Fahd took personal charge, swept aside cost-cutting plans and built the best hospital money could buy. It is now heavily into such advanced disciplines as radioactive cancer treatments.

For other projects, he has locked away beforehand the cost in untouchable accounts.

Prince Mohammad Ibn Fahd, 38, hosted dinner for the JetCapade news team in a beflowered, begoldened palace in Riyadh. A table set for 10 was covered with enough food for 50 — pigeons, meat pastries, noodles, lamb chops, eggplant, salad, dates, lamb with rice. "If I don't have rice every day, I don't feel complete," said the prince, who also likes burgers and fries at McDonald's when he visits the USA. The tall and husky prince manages to look at ease and elegantly dressed in a double-breasted, continental-cut navy blazer, white Arabian robe and white headdress. Prince Mohammad graduated from the University of California at Santa Barbara in 1972 with a B.A. in political science. "Saudis like to study in California because of the weather," he says. His bane: snow in the Northeast. The prince got down to serious topics while smoking a Marlboro and sipping a bitter potion of unroasted coffee and cardamom.*

"The finance ministry doesn't have control, because you know how money people are," the prince said. "They want to trim a little bit here and a little bit there."

Royal family members say they consider it a duty to stay close to the people. The king and prince regularly hold "majlis" — meetings with ordinary folks who ask for favors or redress of grievances.

Up to 100 petitioners are seen in these sessions. "Many times we can solve the problem, such as a land dispute, without sending it to court," the prince said. "It helps me to talk with the people face to face."

Right now the prince's pet project is water: "We recently discovered enough underground water in the north to last us 500 years. It's like discovering oil again."

SOUTH AFRICA

Featured in USA TODAY: April 22

SOUTH AFRICA
AT A GLANCE

Population and land
▶ 29,025,000 people. 471,445 square miles; 27th largest country; 12.9% of U.S. size; about four times the size of Arizona.

Government
▶ Republic. State president elected by members of parliamentary electoral college. Three houses of parliament: white, coloured, Indian. No black house.

The USA and South Africa
▶ About 26,000 South African-born people live in the USA.
▶ Paul Simon's 1986 Grammy Award-winning album *Graceland,* featuring the black South African group Ladysmith Black Mambazo, has sold 3.5 million copies in the USA.
▶ Since 1985,144 U.S. companies, including GM and IBM, have left in protest of the apartheid system. 163 companies remain.

Atlantic Ocean

Angola

0   200
miles

N

Namibia

Largest city
Johannesburg
Pop. 1.7 million

Zimbabwe

Administrative capital
Pretoria

Judicial capital
Bloemfontein

Botswana

Mozambique

Soweto

Swaziland

Indian Ocean

Languages
English and Afrikaans; other principal languages: Xhosa, Zulu, Sesotho.

Major products
Gold, coal, diamonds.

Legislative capital
Cape Town

Lesotho

Durban

South Africa

Crossroads

Khayelitsha

South Africa

Hope and hopelessness; apartheid solid, and soft

Nearly everything revolves around race in this complicated country.

The degree to which racism — apartheid — is practiced varies from issue to issue and place to place. A political stonewall. But socially and economically, the door is ajar. This is why race overrides all else:

▶ 20 million blacks, about 70% of the population. Many are undereducated, underemployed or unemployed. Legacy of long British colonial rule that ended in 1910.

▶ 5 million whites, most "Afrikaner" descendants of Dutch settlers in the 1600s. Feel it's their country and run it their way. Total political and tough police control.

▶ About 3 million "coloured," as the racially mixed are officially termed.

▶ Nearly a million Indians.

Coloureds and Indians seem generally content to have a foot in the door, including their own houses of parliament, albeit little power. But blacks want the door open wide — and now — and are pounding on it or throwing stones at it.

EBDEN: "We'll get there."   THOKOZANI: "Life's horrible."

But even the segregated housing wall is cracking. At the University of Cape Town, nearly 10% of the 13,000 students are black and live in multiracial, coed dorms.

Paul Zwane, 23, senior in personnel management, is one. Grew up in a black township near Durban (pop. 1 million). Won college admission strictly on merit. He has high hopes.

Others with hope, or hopelessness:

Phillip Thokozani, 20, unemployed black in Soweto, suburb of Johannesburg: "Life is horrible here, man, horrible. Sanctions? Man, we want sanctions."

Patricia Ebden, 24, black, sells jewelry in Market Square in Cape Town (pop. 1.5 million): "You can see changes taking place all the time. Slowly, we'll get there."

TUTU: Demands black power now, calls regime evil.   TREURNICHT: "If you share power, you lose control."

Most visible and vocal is **Archbishop Desmond Tutu**, 57, 1984 Nobel Peace laureate. Says the regime of **President Pieter W. Botha** is "un-Biblical, un-Christian, immoral and evil."

The hard right matches Tutu tit for tat. Conservative Party leader **Andries Treurnicht**, 67: "We believe blacks should not have power in politics. If you share power, you lose control."

Socially and economically, the lines are much softer than they are politically. No "back of the bus" syndrome as there was in the South of the USA 30 years ago.

Whites, blacks and coloureds can and do use the same restrooms and water fountains. Enjoy the same beaches and parks. Shop the same shops.

Most blacks live in substandard segregated housing, not unlike Harlem or Watts. In newer black suburban townships and in the country, shanty homes are built of tin and cardboard, not unlike huts in villages of India.

Edith Van der Westhuizen, white, 51, makes clothing and sells it to everyone in Green Market Square: "There's no apartheid left in business."

WESTHUIZEN: Sells to all.

Coloured **Solly Khan**, 42, peddles fruit in the Hout Bay section of Cape Town: "If the blacks take over, we (coloured) will be kicked out. So

KHAN: Likes status quo.

will the whites. The government should leave things as they are."

President Botha, who says he's moderate, tries to walk a fine line between left and right. Botha's view:

"Reform should be evolutionary, not revolutionary. We are being pressured from outside by people who want us to do what international revolutionaries want us to do. That's not acceptable."

That's Plain Talk from South Africa.

CHANGING TIMES: Bob Seddon, his wife, Sylvia Vollehoven, and son, Ryan, live in Woodstock, a multiracial housing area in Cape Town. Interracial marriages were illegal before June 1985.

TIN HUT: Oko Ntetha, 12, watches his family build a wood and tin house. They moved to Khayelitsha, a black township outside Cape Town, from a squatters camp.

MOTHER AND CHILD: Barbara Didloff, 37, carries her 18-month-old son, Eugene, in a blanket wrapped around herself. Many women in Johannesburg use the same method to help carry their children.

ROCKY AND RUGGED: The shoreline abruptly rises into a mountainous coast in the Llandudno area offering its residents a clear view of the Atlantic Ocean.

Allan Boesak, 41
Anti-apartheid leader
Cape Town

"We have run into all kinds of repression: meetings banned, services banned. The police break up meetings. When you go to such public meetings, you take your life in your hands."

Shirley Breed, 47
Secretary
Cape Town

"I think all the races in South Africa should remember to be reasonable. There's a time to protest, but there's also a time to negotiate."

Thelma Ntetha, 47
Maid
Khayelitsha

"It's very hard for us. They tell us where we can move and where we can live and where we can't. We can't buy a house. But we have to live somewhere."

Gert Oosthuizen, 30
Parliament member
Pretoria

"We don't get credit. We just get accused of doing too little, too late. ... We want to do justice for all people, and we need help. But the only help we receive is sanctions."

'We're not a little dictatorship in the bush'

On South Africa's image in the USA:

"South Africa should be seen in the eyes of reasonable Americans as a country worth having as a friend. To a large extent, the misunderstandings and confusion are the result of mischief makers who wish to see that the U.S. and South Africa do not associate properly. Many U.S. citizens are under the impression that we are a little dictatorship somewhere in the bush and that they must now put us right. That is the wrong idea. South Africa is a regional power in Africa."

On relations with President Reagan and other U.S. politicians:

"I have a very high regard for your president. I know he's been critical of South Africa in some respects, but I've found him very reasonable and open-minded. But there are also politicians in the U.S. who apparently want to use South Africa for their internal political fights in the U.S., and I object to that. In South Africa, we don't use the U.S. as an electioneering cry."

On a congressional move for stricter economic sanctions against South Africa:

"Sanctions form part of a march of folly in international affairs. I don't believe in sanctions. I believe in the expansion of trade between nations. The world once started applying sanctions against us on armaments, and they lost the fight. We are producing more and more sophisticated arms, and we are selling them on world markets. Sanctions are not going to harm the regime, as we are called — the government — or the civilized and developed part of our population. Sanctions will harm the less privileged."

On how the foreign media cover South Africa:

"In some cases, television representatives staged and took part in attempts to stage incidents in South Africa and that is why we brought it to an end. I have literally thousands of letters from black people thanking me for the fact that I put an end to this stirring up of mob emotions. But some of the media, while remaining critical, do try to paint a true picture."

On the pace of reforms to apartheid in South Africa:

"You can't measure reform by a yardstick or with a speedometer. Reform should take place, as far as underdeveloped people are concerned, socially and economically, because you can't eat votes and you can't wear votes."

On whether economic reforms signal a shift from political reforms that would grant more rights to blacks:

"Reform is improvement in all directions. Revolutionaries want to destroy that which has been built. And they have nothing to put in its place. That's why they totally made a mess of things in Mozambique. They

Pieter Willem Botha, 72, has been state president of South Africa since 1984 and a politician since 1936. He's called a traitor by the far right, a racist by the far left and a moderate by supporters in his National Party. Both opponents and supporters say he is strong and strict, determined and disciplined. Botha met with the JetCapade news team for 50 minutes in his office, a large room bordered in light-stained wood with a desk to match. He granted no interviews to U.S. journalists in 1987, and had granted only one other U.S. interview in 1988. After refusing numerous JetCapade requests for an interview and for permission to enter the country, Botha relented on April 11. The JetCapade news team left a tour of the South Pacific and flew 30 hours and 13,778 miles from Tahiti to meet with him.*

made a mess of things in Angola. They made a mess of things in other countries in Africa."

On opposition charges that recent government restrictions on the activities of 17 anti-apartheid groups would lead to violence:

"The restrictions had nothing to do with the real intentions and principles of those organizations. We said no organization should be used to do subversive work. All those organizations are continuing with their ordinary work. I don't think any of them will now turn to violence — unless they originally intended to. But that we can deal with."

On Botha's critics within South Africa:

"We have different opposition groups in South Africa. You have yours in America, too. You have your far left. They're always dissatisfied with everything positive. But they can't show us the heaven anywhere that they want to create. And you have your far right opposition. I don't think that they are of any value to a country."

On his opinion of black activist Archbishop Desmond Tutu:

"He is a man of the cloth, but I think he is too politically minded. He is not representative of the vast majority of Christians in South Africa."

On whether he plans to retire:

"Good heavens, why should I retire? I'm healthy. I am strong enough to keep on with public life."

CAPITAL CITY: Zimbabwe's Harare, formerly Salisbury, rises amid the lush green of Southern Africa.

Black-ruled Zimbabwe: Peace and prosperity

Handshakes have replaced grenades and old enemies have taken on new lifestyles in Zimbabwe.

▶ Andrew Nyathi, 35, "Comrade Zebra" during the 7-year Rhodesian civil war that killed 27,000 people, mostly blacks, now manages a farm in a traditionally white area.

"I used to fight around here. What I've always wanted to do was farm. In Zimbabwe, we learn to farm while still in our mother's stomach."

▶ James D. Whyte, 50, born in Scotland, once a soldier in the Rhodesian Army for the ruling white minority, now owns a motorcycle shop. He rates the title "Comrade Whyte" since his family joined the Zimbabwe African National Union (ZANU), the ruling black majority political party.

Zimbabwe — known as Rhodesia before white rule was thrown off — gained a truce between blacks and whites in April 1980.

Guerrillas such as Nyathi literally turned their swords into plowshares. Whites such as Whyte have accepted black majority rule, survived and prospered.

"We made a mistake," Whyte says of the whites' fight

NYATHI: Ex-guerrilla prefers farming to fighting.

WHYTE: Ex-soldier "wouldn't want to live elsewhere."

▶ **ZIMBABWE POPULATION:** 9.2 million — 98% black.

▶ **HEAD OF STATE:** President Robert Mugabe — known as "Comrade Bob."

▶ **RECENT HISTORY:** The British colony Rhodesia declared its independence in 1965 to preserve white rule. Zimbabwe was born when a 7-year civil war between black nationalist guerrillas and the Rhodesian Army ended in 1980.

---

for power. "You can't fight the majority. You can't fight the world."

Whyte says a merger between battling black political factions in December 1987 was important: "I think Zimbabwe is a great country. I wouldn't want to live elsewhere. But it was the unity agreement that convinced me that my family and I should join the ruling party."

"Whites have never had it so good," says Judith Todd, 44, white and head of The Zimbabwe Project, a volunteer organization that has helped ex-combatants return to normal lives. "There is no war, no conflict." Todd, daughter of a former Rhodesian prime minister, was jailed in 1972 for opposing the white minority.

The country on the surface is much like yesterday's Rhodesia.

Airplanes no longer make diving, corkscrew landings to avoid being shot at by guerrillas, but black men in white coats still manicure public gardens in downtown Harare. Black waiters still serve mostly white guests nearby in a fancy restaurant.

The difference now is blacks also run Zimbabwe.

SOUTH KOREA

Featured in USA TODAY: May 24, June 3
Three months before the Summer Olympics

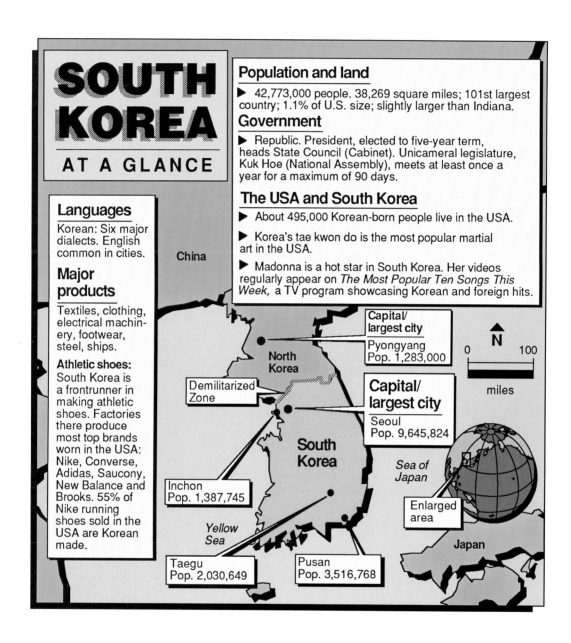

SOUTH KOREA

AT A GLANCE

Population and land

▶ 42,773,000 people. 38,269 square miles; 101st largest country; 1.1% of U.S. size; slightly larger than Indiana.

Government

▶ Republic. President, elected to five-year term, heads State Council (Cabinet). Unicameral legislature, Kuk Hoe (National Assembly), meets at least once a year for a maximum of 90 days.

The USA and South Korea

▶ About 495,000 Korean-born people live in the USA.

▶ Korea's tae kwon do is the most popular martial art in the USA.

▶ Madonna is a hot star in South Korea. Her videos regularly appear on *The Most Popular Ten Songs This Week*, a TV program showcasing Korean and foreign hits.

Languages

Korean: Six major dialects. English common in cities.

Major products

Textiles, clothing, electrical machinery, footwear, steel, ships.

Athletic shoes: South Korea is a frontrunner in making athletic shoes. Factories there produce most top brands worn in the USA: Nike, Converse, Adidas, Saucony, New Balance and Brooks. 55% of Nike running shoes sold in the USA are Korean made.

China

North Korea

Demilitarized Zone

Capital/ largest city
Pyongyang
Pop. 1,283,000

N
0   100
miles

South Korea

Capital/ largest city
Seoul
Pop. 9,645,824

Inchon
Pop. 1,387,745

Sea of Japan

Enlarged area

Yellow Sea

Taegu
Pop. 2,030,649

Pusan
Pop. 3,516,768

Japan

Olympics: Showoff time; will tension ease?

Three billion people worldwide will watch this Hermit Kingdom's coming-out party when the Olympics are on TV next September. Everyone here realizes it's showoff time.

In this young democracy, fierce political infighting and often-tragic student protests have become regular fare. But nearly all factions seem hopeful the tensions will take at least a temporary back seat in September.

President Roh Tae Woo, former chairman of Korea's Olympic Organizing Committee and avid sports fan, is reassuring: "I don't see any likelihood of a major disturbance." Tens of thousands of Koreans are directly involved in the Olympics, most volunteers. Hopeful teenage competitors are among the most enthusiastic.

Seo Mi Sook, 18, and **An Een Kyong**, 17, are being coached to carry equipment and cater to others' needs as "go-fers" for gymnastic competitors. They chose that category because they both have been training 12 hours daily as aspiring future Olympic gymnasts.

SEO, AN: "Go-fers" train at Olympic complex.

"We believe if we try hard enough, we can do anything. In Korea, we never think 'we cannot,' only 'we can,' " says An.

People here fall into four divergent categories:

▶ Young teen-agers, most full of hope and enthusiasm.

▶ College and university students, many patriotic but a strong, vocal segment with anti-establishment and anti-American feelings. Many here think that protestors are led by communist Pied Pipers from North Korea.

▶ Young and middle-aged adults, most fiercely anti-communist and determined to work to make Korea succeed politically and economically.

▶ The elderly, generally happy and grateful that the USA and others saved them from communist takeover.

Two distinctly divergent views:

▶ **Nam Hyun Young**, 22, literature student at Seoul's Yonsei University (enrollment 19,566):

"The governments of the U.S. and Japan are the main obstacles to a reunified Korea. The U.S. takes advantage of us as a front line against communism. In a University poll, 65% said the U.S. should get out of Korea. I agree."

NAM: The USA should get out of South Korea.

AN: MacArthur, USA saved people's lives.

▶ **An Yun Kun**, 85, a retired rice farmer who came south from Pyung-An province in North Korea 35 years ago:

"Under the communists, life was not good. MacArthur and the U.S. saved a lot of people's lives. I'm quite happy with the way things are."

Here's the way things are militarily:

▶ A 4,400-yard-wide, 155-mile-long demilitarized zone separates communist North Korea from democratic South Korea.

▶ An estimated 838,000 North Korean military, bolstered by Soviet troops and equipment, are north of the line.

▶ About 600,000 South Koreans, augmented by 43,000 U.S. military, face off against them south of the zone.

A temporary "armistice" was signed July 27, 1953. But no permanent peace treaty. The two sides fought to a "draw" and technically are still at war. Tension is thick at the DMZ.

Most U.S. military serve one-year tours of duty. **Capt. Don Kell**, 36, from Dunlap, Tenn. — 6'7" and every inch a soldier — came here last August, leaves this August.

KELL: On guard at "scary" DMZ.

Says Kell, armed with a loaded .45-caliber automatic and fingering the barbed wire fence:

"It's scary here. The North Koreans are unpredictable. Most people in the States don't realize that it's not really over, over here."

That's Plain Talk from South Korea.

PREPARING FOR COMPETITION: A member of the Korean Army cycling team practices inside the Olympic Velodrome, one of two main sports complexes built for the Summer Olympics.

AT EASE, SOLDIER: U.S. Army Staff Sgt. Keith Fowler, 28, pets his dog while taking a break from mortar practice in the demilitarized zone in South Korea. "You get a nervous feeling sometimes," says Fowler, of Muskegon, Mich. He's on his second one-year tour in South Korea.

TEMPLE TOURISM: Historic temples are popular attractions. The Temple of Heaven (Hwanggung-u) is a remnant of the impressive Won-gudan Altar in Seoul, where Korean kings brought offerings and assumed the title "emperor." More than 1.5 million tourists visit South Korea each year — 326,000 from the USA.

BY NIGHT: Itaewon, the Seoul shopping district and streets adjacent to the military headquarters of the U.S. 8th Army (Yongsan), caters to the foreign community but also attracts many Koreans.

TEAM SPIRIT: Children from the Sessac Montessori School in Seoul cheer on their country's Olympic hopefuls during a practice session.

Chun Byung Tak, 32
Flower shop owner
Seoul

"Koreans are a most diligent people. One reason people work so hard is they've been so poor for so long. Now they're getting richer."

Huh Hyun Nam, 42
Housewife
Seoul

"I get concerned about prices going up on necessary items and about land prices going up. But Korea has to expect such things if its people want to have a better life."

Ma Young Hwa, 46
High school teacher
Inchon

"My hometown is in North Korea. I came here when I was 5. I miss my home. My relatives are still there. But I'll see them again – I think the North and South will reunite someday."

Chi Chumo-Ku, 56
Gallery manager
Kyongiki-do

"Although our potters are many, every potter's work is different. It is like family recipes — none are the same, all are secret."

'We built a nation from ashes of war'

On arrangements for the Olympics:

"In the U.S., you've hosted the games three times — the last being in Los Angeles. This is the first time for Korea. This is the forefront of the confrontation between the free world and the communist world. The fact that we can have this festival of peace here means that we can overcome the danger of war. I think the Seoul Olympics is the most comprehensive ever. The last two or three games were marred by boycotts. I hope these games will be the most successful."

On security at the Olympics:

"We don't see any likelihood of a major disturbance. Infiltration and sabotage are another matter, however. The Soviet Union, China and Eastern European nations are participating in the Olympics. Their presence is something of a guarantee that dramatic things will not happen."

On profits from the Olympics:

"We have a contract with NBC. We're guaranteed $300 million. We will not be in the red. Whatever profit we make, we will invest to make it comfortable for the athletes, the officials and visitors."

On relations with North Korea:

"The danger from North Korea has not diminished. It continues to exist. Since the armistice, we have lived under that threat. As long as North Korea maintains its policy of reunification by force and communism, we will have to be prepared. We have been able to build up our defense and are now spending 6% of the GNP on defense. Although North Korean (relations) are cooling with China, the Soviet Union is coming in very strong. Altogether, the Soviet military power is stronger in this region than overall U.S. military power here."

On relations with the USA:

"Korea was devastated in the 1950s during the war. The U.S. came to our aid. We are allies forged in war. We built our nation from the ashes of war. We've achieved spectacular economic results and we are approaching a more mature democratic republic. We are one country you can be proud of contributing your efforts to."

On dealing with a National Assembly controlled by the opposition:

"I didn't seek President Reagan's advice, but I've watched with admiration how he exerts his influence over Congress. He has given me a good example. This is the first time in our history that the opposition party enjoys more seats than the government party. The people are worried. I look forward to much more mature negotiations. From now on, we will have to rely on compromise and dialogue. I will look to Washington for good examples."

President Roh Tae Woo, 55, was elected to a five-year term in December 1987. He held a number of posts in the previous Chun Doo Hwan regime, including minister of political affairs, minister of home affairs and chairman of the Seoul Olympic Organizing Committee. Roh wears a small pedometer on his belt to count the steps he takes each day around the presidential palace, once the Korean Dynasty's summer residence. Daily average: 4,000. Roh met with the JetCapade news team in his office, which is decorated with antiques and chandeliers.

SOVIET UNION

Featured in USA TODAY: Sept. 9

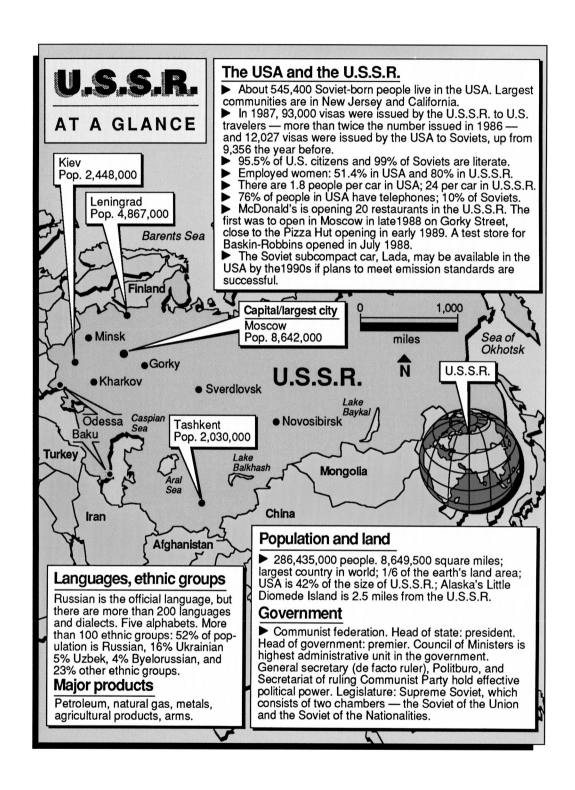

U.S.S.R.

AT A GLANCE

Kiev
Pop. 2,448,000

Leningrad
Pop. 4,867,000

Barents Sea

Finland

● Minsk

●Gorky

● Kharkov

● Sverdlovsk

Odessa
Baku
Caspian Sea

Turkey

Capital/largest city
Moscow
Pop. 8,642,000

Tashkent
Pop. 2,030,000

Aral Sea

Iran

Afghanistan

0   1,000

miles

U.S.S.R.

N

● Novosibirsk

Lake Baykal

Lake Balkhash

Mongolia

China

Sea of Okhotsk

U.S.S.R.

The USA and the U.S.S.R.

▶ About 545,400 Soviet-born people live in the USA. Largest communities are in New Jersey and California.
▶ In 1987, 93,000 visas were issued by the U.S.S.R. to U.S. travelers — more than twice the number issued in 1986 — and 12,027 visas were issued by the USA to Soviets, up from 9,356 the year before.
▶ 95.5% of U.S. citizens and 99% of Soviets are literate.
▶ Employed women: 51.4% in USA and 80% in U.S.S.R.
▶ There are 1.8 people per car in USA; 24 per car in U.S.S.R.
▶ 76% of people in USA have telephones; 10% of Soviets.
▶ McDonald's is opening 20 restaurants in the U.S.S.R. The first was to open in Moscow in late1988 on Gorky Street, close to the Pizza Hut opening in early 1989. A test store for Baskin-Robbins opened in July 1988.
▶ The Soviet subcompact car, Lada, may be available in the USA by the1990s if plans to meet emission standards are successful.

Languages, ethnic groups

Russian is the official language, but there are more than 200 languages and dialects. Five alphabets. More than 100 ethnic groups: 52% of population is Russian, 16% Ukrainian 5% Uzbek, 4% Byelorussian, and 23% other ethnic groups.

Major products

Petroleum, natural gas, metals, agricultural products, arms.

Population and land

▶ 286,435,000 people. 8,649,500 square miles; largest country in world; 1/6 of the earth's land area; USA is 42% of the size of U.S.S.R.; Alaska's Little Diomede Island is 2.5 miles from the U.S.S.R.

Government

▶ Communist federation. Head of state: president. Head of government: premier. Council of Ministers is highest administrative unit in the government. General secretary (de facto ruler), Politburo, and Secretariat of ruling Communist Party hold effective political power. Legislature: Supreme Soviet, which consists of two chambers — the Soviet of the Union and the Soviet of the Nationalities.

What does it all mean to Ivan and Katrina?

The last time I saw the Soviet Union was in 1979. Before *glasnost* (openness). And *perestroika* (reform). And **Mikhail** and **Raisa Gorbachev**.

Much has changed. Much remains the same.

Then, most Soviets on the streets seemed sullen and surly, suffering from self-pity.

Now, most still look a bit grim. But many seem hopeful. Some are actually happy.

Then, the streets of Moscow were clear of everyone except drunks and derelicts after 10 p.m.

Now, the drunks and derelicts have disappeared. There is late supping and sipping by Soviets and foreigners alike.

Then, the only food you could count on at state-owned restaurants was borscht, boiled fish, boiled potatoes.

Now, cooperative, private, profit-making restaurants offer fare ranging from steak tartare to crepes suzette.

NATALIA, 57, AND GRANDDAUGHTER: Peace hopes better for future.

Then, most facilities and utilities from telephones to rest rooms to elevators were third-rate, and nobody seemed to care.

Now, they're still third-rate, but Soviets apologize and assure you things will get better.

Then, most Soviets shied away from any discussion of politics or world affairs.

Now, many initiate or welcome discussion and debate. About capitalism and communism. War and peace.

What does glasnost and perestroika really mean to the Ivans and Katrinas across the vast U.S.S.R.? And, to Janes and Joes in the USA and people around the globe?

Some answers in the words of Soviets themselves, the hopeful and the hopeless:

Yevgeny Gorayachev, 25, and **Vera**, 26, are newlyweds. He's a Moscow meat salesman. She did the talking: "We don't feel any improvements yet as a result of perestroika. We live with his parents. It's not easy to start a marriage. We still can only dream of a flat of our own."

Natalia Derugina, 57, a pensioner in Leningrad, strolled the park with her 8-month-old granddaughter, **Catherine**. "With our leaders meeting four times, chances have increased for our grandchildren to live in peace. We are very encouraged by what has happened."

Boris Kalensky, 68, a lawyer in Kiev. Lost his leg as a Soviet pilot in World War II. "I remember flying alongside American pilots as we fought to defeat the Nazis. There was no difference between us then. I'm glad we're returning to the spirit of the friendship of that time."

Dimitri Bakayev, 16, Moscow high school student. "People spoke frankly during the special party conference. It was much more open than meetings have ever been. There is a lot of talk but you can also see things happening."

Galina Shumskaya, 27, attractive Moscow model who wears fashions that friends send her from Vienna and Paris. Her father is an aircraft engineer, her mother a former Bolshoi ballet dancer. Galina, in fluent English, says: "It's all talk. Just talk. Nothing has changed."

Father Valentin Dronov, 35, Holy Danilov Monastery in Moscow. "It's very difficult to be a priest here. Even now that the government admits the church has a place in a socialist country, the local bosses continue to deal from the point of view of the old anti-church positions."

Vera Kuzmanova, 32, park vendor, is part of a 15-member cooperative. Sells juice of the klyukva, a Siberian berry. "When I worked in a state factory, I made 200 rubles ($312 U.S. dollars at official exchange rate) a month. Now I can make 500 to 600."

Cooperatives were legalized by the government a little over a year ago. There are now about 150 co-op cafes or restaurants in Moscow. The partners keep the profits, pay only 5% to the state.

Generaloff Slawa, 40, is deputy chairman of the group that runs 36-CO-OP, Moscow's first cooperative restaurant. It opened in March 1987 and is thriving.

Says Slawa: "This started because of perestroika and glasnost. We are taking the best of capitalism and putting it into this communist society. This is only the beginning."

That's Plain Talk from the Soviet Union.

SLAWA: Communist businessman seeks capitalist profits.

BASIL'S BY MOONLIGHT: The moon spotlights the colorful domes of St. Basil's Cathedral, the jewel of Moscow's Red Square architecture. Red Square is the traditional site of Soviet state celebrations and mourning.

REAGAN WAS HERE: Moscow's Arbat Street was the scene of a surprise visit from President Reagan during his summit meeting with Mikhail Gorbachev in June 1988.

MIMING FOR LAUGHS: A clown breaks the language barrier with his pantomime act at a Moscow circus. The one-ring show is a popular attraction for Muscovites and visitors. The audience dresses in evening attire to watch the circus featuring horses, bears, goats and pigeons.

STREET STEW: Vendors at Kiev's Besarabsky farmers' market sell potatoes, meats and flowers. The Soviet Union has more farmland than any other country — about twice as much as the USA. However, fresh produce remains a scarcity on menus at restaurants, hotels and homes.

SCENIC PRACTICE SITE: A practice ski jump for children overlooks Moscow.

READY FOR MARKET: A shipment of beef arrives in one of Moscow's busiest shopping areas, the Arbat District. Still, Soviet citizens say it is easier for tourists to obtain meat than for the average Muscovite.

THE HARVEST: Nikolai Roal, 22, works at Bortnytchy collective near Kiev. The tractor driver's goals: "To become an experienced worker, to meet a beautiful girl, to marry and have a family."

RELICS OF ROYALTY: The distinctive golden "onion" domes of New Maiden's Convent, left, and Annunciation Cathedral rise above Moscow. The cathedral is part of the Kremlin's massive Cathedral Square, where czars were baptized and married. The churches no longer are used for services.

SILENT GIANT: Behind Moscow's Cathedral Square is the largest bell ever cast — the 200-ton Czar Bell. The bell was never rung. Its shell cracked during a fire when it was doused with water.

BRIDAL TRADITION: Moscow's new brides lay flowers at the Tomb of the Unknown Soldier and stroll with their husbands past Lenin's mausoleum.

CHERNOBYL VETERAN: Fireman Lt. Col. Leonid Telyatnikov, 37, shown here at the Chernobyl Museum in Kiev, was at the Chernobyl nuclear power plant after disaster struck April 26, 1986. Of 28 men on his team, six died. Telyatnikov contracted hepatitis, suffered hair loss and other symptoms of radiation sickness. He's now deputy chief of the Kiev Fire Department. "I am an optimist. How many people did we save that day? Who counted?" Telyatnikov says.

Pyotr Zborovsky, 74
Retired teacher
Kiev

"I was a Soviet artillery sergeant during the war. War is killing and grief. The U.S. hasn't suffered an invasion in 200 years. Let me wish that your country does not suffer our experience."

Nora Ivanova, 47
Gypsy singer
Moscow

"To be a Gypsy is to be rich in creativity. I write 'Gypsy' on my passport because I'm proud. The worst thing that can happen to us is assimilation, because we would lose our identity."

Gennady Yatsenko, 46
Physician
Moscow

"I think that the people of the U.S. are still a mystery for the Soviet people and vice versa. We know quite little about each other and that's a pity."

Yevgeny Kostoglodov, 28
English teacher
Novosibirsk, Siberia

"It's old people who are against perestroika. They got used to living in the old way and don't want to change. Young people want it changed right now, right here."

Neither East nor West united in reaction to changes

The advent of Mikhail Gorbachev and the Reagan-Gorbachev summit that ended June 2, 1988, changed U.S.-U.S.S.R relations and the superpowers' relations with the world. Here's my assessment published in USA TODAY *Sept. 9, 1988.*

One hundred days after the latest Reagan-Gorbachev summit meeting, what's the mood in Moscow and around the world?

▶ Soviet politicians are proud and positive.

▶ Our U.S. envoy in Moscow warns against "euphoria."

▶ Western world leaders voice reflections ranging from gushy to guarded.

Britain's Prime Minister Margaret Thatcher says, "We are fortunate there is a person (Gorbachev) with such vision and courage." But West German Chancellor Helmut Kohl urges we "remain sober and have no illusions."

▶ Chiefs of some communist countries express admiration, others remain aloof.

Cuba's President Fidel Castro says Mikhail Gorbachev "is a communicator. He's nice. He has a direct style."

But China's General Secretary Zhao Ziyang is unconvinced. "We don't think the international situation has really been relaxed."

President Reagan and General Secretary Gorbachev have been lying low — especially the past month — on superpower relations since they said goodbye in Moscow June 2.

Reagan's attention has been directed toward helping Vice President George Bush succeed him in his job and to a 10-day California holiday of horseback riding and wood chopping.

Gorbachev literally sneaked away unannounced July 30 for a five-week-plus sabbatical in the sun of the Crimea. Nothing official was heard from him. He arrived

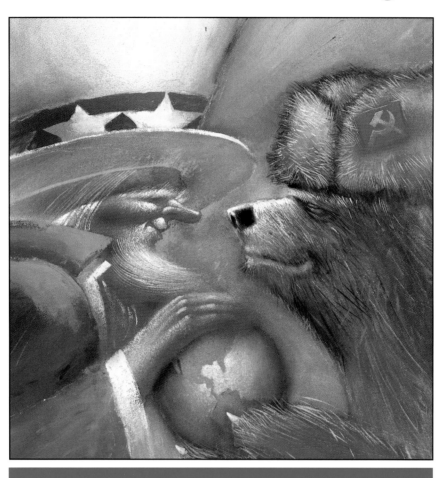

back unannounced Tuesday night, returned to work at Thursday's Politburo meeting.

While the key summit players have been offstage, others in both countries have been busy with follow-up or basking in the afterglow.

During our JetCapade stop in Moscow, Soviet Foreign Minister Eduard Shevardnadze talked with us for an hour: "The recent deeds of our countries have deeply influenced the general sentiments on the entire planet. If we stop or pause in our new relations, the people of the world will not forgive us."

Outside Shevardnadze's office, aides monitor the Cable News Network nonstop for news from the USA.

Anatoly Dobrynin, Soviet ambassador to the USA for 24 years until 1986, now a key Gorbachev adviser on relations with us, waxes with even more enthusiasm:

"Before our relations were always see-saw. Now I feel very much better. Can you imagine touring each other's most secret military places? And there will be more of this."

His office doorway is flanked by maps of the USA and U.S.S.R. A corner table in his waiting room is stacked with publications from the USA.

But at the U.S. Embassy — getting a $35 million renovation to make it liveable a few more years while the new $200 million one the Soviets bugged is torn down and rebuilt — Ambassador Jack F. Matlock Jr. was restrained, reserved:

"Relations have been moving in a more positive direction. But I hope the people in the U.S. don't go into euphoria as in the past when things improved. Let's make sure the goals are translated into reality before we celebrate too much."

Elsewhere around the world, these are summit assessments given to us on JetCapade visits:

SOVIET UNION: CLOSE-UP OF FOREIGN RELATIONS

▶ Britain's Thatcher, while saluting Gorbachev, added this self-tribute: "I was the first to meet with Mr. Gorbachev and say, 'He's a man I can do business with.' I was the first to publicly encourage reforms."

▶ West Germany's Kohl supplemented his suggestion of sobriety: "Gorbachev doesn't want to do away with communism; he wants to make it more effective."

▶ France's President Francois Mitterrand, leader of the world's sixth largest defense spender, favors "reducing over-arming" but opposes "disarmament." He reaffirms his belief in "watchfulness and vigilance ... because the lust for power and the spirit of intolerance could rise again."

GOVERNMENT GATEWAY: The Old Trinity Tower entrance to the Kremlin, the seat of power of the Soviet Union.

even believe he'll turn to capitalism. Of course, he won't do that. He knows the Western mind."

▶ Poland's Gen. Wojciech Jaruzelski, with whom Gorbachev spent six days in July after the summit with Reagan, says, "The Moscow meeting proves there is an opportunity to get closer."

Jaruzelski hopes to be invited to Washington. "The U.S. is such a fantastic country and to get to know it better would be an extremely valuable thing for me and for Poland."

▶ China's General Secretary Zhao, leader of 1 billion-plus people in the world's most populous country, reflects the coolness of predecessor Deng Xiaoping toward the U.S.S.R.

During an hour-long session with JetCateers, Zhao emphasized what he calls communist China's "non-aligned" status. He clearly is more interested in "technology transfer" from the USA to China than he is in cozying up to the U.S.S.R.

▶ Indian Prime Minister Rajiv Gandhi, leader of the world's second most populous nation, sees the new U.S.-U.S.S.R. era as substantiation of his stance:

"The world needs to break down artificial barriers it has built up. Capitalism vs. communism. North vs. south. If the world is to progress, these barriers must be removed. The concept of power blocs must end. The only way to end power blocs is to be non-aligned."

Among leaders of other communist countries, reactions range from clear reflection to cool rejection of Gorbachev's game plan:

▶ In Vietnam, where economic woes dwarf those facing the Soviet Union, Foreign Minister Nguyen Co Thach takes a mini-Moscow posture:

"We have taught that everything from capitalism is corrupt. This is false. Without some capitalism, there would be no socialism."

▶ Castro, though miffed he has not been in on missile talks, doffed his army fatigue cap to the man who controls Cuba's economic lifeline during a six-hour, dark-of-the-night JetCapade interview. "(Gorbachev has) honestly analyzed problems in the Soviet Union. Some

Perhaps the most outspoken suspicions of the two leaders come from Costa Rica. President Oscar Arias Sanchez, 1987 Nobel Peace Prize winner, simplifies — or oversimplifies — his summit visions. Leader of a country that has had no standing army since 1948, Arias says:

"Spending money on arms is incompatible with economic and social growth. We had to choose between rifles and bread, machine guns, tanks, helicopters, airplanes, and schools, hospitals, and secondary roads."

Arias scoffs at suggestions that either Reagan or Gorbachev — or both — might be considered for the 1988 Peace Prize: "The (prize) is for people who make peace. Mr. Gorbachev and Mr. Reagan make wars." He cited Afghanistan, Angola, Grenada, Nicaragua.

That's a mini-view of the multifaceted mood of the world about the two superpowers and their leaders.

Soviets are closing the gap as U.S. space program stalls

While NASA labors to get the USA's shuttle back into space, the Soviet Union is plunging ahead to put what remains of a space race out of reach.

"The Soviets have been running over the top of us," says former U.S. astronaut Deke Slayton, one of the Mercury Seven who raced the Soviets to reach the stars nearly three decades ago.

Despite setbacks, the Kremlin's goal is clear.

"We do not intend to lose our vanguard positions in the conquest of space," says Soviet leader Mikhail Gorbachev.

NASA hoped to return the challenge by launching Discovery in late September. The USA's 26th shuttle mission would be the first since the 1986 Challenger

HOME OF COSMONAUTS: Gen. Vladimir Dzhanibekov lives and trains with other cosmonauts in Zvyozdny Gorodok (Star City), 19 miles northeast of Moscow.

disaster that killed seven crew members.

In December 1988, two Soviet cosmonauts aboard the orbiting Mir (peace) station were to attempt to set a new space endurance record of 365 days, eclipsing the old Soviet mark of 326. And engineers are putting final touches on a shuttle that looks exactly like NASA's, hoping for an unmanned maiden flight before the end of 1988.

Meanwhile, NASA is trying to pry enough money from Congress to begin building an $18 billion space station in the mid-1990s.

The Soviets are building on a bumper year of space success in 1987 in which they:

▶ Launched 95 missions. The USA, Europe, Japan and China sent up 15.

▶ Established Mir as a permanent station by sending up relief crews.

▶ Introduced the heavy-lift Energia rocket that will help build a bigger station. The USA is six to eight years from launching a similar booster.

▶ Began a commercial program by launching a satellite for India.

Have the Soviets passed the USA? Experts rate the U.S.S.R. ahead in man-years in space — 14 to 5 — and heavy-lift rockets. But the USA has the edge in optics, high technology and deep-space exploration.

JetCapade toured Star City, the Soviet cosmonaut training center. In an exclusive interview, senior cosmonaut Vladimir Dzhanibekov said that the Soviets' major goal — and current lead — is long-duration spaceflight.

"From the very beginning, our main task and aim was to create a long-living station in orbit," he said.

"In technological know-how, you're ahead. But we know how to prepare people for long flights," said Dzhanibekov. "Your know-how is metal, not people. You'll have the same problems we had years ago when you train for long flights."

Much of the Star City training center remains closed to the public. But like NASA's Johnson Space Center in Houston where U.S. astronauts train, Star City has a shuttle simulator, control panels for practice flights, gravity-force testing machines and a museum.

Despite the differences between the Soviet and the U.S. systems, Dzhanibekov — like many U.S. astronauts — believes cooperation, not competition, should be the rule. He would like to see a repeat of the 1975 Apollo-Soyuz mission where three astronauts and two Soviet cosmonauts joined their capsules in space.

But this time, Dzhanibekov believes, a joint mission should fly to the moon and on to Mars.

"We need to learn that space is not a stadium," he said. "It's not for competition. It belongs to no one. Let's work for the common good."

More voices find their way into Soviet newspapers

On the palace grounds where Peter the Great played as a child, Soviet citizens young and old sit reading newspapers on a sunny Sunday morning.

"That is new. Now people read newspapers, instead of fiction," says Masha Shestakova, 34, a tour guide at the Kolomenskoe Palace grounds in Moscow's outskirts.

"Now newspapers are interesting, with all different points of view."

Soviet leader Mikhail Gorbachev's perestroika policy of reform has brought new freedom to the Soviet press. The result: a boom in newspaper circulation and surprising comparisons with the U.S. press. The new look shows in many ways.

▶ Foremost is in news coverage: In dramatic reports of the cosmonauts' close encounter with disaster in space in September 1988. In aggressive economic, environmental and investigative reporting, especially by progressive weeklies.

▶ In bagfuls of letters to the editor. An estimated 1,500 to 2,000 a day pour in at *Izvestia,* the daily newspaper of the Supreme Soviet. That compares with 35-50 a day at USA TODAY, 100 at *The New York Times.*

Published letters comment — critically or otherwise — on everything from Gorbachev's policies and personality to long lines and short supplies at stores. And Soviet editors claim special delight in publishing ones that begin: "I know you won't print this . . ."

▶ In more aggressive editing and promotion. Full-year subscription rules have been cut back; promotions are used as fillers in news columns. *Izvestia* Editor in Chief Ivan D. Laptev says: "The newspaper must advertise itself, say by its content why you must read it. . . . People must think this is their newspaper."

▶ In the return of advertising. Ads are due to appear in 1989 for the first time in more than 50 years. Laptev hopes to increase his newspaper by two pages of ads,

NEWSMEN COMPARE: USA TODAY Editor in Chief John C. Quinn talks shop with *Izvestia* Editor in Chief Ivan D. Laptev.

first from technology suppliers; later, from makers of household goods.

▶ In modernizing of printing plants. *Pravda,* the Communist Party journal, has new electronic typesetting and page layout equipment. *Izvestia* expected new typesetting by the end of 1988 and planned for a 107-million-ruble ($167 million) suburban plant.

Laptev is pleased with the progress the newspaper has made since he took charge four years ago. "Our circulation was slipping. We told the staff that if you want to make a newspaper for the people, not for the bosses, you have to face the problems that are bothering the people. That was risky at the time."

Izvestia's editors discovered news for the people sells newspapers: Laptev says circulation jumped about 500,000 in each of his first two years, 1 million the third year and 3 million in 1987, to 11 million.

"If we could print 13 million, there would not be a single copy left." Paper shortages still limit circulation.

Laptev credits diversity of news and views for the growth. "For a long time we were all talking the same thing. Now a person has to say what he sees and knows. We are not censored anymore."

Pravda's editor in chief, the more traditional Viktor G. Afanasyev, 66, is even more frank about the changes.

Afanasyev admits the old limits were frustrating: "I knew these things should be criticized, but I couldn't. . . . You could not criticize Moscow. We called it the city of the future and nothing bad could be written about it."

Afanasyev concedes there still are limits. Can *Pravda* criticize Gorbachev?

"We can, but we wouldn't dare yet. . . . We want to support this especially in this very difficult time. . . . We try to help. We are the front line of perestroika."

'Conditions are right for better relations'

Mikhail Gorbachev's first three years as the top leader of the Soviet Union have been nothing short of revolutionary.

Before Gorbachev became general secretary of the Communist Party in March 1985, who would have thought of glasnost (openness) and perestroika (reform) as being official policies in the U.S.S.R.?

Gorbachev clearly represents a new generation.

At the party conference in June 1988, he said:

▶ "The existing political system proved incapable of protecting us from stagnation in economic and social life."

▶ "(Free speech) is a real guarantee that any problem of public interest will be discussed from any angle."

▶ "It is time we introduced democratic restrictions on the duration of service in elective offices."

Since Gorbachev has been in power, the U.S.S.R. has:

▶ Signed the Intermediate Nuclear Forces Treaty with the USA.

▶ Begun a withdrawal of forces from Afghanistan.

▶ Accelerated its opposition to the USA's "star wars" or Strategic Defense Initiative.

But Gorbachev is not without strong opposition. Yegor K. Ligachev, 67, No. 2 man in the Communist Party, reminded delegates at the party conference that Gorbachev's selection as party leader was a close call. Regarding Gorbachev's reform policies, he warned:

"Policy making is not as easy as slurping cabbage soup. Caution should be combined with decisiveness."

Gorbachev's key leaders, Soviet Foreign Minister Eduard Shevardnadze and International Adviser Anatoly Dobrynin offered their views on issues:

On U.S.-Soviet relations:

Shevardnadze: "Everything in U.S.-Soviet relations represents a process toward putting our relations on a solid foundation. Look at what's happened in the last two and a half to three years — four summit meetings, 28 meetings at the foreign minister level . . . unprecedented meetings of the ministers of defense. We have not overcome suspicion, but there is more confidence now."

Dobrynin: "Conditions are right. We have good prospectives for improvements."

On the arms race:

Shevardnadze: "There is a need to save civilization, to eliminate nuclear weapons, to ban chemical weapons. The major way these tasks can be resolved is through better Soviet-U.S. relations."

On the impact of a new U.S. president on relations:

Shevardnadze: "The progress will continue. I

General Secretary Mikhail Gorbachev

Foreign Minister Eduard Shevardnadze

International Adviser Anatoly Dobrynin

Mikhail Gorbachev, 57, the educated son of Russian peasants, joined the Communist Party in 1952 and steadily rose through its ranks. He is the youngest leader of the Soviet Union's Communist Party since Joseph Stalin, at age 45, succeeded Vladimir Lenin in 1924. The image he has set is new, too. The Western media have dubbed him and his wife, Raisa, the "Gucci Comrades" because of their stylish dress. Two of Gorbachev's key leaders — Eduard Shevardnadze, 60, foreign minister, and Anatoly Dobrynin, 58, ambassador to the USA from 1962 until he became chief of the Communist Party's International Department in 1986 — met with the JetCapade news team.

have not met Mr. Michael Dukakis, but I have been following his policy statements. It's difficult to say what the turn of events will be. But good groundwork has been laid, so no matter who the president is, the policy of normalizing Soviet-U.S. relations will continue, including further arms control. If a new president is going to pursue a different policy running counter to what has been done at Geneva, Reykjavik, Washington or Moscow, it will pose a problem to the entire world."

Dobrynin (jokingly): "I hope both of them win. What is your guess?"

On how Soviet people feel about improving relations:

Shevardnadze: "I would be hard put to say there is a generation against normalization of Soviet-U.S. relations. Everything has enjoyed the support of all the people. . . . I understand that there are public opinion difficulties in the U.S. I think this trend can be overcome. In the U.S. there is a stronger sentiment among the general public to put an end to the arms race."

SPAIN

Featured in USA TODAY: July 15

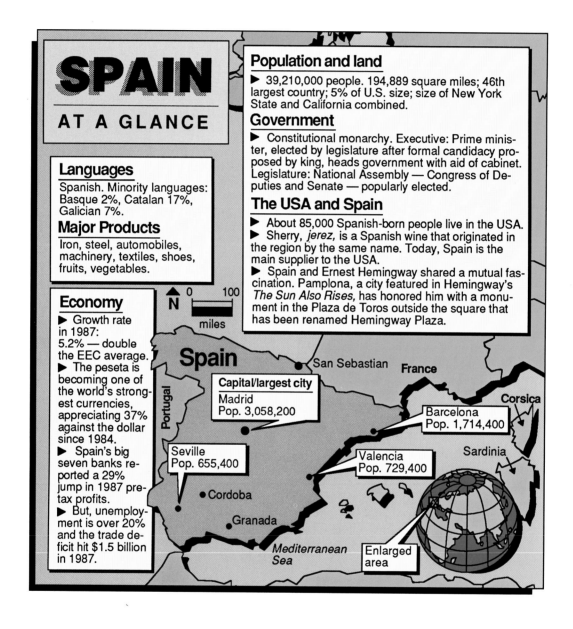

SPAIN
AT A GLANCE

Languages
Spanish. Minority languages: Basque 2%, Catalan 17%, Galician 7%.

Major Products
Iron, steel, automobiles, machinery, textiles, shoes, fruits, vegetables.

Economy
▶ Growth rate in 1987: 5.2% — double the EEC average.
▶ The peseta is becoming one of the world's strongest currencies, appreciating 37% against the dollar since 1984.
▶ Spain's big seven banks reported a 29% jump in 1987 pre-tax profits.
▶ But, unemployment is over 20% and the trade deficit hit $1.5 billion in 1987.

Population and land
▶ 39,210,000 people. 194,889 square miles; 46th largest country; 5% of U.S. size; size of New York State and California combined.

Government
▶ Constitutional monarchy. Executive: Prime minister, elected by legislature after formal candidacy proposed by king, heads government with aid of cabinet. Legislature: National Assembly — Congress of Deputies and Senate — popularly elected.

The USA and Spain
▶ About 85,000 Spanish-born people live in the USA.
▶ Sherry, *jerez,* is a Spanish wine that originated in the region by the same name. Today, Spain is the main supplier to the USA.
▶ Spain and Ernest Hemingway shared a mutual fascination. Pamplona, a city featured in Hemingway's *The Sun Also Rises,* has honored him with a monument in the Plaza de Toros outside the square that has been renamed Hemingway Plaza.

N 0 — 100 miles

Spain

Portugal

San Sebastian   France

Capital/largest city
Madrid
Pop. 3,058,200

Barcelona
Pop. 1,714,400

Corsica

Valencia
Pop. 729,400

Sardinia

Seville
Pop. 655,400

● Cordoba

● Granada

Mediterranean Sea

Enlarged area

Old tree, new branches greening for '92 showoff

Bullfighting is still bravado. Gypsy flamenco dancers still sing of sadness and gladness.

But, without forsaking their folklore, Spaniards are now getting a fix on the future.

After a long isolation, including 36 years of dictatorship under Francisco Franco, Spain has rejoined the world.

It has a partnership with the USA in everything from NATO to NASA, although strong anti-nuclear sentiment is forcing withdrawal of our nuclear-capable fighter-bombers.

Six years under the premiership and presidency of **Felipe Gonzalez Marquez**, 46, in a comfortable combine with **King Juan Carlos I**, 50, and Spain is poised to showcase itself.

Target: 1992. On that year's agenda:

▶ 500th anniversary celebration of Columbus' journey from Spain to discover America.

▶ First-ever Olympics in Spain. Barcelona, 2nd largest city, will be the host.

▶ A World Trade Fair in Seville, 4th largest city.

▶ Madrid, capital and largest city, becomes "Culture Capital of Europe," so designated by the European Economic Community.

▶ Spain becomes fully integrated into the EEC.

"We are like an old tree with old roots, but with new branches flowering very strongly," says Gonzalez.

While the political, economic and social rejuvenation is in the forefront, traditional fun and games are not forgotten.

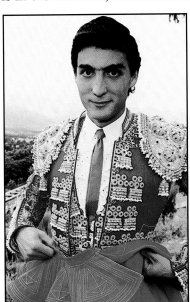

CAMINO: Spaniards worship macho bullfighters as heroes.

Bullfighting coliseums in major cities drew 35 million spectators in 1987. Smaller rings in towns and on farms train bullfighters.

One such backyard bullring is on the 450-acre ranch of **Paco Camino**, 46, outside Talavera, 150 miles southwest of Madrid. A legendary bullfighter here for 20 years, Camino retired in 1982. Now he's coaching his son **Rafael**, 19, one of Spain's top young bullfighters.

"This is an art, but you must prepare for it like an athlete," says the teenage matador. Spaniards understand the art of bullfighting, but Americans don't. Here, the bullfighters who make it are worshipped and make a lot of money. I hope to be one of them."

While Spanish macho is manifested in the bullring, the sentimentality of Spaniards is expressed by the fabled flamenco dancers.

Spain's poet laureate **Federico Garcia Lorca** said flamenco was "born of the first cry and the first kiss."

Flores Amaya, 56, known as La Chunga, one of Spain's most noted flamenco dancers, has been performing since age 6. "When I dance, I am in a cloud. Sometimes it is a sad cloud. But if I am happy, I dance to show my happiness."

Pilar Rospide, 22, one of the young stars says, "We dance our emotions." Then, she sings these emotions, over and over:

ROSPIDE: Dances all her emotions.

I gave you the most wonderful thing I have . . . myself.
But now you act like you don't know me.
Why do you break my heart? . . .

The folklore of the past and the hopes for the future are overshadowed by the realities of the present for some 12,500 U.S. military here.

Our 401st Tactical Fighter Wing with 72 F-16 planes and personnel is being kicked out and relocated in Italy.

U.S. Sgt. Raul Denis, 24, Newark, N.J., resents the cold shoulder. "What people here forget is that every U.S. squadron sponsors an orphanage each year. We donate $5,000 to $25,000. We're not all bad. We're here to help them."

But **Aurora Jordan**, 54, a native homemaker near the Torrejon base, counters:

"Do you know what it's like to live with your windows shaking, with nuclear weapons in your back yard? No more bases here. We've been too nice too long."

That's Plain Talk from Spain.

200-YEAR-OLD TRADITION: Bullfighting is big business in Spain. Revenues reached $300 million in 1987; 30,700 bulls were killed. Best time for bullfights: May, during the monthlong festival of San Isidro, honoring Spain's patron saint.

MOORISH MINARET: Part of this tower adjoining the Seville Cathedral was built in the 12th century by the Moors. A mosque once occupied the cathedral site.

CELEBRATING THE PAST: Children pose in front of a monument built in Seville in 1892 to mark the 400th anniversary of Columbus' discovery of America. It was restored by dictator Franco in 1961.

ARTISTS' HAVEN: Guillermo Sanchez Robles, 34, paints the Parque del Retiro in Seville. An artist who once studied to be a lawyer, Robles is one of many street painters trying to capture the park's beauty. He signs his paintings "Guisaro," combining the first syllables of his three names.

GUITAR MAKER: Antonio Ariza, 49, makes classical and flamenco guitars in his tiny workshop in Alhambra. Cost: 100,000 pesetas (about $895) or more.

Maria Dolores Diaz Cuevas, 15
Student, Madrid

"Our cultural life has improved as we become more integrated with Europe. We do feel there have been changes under democracy, but there is still some censorship."

Julio Cuesta, 40
Expo '92 official
Seville

"The place is right, the occasion is right, the year is right. Spain has done great things in history. Why not again?"

Manuel Pujol Baladas, 40
Artist
Barcelona

"Spain has to quit thinking of herself as the mother country of others, especially those in the Western Hemisphere. We have to quit selling history and deal in reality."

Juan Carlos Frieben, 24
Merchant
Madrid

"When I travel outside Spain, I notice many in Europe still don't think of us as a democratic nation. They think we're just bullfights, wine and flamenco. But we're more than that."

'We have the greatest potential in Europe'

On the image of Spain:

"Spain has managed to accomplish a peaceful revolution (after the 1939-1975 Franco dictatorship) — a democratic revolution — which hasn't been normal during our history. This democratic transformation, done peacefully without any vengeance or civil confrontation, has been accompanied by a spectacular opening of our borders. Spain is the fifth country in importance in the European market. All this has taken place in just one decade. This is a country which is beginning to flourish economically. It was traditionally considered a poor country. Now, it's considered the country with the greatest potential for growth and development in Europe. I need to make that image known."

On Spain's future:

"The year 1992 is becoming an important point of reference for Spain. First, as a European country that forms part of the Economic Community, we have an important challenge in establishing with the countries an inner market for all our 330 million inhabitants. We still have a standard of living below that of the Federal Republic of Germany. But, whereas its economy grows at a rate of 1.5% a year, we are growing at a rate of over 5%. Apart from this, Spain is going to host the 1992 Olympic Games. This means for Spain what it meant for the United States when Los Angeles hosted the Games."

On negotiations to keep U.S. military bases in Spain:

"For 30 years the U.S. operated the bases as a land lease, which was possible within a dictatorial regime. But when a democratic change takes place, bilateral relations must adjust. It is fundamental to keep in mind that the bases are being used jointly by the U.S. and Spain."

On Gonzalez's internal challenges:

"Undoubtedly, the most important challenge to Spanish society is the elimination of unemployment. At the same time, there is also the growth of the working population, especially women. We must maintain the rate of growth and accelerate it. We must also incorporate young people into the work force. That is where we seem to encounter the greatest difficulty. We also must finish off what remains of terrorism. This is our second concern. It is also true that we still have the problem of sharing power (with regions). Before we were highly centralized and now have an almost entirely federal system. Perhaps the problem in Spanish society in political terms — and that is why they speak of the year 2000 — is that we see no organized alternative to the present government. That may please the politicians from my own party, but from the democratic viewpoint, it's not healthy. I would like to have a competitor or a set of

Felipe Gonzalez Marquez, 46, has been prime minister of Spain since 1982. He is a member of the Socialist Workers Party, which, like many other socialist parties in Europe, has shifted from pure Marxist to middle-of-the-road positions. Gonzalez's party has no unified, strong opposition, and he is expected to be re-elected in 1990. Because of his age and his popularity, Gonzalez is considered the only European leader likely to still be holding his position at the turn of the century. During the interview with the JetCapade news team, Gonzalez sat comfortably in a garden chair outside the prime minister's palace on the outskirts of Madrid.

competitors with reasonable opportunities for success in the next election."

On whether criticism of the USA stems from the Franco years:

"Undoubtedly. That is the main root of the problem. It is difficult to imagine President Reagan visiting the Chile regime, but nonetheless the Cold War resulted in President Eisenhower visiting Franco."

On the image of the USA in Spain:

"It is still profitable for a Spanish politician to talk harshly about the United States. It is not a country that is loved from a general point of view. The Americans want to be loved and that is much more difficult if you are powerful."

SWEDEN

Featured in USA TODAY: July 8

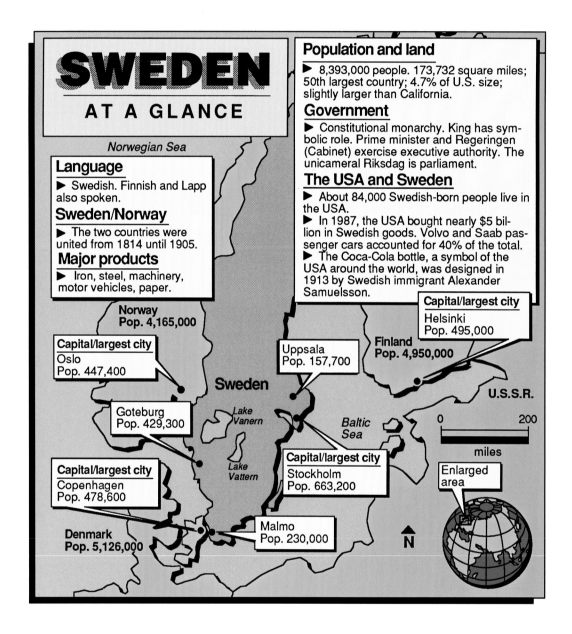

SWEDEN

AT A GLANCE

Norwegian Sea

Language
▶ Swedish. Finnish and Lapp also spoken.

Sweden/Norway
▶ The two countries were united from 1814 until 1905.

Major products
▶ Iron, steel, machinery, motor vehicles, paper.

Population and land
▶ 8,393,000 people. 173,732 square miles; 50th largest country; 4.7% of U.S. size; slightly larger than California.

Government
▶ Constitutional monarchy. King has symbolic role. Prime minister and Regeringen (Cabinet) exercise executive authority. The unicameral Riksdag is parliament.

The USA and Sweden
▶ About 84,000 Swedish-born people live in the USA.
▶ In 1987, the USA bought nearly $5 billion in Swedish goods. Volvo and Saab passenger cars accounted for 40% of the total.
▶ The Coca-Cola bottle, a symbol of the USA around the world, was designed in 1913 by Swedish immigrant Alexander Samuelsson.

Norway Pop. 4,165,000

Capital/largest city
Oslo
Pop. 447,400

Goteburg
Pop. 429,300

Sweden

Lake Vanern

Lake Vattern

Uppsala
Pop. 157,700

Finland Pop. 4,950,000

Capital/largest city
Helsinki
Pop. 495,000

U.S.S.R.

Baltic Sea

Capital/largest city
Copenhagen
Pop. 478,600

Capital/largest city
Stockholm
Pop. 663,200

Denmark Pop. 5,126,000

Malmo
Pop. 230,000

N

0   200
miles

Enlarged area

A smooth playing field, stiff admission price

There is no poverty here as we know it. And no really great wealth. Everyone is somewhere near the middle.

The socialist government's policy is to level things out. Playing on such an even field has its payoffs. And price tag.

Some of what the Swedes get:

▶ Free education, kindergarten through college.

▶ Free national health insurance.

▶ Free day care for children.

▶ Five weeks minimum annual vacation.

But they pay:

▶ World's highest income tax, a top of 80%. (USA's maximum is 28%).

▶ 23% sales tax on everything, including food (USA state sales taxes average 5%, with many necessities exempt).

Naturally, there is some grumbling about high taxes. When we asked **Prime Minister Ingvar Carlsson** about that he replied: "I wish you would ask me about our high standard of living."

The standard of living is high:

▶ Per capita annual income: $11,989. (USA: $15,340.)

▶ Unemployment: 1.6%. (USA: 5.6%.)

Swedes reflect their role as the largest and leading Scandinavian country. At peace with themselves. Their country's non-aligned and neutral stance has kept them out of war for 174 years. They generally seem happy, laid-back, friendly, free-spirited.

There are peaks and valleys. Summer sunshine and nearly 20 hours of daylight keep Swedes on a high. Winter's heavy snows and 20 hours of darkness put them on a low. Not unlike Alaska. Here, as there, wintertime alcoholism and suicides are a problem.

But now, summertime spirits surge. Fishing, relaxing and romancing reign. Examples:

Leif Bjur, 70, retired telephone worker, is on Strommen Bay with his rod and reel early each morning:

"Here, anybody can fish. No license. No fees. Fishermen are the happiest people in Sweden. I think the king watches me out of the corner of his eye and wishes he were me down there."

The Baltic Sea, Gulf of Bothnia and thousands of lakes and parks make this a fisherman's paradise. Also a harbor for amour.

Sweden has a reputation for free love. A misnomer. Not free, in terms of prurient promiscuity. But very open and uninhibited. Live-in loving is in.

Conversations with randomly selected young men and women or couples found most are unmarried, but living with a mate.

Ann Lindquist, 21, nurses' assistant, has been living with interior designer **Peter Reijto**, 26, for 3½ years. Says Ann: "Our generation doesn't want to get married.

Divorce is a sad thing and we want to avoid it. This way you could break up without shattering a marriage."

Adds Peter: "We now have yuppies in Sweden. First, you live together for five to six years for fun. Then maybe you start thinking seriously — about living together even longer."

Ann, beautiful, blue-eyed and blond, is typical of young women in Sweden. Catch your eye everywhere, said **Sylvester Stallone**, in

PETER, ANN: Yuppie live-in lovers.

Stockholm promoting his new film *Rambo III:* "They're everywhere. Without a doubt, these are the most genetically gorgeous people in the world."

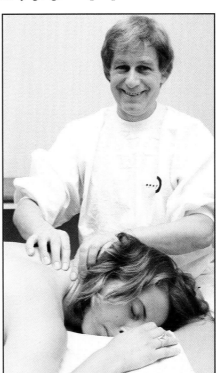

AXELSON, ELMSTROM: Floating on a cloud from relaxing massage.

The laid-back loveliness of Swedes may have something to do with their world renowned Swedish massage. Axelson's Gymnastiska Institute, Sweden's oldest and largest massage school, has over 2,000 students, including many from the USA.

Says head instructor **Hans Viking Axelson**, 54, as he works on student-masseuse **Eva Elmstrom**, 23:

"People are becoming more body-minded, health-minded. Stress is higher. So massages are coming back. The Swedish massage is different and deeper. You space out and go into a dreamlike state. It's like floating on a cloud. When you land, no more stress."

That's Plain Talk from Sweden.

SNOWY PEAKS: The rugged wilderness of Northern Sweden is a land of lakes and snow-capped mountains. Mount Kebnekaise rises 6,926 feet above sea level. Located in the Lapland region, it is Sweden's highest mountain.

CHERISHED CHILDREN: These Stockholm youngsters are the picture of health. It lasts. Sweden has the world's highest life expectancy rate, 76.8 years.

TOURIST TEMPTATIONS: More than 225,000 tourists visit Sweden annually, spending an average of $125 per person daily. This scene is in Stockholm.

OLD CHARM: Although Stockholm is famous for its modern architecture, narrow brick streets and alleys are common in Gamla Stan (Old Town), the heart of the city.

ISLAND CITY: Stockholm, the capital and largest city in Sweden, covers 14 islands connected by 50 bridges. More than 1.5 million people live in the metropolitan area, Sweden's commercial and cultural center. This view overlooks Strommen Bay.

Belay Zewdie, 32
Student in Stockholm
Addis Ababa, Ethiopia

"Swedes have never had to worry about tomorrow, or scramble for their daily bread. Because Swedes are secure, you can be yourself, and they will accept you."

Anna Lindh, 30
Lawyer
Stockholm

"Sweden isn't the country of "free love" — and never was. Even when marriage was not popular, people living together came up with some pretty sophisticated financial agreements."

Leif Kihlberg, 45
Union official
Stockholm

"There's a word, 'lagom,' that's as Swedish as smorgasbord. It means getting along with not too much, not too little. The story of Sweden's evolutionary progress is wrapped up in that word."

Allan Johansson, 77
Retired watchmaker
Goteborg

"We have a king and queen. They guide the ship. In other countries, royalty are like gods. Here, they're more like everybody else. It has to do with our sense of democracy."

Nordic neighborhood: Close ties, allies

On the U.S.-Soviet summit:

"I'm a bit split. I had hoped there would be an agreement on strategic nuclear weapons. On the other hand, TV was sending the pictures directly into American homes from Moscow. In that way, I think this could mean something very important for the future."

On superpower relations:

"They are improving. Sweden can be affected if there is a cold war or a possibility of detente. The fact that the Soviet Union and the United States are now in a cooperative mood will lead to further successes. You cannot solve any problems without an understanding between the United States and the Soviet Union."

On whether Sweden will try to join the European Economic Community:

"Our attitude here is very clear. We want to take part in the cooperation in all aspects with the exception of foreign policy and security. We need the trade. But we are not going to ask for full membership, because of our neutrality."

On Vietnam draft resisters who went to Sweden:

"I don't have any statistics. I can only say that some of them are now Swedish citizens, some of them wanted to go back to the United States as soon as they could, and some of them probably went to Canada and later to the United States."

On the unsolved assassination of former Prime Minister Olof Palme in 1986:

"It's quite difficult to understand. Sweden had not had a political murder in 700 years. Theoretically, we knew this could happen but still we were not prepared. After more than two years, we have not been able to catch the murderer. This is kind of an open wound. We don't know if it was a conspiracy or not."

On Sweden's high tax rate:

"We will most probably have tax reform, but still we have public sector needs in housing, schooling, universities and research. The difference really is between paying for your children's education with high fees or paying taxes. You pay one way or the other, but our system gives a guarantee that certain individuals will not be left aside."

On how he likes his job:

"I've been involved in politics for 30 years. It's impossible to have a job of this kind if you don't like it. I still play soccer and ski, but this must be a mixture of job and hobby. If you don't look at it this way, you would be overly tired in a few months."

*Sweden is the biggest and most populous Scandinavian country. It prides itself on its close relationship to the USA. In 1783, Sweden became one of the USA's first trading partners. The closeness continues under **Prime Minister Ingvar Carlsson**, 53. "Sometimes in Sweden, they say we are the most Americanized country in the world. It's true. We have been very influenced by the United States," Carlsson said.*

But also true: Sweden and the USA have agreed to disagree on several major issues, including Central America, South African trade and nuclear disarmament.

Carlsson, youthful and athletic-looking, met with the JetCapade news team in his garden at his idyllic, lakeside summer home 60 miles north of Stockholm.

The meeting followed a gathering of prime ministers from four surrounding Scandinavian countries — Denmark, Norway, Finland and Iceland. "We have closer political cooperation among our countries than perhaps any other region in the world. We know each other as people as well," Carlsson said.

SWITZERLAND

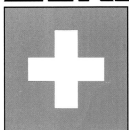

Featured in USA TODAY: June 24

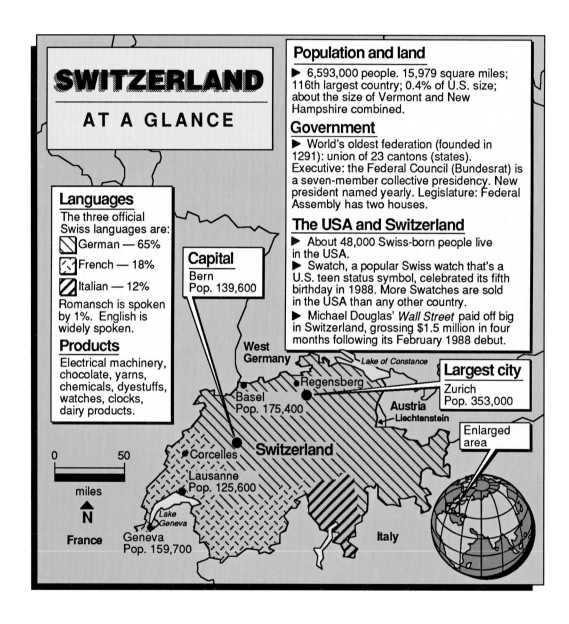

SWITZERLAND

AT A GLANCE

Languages
The three official Swiss languages are:

- German — 65%
- French — 18%
- Italian — 12%

Romansch is spoken by 1%. English is widely spoken.

Products
Electrical machinery, chocolate, yarns, chemicals, dyestuffs, watches, clocks, dairy products.

Capital
Bern
Pop. 139,600

Population and land
▶ 6,593,000 people. 15,979 square miles; 116th largest country; 0.4% of U.S. size; about the size of Vermont and New Hampshire combined.

Government
▶ World's oldest federation (founded in 1291): union of 23 cantons (states). Executive: the Federal Council (Bundesrat) is a seven-member collective presidency. New president named yearly. Legislature: Federal Assembly has two houses.

The USA and Switzerland
▶ About 48,000 Swiss-born people live in the USA.
▶ Swatch, a popular Swiss watch that's a U.S. teen status symbol, celebrated its fifth birthday in 1988. More Swatches are sold in the USA than any other country.
▶ Michael Douglas' *Wall Street* paid off big in Switzerland, grossing $1.5 million in four months following its February 1988 debut.

Largest city
Zurich
Pop. 353,000

Enlarged area

West Germany

Lake of Constance

Regensberg

Basel
Pop. 175,400

Austria
Liechtenstein

Switzerland

Corcelles

Lausanne
Pop. 125,600

Lake Geneva

France

Geneva
Pop. 159,700

Italy

0   50
miles

N

A peaceful cubbyhole that's rich and ready

What's it like to live in the richest and most peaceful nation in the world?

Most people in Switzerland will tell you it's the closest thing to heaven on earth. They cite:

▶ No. 1 per capita annual income: $17,680. USA: $15,340. West Germany: $12,080. Great Britain: $8,870. Halfway around the world, in the Philippines it's $560.

▶ Unemployment: 1%. USA: 5.6%.

▶ Inflation: 1%. USA: 5%.

▶ Not involved in a war since 1815. The USA has been in eight during that time.

This rich land-locked haven surrounded by the often-troubled and warring nations of Europe and the Middle East didn't get that way by chance.

It's been planned with Swiss pragmatism and precision — untouched by worldly ambitions or romantic notions of its much bigger neighbors — France, Germany, Italy.

While Switzerland sits out wars, it's heavily armed and has the most elaborate civil defense system in the world.

Underneath schools, other public buildings, athletic fields, even gingerbread chalets are concrete shelters filled with first aid, food, bunks, baths. The goal is to have nuclear-safe space for every one of its 6.6 million people by the year 2000. An estimated 83% of the population already has access to such shelters.

We asked **President Otto Stich** why such precaution and preparedness: "Don't you trust superpowers?" He replied, laughing: "It pays to be careful. You never know."

All Swiss males must serve in the army for one year at age 20 and remain in the reserves, with annual renewal training, until age 50. They keep their uniforms and weapons at home. 640,000 could be mobilized in 48 hours.

Sgt. Wirth Roland, 28, a reserve on three weeks duty at Kloten Army Base in Zurich, says: "We're a defending army, not an attacking one. You can have your own army in your own country, or you'll have an enemy army. We prefer our own."

SGT. ROLAND: Ready to defend, like 640,000 others.

While it maintains its neutrality, Switzerland serves as the meeting place for those with differences or disagreements. **President Reagan** first met the Soviet's **Gorbachev** there in Geneva in 1985.

And while the rest of the world is often otherwise occupied, the Swiss go about their business of banking big money — $600 billion in deposits — making and selling cheese, chocolates, Swiss army knives, watches.

Bucherer is a leading Swiss jeweler. **Margrit Botsche**, 47, a manager at the Bucherer store in Zurich, says: "You can tell a person's class by their watch. If you wear a Piaget or a Rolex, you are upper class. A Rado, middle class. If you wear a Swatch you are young or maybe lower class. But all our watches are better than anything the rest of the world has."

The Swiss work hard. A 44-hour week is standard. But they also play a lot. The majestic Alps offer year-round pleasure.

BOTSCHE: A watch tells class.

Some who work there consider it play. One such is **Ulrich Inderbinen**, 88, the oldest working mountain guide in Zermatt, a quaint, seductive town in the shadow of the Matterhorn.

Thousands, mostly foreigners, come to try to climb the Matterhorn each year. Last year, 31 died in the attempt, three are still missing, 136 had to be rescued by helicopters of Air Zermatt or the Red Cross.

Inderbinen stopped climbing the Matterhorn six years ago, at age 82. But he still guides others in the shadows of the highest Alps.

INDERBINEN, 88: A lifetime reaching for the mountaintop in the Alps.

He explains how you learn to reach upward: "As a boy I was tending cows in my father's pasture. I saw a flower blowing in the wind, very high up in the rocks. So I had to climb up to get it. That's how you learn to climb mountains."

That's Plain Talk from Switzerland.

SWITZERLAND: PEOPLE AND PLACES

MEDIEVAL VILLAGE: Restoration work continues in Regensberg, north of Zurich. Much of the village was rebuilt after a fire centuries ago. Regensberg's architectural focal point is the Regensberg Castle, a relic of the 13th century.

SHELTER SAFETY: The Swiss government's goal is to have bomb shelters available for all of its 6.6 million people by 2000. This Zurich shelter can house 500 people.

HIDDEN WEALTH: Private banking is a Swiss institution. Bank president Hans J. Bar is shown inside a vault at Bank Julius Bar & Co. in Zurich.

MAJESTIC MOUNTAIN: In the 13th century, most residents of Zermatt thought "ghosts and gods" lived atop the Matterhorn. Climbers reached its 14,700-foot summit in the 1860s. In the Matterhorn's shadow, Zermatt has become a boutique and skiing boomtown.

SPRY AT AGE 79: Anna Neeracher and her four cats live in a restored medieval house in Regensberg. There's no senior citizens' residence planned for Neeracher's future: "I never want to go to one," she says.

TRANQUILITY TRAIL: Parachutists dive off 7,000-foot Mount Pilatus, near Lucerne.

Langer Hermann, 47
Pharmacist
Zurich

"Even children here work hard. They attend school from 7 o'clock in the morning until 6 in the evening. It trains them. If you see hard work as a child, you can do it as an adult."

Annemarie Hofstetter, 53
School secretary
Regensberg

"The Swiss take care of things. The phone in this office was here when I came 31 years ago. When it needs repair, they send one of the older men. Young ones don't know how it works."

Dominique Loiseau, 39
Watchmaker
Corcelles

"The Swiss contribution to watchmaking is precision. They learned early how to manufacture tiny, tiny pieces. One must have a calm environment to make watches and clocks."

Hans Ochsner, 28
Stockbroker
Zurich

"A successful Swiss banker has to work outside Switzerland to get ahead. Spending time in New York, London or Tokyo will put the average Swiss banker ahead of the rest."

'We're independent but not isolated'

On whether Filipino ex-President Ferdinand Marcos has money "stashed away" in Swiss banks:

"Whether and how much money ex-President Marcos has really hidden in Swiss bank vaults, I don't know. The secrecy of the banks is anchored in our laws. But we do have strict rules and regulations for the acceptance of large sums of money from abroad. In final instances, it will be up to the Swiss courts to decide where the money comes from and whether these are really illegal funds."

On the recent Reagan-Gorbachev summit:

"I'm happy about the dialogue between the superpowers. That is one of the preconditions of peaceful coexistence. If you know somebody, you may trust him. If you do not know him, you may distrust him."

On why Switzerland, a country known for neutrality, has an army:

"We do have an army, and it is the expression of our wish to be independent."

On Switzerland's stability, despite its diversity of language, culture and political subdivisions:

"We have a direct democracy in Switzerland. All our laws are decided upon by the citizens on the grass-roots level. Many things are delegated to the cantonal (state) level. The cantons have much freedom on cultural and religious levels, and many things are just their business. Probably that helps ease tensions."

On Switzerland's rotating one-year presidency:

"The office of president brings about additional work and, as we are only seven, we have quite a bit of work already. So I am quite happy to pass on my office to a colleague next year. . . . We do not want one of us to become too strong or dominant."

On how the Swiss feel about prospects of having their first woman president (Councillor Elisabeth Kopp is to assume the position in 1990):

"I don't think there are any bad feelings about a woman being president. Women got the right to vote in 1971. When I was elected a federal councillor, it was a woman who was running as a candidate for my party. She was not elected. The time was not yet mature for a woman. This is not a problem any longer. Now women are cantonal ministers. They hold important jobs, and people welcome this."

On whether Switzerland's absence from the European Economic Community and the U.N. signals isolationism:

"We do not feel isolated. We need good relations with other countries and I think we have them. We meant to become a member of the United Nations and then the people wouldn't have it (in a referendum). We were

Otto Stich, 61, is one of seven federal councillors who each assume the Swiss presidency for one calendar year. In 1990, Switzerland will have its first woman president when Elisabeth Kopp, 52, federal councillor for justice and police, assumes office. Stich, Switzerland's finance councillor, was interviewed by the JetCapade news team in his simply decorated finance office. He uses it in both his roles as president and councillor.

quite astonished by this negative stance. We try to help in various ways without giving up our independence."

On how much Swiss chocolate he eats:

"I don't think I'm fulfilling my duty in this field. I do not quite reach the standard. I prefer other things and besides, there might be weight problems."

UNITED KINGDOM

Featured in USA TODAY: Sept. 2

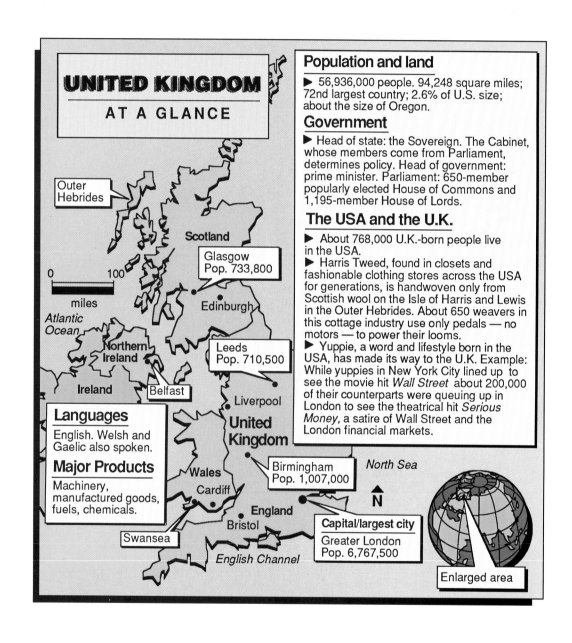

UNITED KINGDOM
AT A GLANCE

Outer Hebrides

Scotland

Glasgow
Pop. 733,800

0   100
miles

Atlantic Ocean

Edinburgh

Northern Ireland

Leeds
Pop. 710,500

Ireland

Belfast

Liverpool

Languages

English. Welsh and Gaelic also spoken.

United Kingdom

Major Products

Machinery, manufactured goods, fuels, chemicals.

Wales

Cardiff

Birmingham
Pop. 1,007,000

North Sea

N

Swansea

England

Bristol

Capital/largest city

Greater London
Pop. 6,767,500

English Channel

Enlarged area

Population and land

▶ 56,936,000 people. 94,248 square miles; 72nd largest country; 2.6% of U.S. size; about the size of Oregon.

Government

▶ Head of state: the Sovereign. The Cabinet, whose members come from Parliament, determines policy. Head of government: prime minister. Parliament: 650-member popularly elected House of Commons and 1,195-member House of Lords.

The USA and the U.K.

▶ About 768,000 U.K.-born people live in the USA.

▶ Harris Tweed, found in closets and fashionable clothing stores across the USA for generations, is handwoven only from Scottish wool on the Isle of Harris and Lewis in the Outer Hebrides. About 650 weavers in this cottage industry use only pedals — no motors — to power their looms.

▶ Yuppie, a word and lifestyle born in the USA, has made its way to the U.K. Example: While yuppies in New York City lined up to see the movie hit *Wall Street* about 200,000 of their counterparts were queuing up in London to see the theatrical hit *Serious Money,* a satire of Wall Street and the London financial markets.

Our Mother Country is a proud Mom again

Nearly 50 million of the USA's 241 million people trace their ancestry to England. Another 11 million have roots in Scotland or Wales.

Great Britain is indeed the Mother Country.

For nearly 40 years after World War II, Mom wasn't doing too well. Steady decline in economic and political power. But now proud Brits say the "great" belongs back in Britain. Some economic reasons:

▶ In three of the last five years, the U.K. had the highest economic growth among the top seven Western nations, including the USA.

▶ British investments in the USA last year out-paced Japan's by 2 to 1.

▶ Britain's industrial productivity is rising faster than that of West Germany, long Europe's postwar power-house.

▶ Personal earnings are up 8.25%, about twice the rate of inflation.

Apart from matching us in many money matters, person-to-person relations between the USA and the U.K. have never been better.

It starts at the top. **President Reagan** and **Prime Minister Margaret Thatcher** have become close political pals during his seven and a half years in office. She's been prime minister for over nine.

Reagan stopped here on his way home from the summit with **Gorbachev** in Moscow in June 1988 and praised Thatcher as a "world lead-

CLAIM TO FAME: Big Ben clock and double-decker buses.

er." She saluted him with *God Bless America.*

The friendly feelings flow right down the line. More people from the USA visited the U.K. in 1987 than any country outside of North America — 2.7 million.

They come to see and taste: Buckingham Palace, Big Ben, double-decker buses, warm beer, hot tea.

Penny Wright, 45, has been a fruit vendor for 16 years at Westminster Bridge, across from Big Ben.

"The world goes by Big Ben time. It has a larger-than-life reputation. Many people who come to see it are dis-

appointed it's not bigger than it is. Anyway, I wouldn't want to carry it around on my wrist, would you?" Wright asks, pointing to the clock.

Roger Auclair, 35, has been conductor on a double-decker bus for 14 years.

"It's nostalgia, simple as that. Whenever people see old movies of England, they see double-decker buses. When I stroll down the aisle, people look at me as though they expect me to break out in song," says the handsome, happy Auclair.

While most of England's venerable institutions remain, some are changing. English pubs traditionally had mahogany bars, wooden chairs and tables, darts and dominoes. Now, many have become glitzier.

Jerry Beggs, 46, leaned on a wooden bar at the Globe Tavern, sipped his warm dark ale and reminisced:

"True pubs are becoming an endangered species. They are being changed into flash for yuppies. Some pubs now serve dinner. A real pub isn't a place for dinner. It's a place to drink and socialize, then you go home for dinner."

Beggs doesn't object to a new law that permits pubs to stay open uninterrupted all day long. Before, they had to shut down from 3 p.m. to 5:30 p.m. because that was tea time.

But tea time still occupies a part of every day for many Brits. **Olive Heaven**, 56, runs a tea room in Swansea, Wales. Things have not changed there and she doesn't think they will. Heaven's tea leaves tell her:

"If you're worried, the first thing you

BEGGS: True pubs endangered.

HEAVEN: Tea time still strong.

should do is have a cup of tea. It calms you down and gives you energy. Drinking tea is THE British tradition. You Americans should know that. You all threw it into the water, didn't you now?"

That's Plain Talk from the United Kingdom.

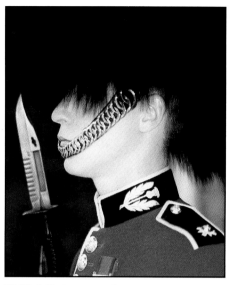

PAGEANTRY REVISITED: John Main, 57, Stratford-on-Avon, poses at Warwick Castle. The stunt man talks to tourists about medieval times. "Romantic, isn't it?" he says.

UNFLINCHABLE: Guards at Buckingham Palace are trained to ignore distractions. Women slip phone numbers into their pockets and tourists trample their feet without getting a response.

LONDON'S BEEFEATERS: John Maher, 58, guards the Tower of London. Why are guards called "beefeaters"? A good guess: They were used as royal tasters to prevent poisoning.

VIEW FROM THE THAMES: The dome of St. Paul's Cathedral towers above the City of London. The Cathedral has become a symbol of British determination. It survived the German bombing raids of World War II while much of London burned. It is the traditional site of British thanksgiving services after national triumphs in battle and in sports.

STREET MUSIC: Liverpool's Penny Lane inspired the Beatles' song of the same name. A tour takes visitors past the street's "shelter in the middle of a round-about" from the song.

ROYAL RESIDENCE: Westminster's Buckingham Palace has been the residence of the royal family since Queen Victoria moved there in 1837. In addition to the mews and state apartments, the mansion shelters Queen Elizabeth II's collection of art masterpieces. Although not open to the public, tourists flock to its gates twice each day to watch the changing of the guard.

BOBBIES AT PICADILLY: Constables Stephen Beattie, 22, and Paul Lovell, 21, patrol London's Picadilly Circus. Lovell says, "Any English person is friendly when the sun is shining. But when it's raining, when his soccer team has lost, or the clouds are hiding the sun, you won't find a smile anywhere in London."

Kasia Malewska, 18
Student
London

"London's always been a multiracial, continental city. We get to know many different cultures. It helps us to understand people better. It also makes us more broad-minded than most."

Brian Simpson, 62
Former rugby player
Swansea, Wales

"You need guts to play rugby. If you're a little chap running toward a big chap, you've got to tackle him and not flinch. To play rugby, you've got to have it in you."

Geoffrey Nicholsby, 41
Kilt designer
Edinburgh, Scotland

"I can discuss everything about the kilt except what a Scotsman wears underneath it. What you wear under it depends on how true a Scotsman you are. And how much you want to show off."

John Hume, 51
Parliament member
Londonderry, N. Ireland

"The territory of Ireland is already united. It's the people who are divided. And you can't unify people through violence. An 'eye for an eye' leaves everyone blind."

Thatcher: Politics isn't just public relations

On the relationship between the U.K. and the USA:

"I've always felt that the center of the free world is the Atlantic Basin. America and Britain have always had one another and, of course, together we liberated Europe."

On her relationship with President Reagan:

"It has been as close a relationship as ever one will get between leaders of two countries. We passionately believe in similar ideas. Our closeness has benefited both our countries and the free world."

On how people in the U.K. feel about the USA:

"We all owe an enormous debt to the United States and the way she defends freedom and justice the world over. Whenever I say that (in U.K. speeches) I get spontaneous applause."

On movement toward personal freedom in the communist world:

"They've realized that if you treat people as a unit of labor, you don't get results."

On causes for these changes:

"They've realized that the might of the Soviet Union as a superpower is dependent only on its military might. Not upon the standard of living, or social services, or housing or technology. I was the first to meet with Mr. Gorbachev and say, 'He's a man I could do business with.' I was the first to publicly encourage reforms. We are fortunate there is a person with such vision and courage there."

On the military response she ordered after Argentina's 1982 invasion of the U.K.'s Falkland Islands:

"It was something that I never contemplated. But let me say, it was a practical expression of the wise advice, 'Never rely for your defense on the rightness of your course alone.' For sure defense, it's men, materials and skill. If we didn't have that, we could not have upheld international law."

On advice to politicians:

"You really have to think out what you believe and why you believe it. Some think politics is only public relations. That is just the packaging. You first have to get the content right."

On the family role of a female politician:

"In a country with enormous distances, if you have a young family, it's much more difficult for a woman. Even in a country this size, had my husband's job been in Glasgow, in Aberdeen, in Exeter . . . I don't think as a wife with young children I would have been prepared Mondays to leave and come down to London to sit in Parliament and then go back late Thursday night or Friday morning."

She was prompt, poised, prepared. The world's most powerful woman walked winsomely into a small press office in the basement of No. 10 Downing St. Her office upstairs is being renovated and repainted. But the "flat" in which she and husband Dennis live, a floor above, isn't being touched. **Prime Minister Margaret Thatcher,** *62, was scheduled to meet with the JetCapade news team at 4:30 p.m. At exactly that moment, she entered the room, exchanged greetings graciously, accepted a cup of coffee (not tea) from an aide. She settled back in an overstuffed chair next to the fireplace. For a minute or two she exchanged small talk. Then she shifted forward to the edge of the chair and shifted to business, all business — accentuating the positive and aiming to eliminate the negative. For the next hour she sat erect at the edge of her chair. Answered, with obvious good nature, every question we asked about the United Kingdom, the USA, the world, her personal life. She balked only once, when we asked her to compare the campaigns and elections in the USA with the United Kingdom's. "You are asking a question which I anticipated. Interviewers usually tempt or provoke one to make unwise comments about other people's politics. You will not be successful in your efforts." She laughed. But the "Iron Lady" had sharply shown her steely side.*

On reflections about her work:

"I'm grateful that I'm able to do it — that I have the health, the strength. . . . We're coming up to a time when I hope that (my) cumulative experience will help the whole of the free world — I hope that doesn't sound pretentious, it's not meant that way — in discussion and debate to come to the right decisions which take us all forward."

On her views of the media:

"The medium is not the message. There are some (in the media) who think their only job is to debunk and undermine. That is absolutely absurd. . . . But when I've been treated unfairly, I've given as good as I've got."

On how she goes through life, day by day:

"I'm always looking ahead. I'll be looking ahead until the day I die."

PROTESTING CHILDREN: Picketers — none the children of jailed Martha Monaghan — urge her release.

Tension never lets up in Northern Ireland

A good day in Northern Ireland is when no one dies for a partisan cause.

The struggle between Catholics seeking independence from British rule and Protestants trying to keep it continues to breed violence.

In 1987, some 217 bombings and 80 murders in Northern Ireland were blamed on Irish Republican Army activities. 1988's death toll from the political turmoil reached 70 through the first seven months.

You can't escape the tension.

▶ One afternoon, a small ring of adults and children blocked a main intersection in Belfast to protest the detention — without bail — of Martha Monaghan, 28, mother of five. She was arrested after soldiers of the Royal Ulster Constabulary said they discovered explosives in her house.

▶ The 10,000 British soldiers patrol in armored cars, behind a thick wall of suspicion.

In Catholic West Belfast, the fading, bargain-rack

ADAMS: British will get tired, eventually leave.

McCUSKER: British departure wouldn't end violence.

▶ **POPULATION:** 1,592,000. About two-thirds are Protestant, one-third Catholic.

▶ **POLITICAL FACTIONS:** Protestant parties include the Unionists and the Democratic Unionists. The Catholic majority party is the Social and Democratic Labor Party. The minority party is Sinn Fein, the political arm of the outlawed Irish Republican Army.

clothes of the residents contrast with the crisp, new camouflage uniforms of British patrols.

Even Rhonda Paisley, 28, whose Unionist Party supports continued allegiance to the British government, criticizes those in charge of security: "You actually see British soldiers with maps trying to figure out where to go."

Paisley says her hopes for a solution soar one day, but are dashed the next. "When there's been another atrocity — a couple of soldiers you've known are blown up, or a friend is killed who's only 21 — you think there's no hope for this country."

British Parliament's Gerry Adams, 39, president of Sinn Fein, says the British "will eventually leave after growing tired of the burden."

But even that won't end the violence, says Unionist Parliament member Harold McCusker, 48: "People think if the British leave, we'll be back in the streets, dancing a jig. It wouldn't be like that. It would be closer to Cyprus, Israel, Lebanon."

VIETNAM

Featured in USA TODAY: June 10

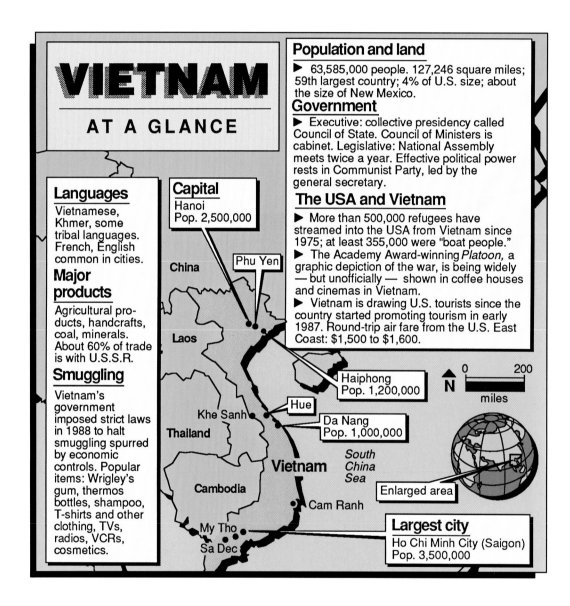

VIETNAM

AT A GLANCE

Languages
Vietnamese, Khmer, some tribal languages. French, English common in cities.

Major products
Agricultural products, handcrafts, coal, minerals. About 60% of trade is with U.S.S.R.

Smuggling
Vietnam's government imposed strict laws in 1988 to halt smuggling spurred by economic controls. Popular items: Wrigley's gum, thermos bottles, shampoo, T-shirts and other clothing, TVs, radios, VCRs, cosmetics.

Capital
Hanoi
Pop. 2,500,000

Population and land
▶ 63,585,000 people. 127,246 square miles; 59th largest country; 4% of U.S. size; about the size of New Mexico.

Government
▶ Executive: collective presidency called Council of State. Council of Ministers is cabinet. Legislative: National Assembly meets twice a year. Effective political power rests in Communist Party, led by the general secretary.

The USA and Vietnam
▶ More than 500,000 refugees have streamed into the USA from Vietnam since 1975; at least 355,000 were "boat people."
▶ The Academy Award-winning *Platoon,* a graphic depiction of the war, is being widely — but unofficially — shown in coffee houses and cinemas in Vietnam.
▶ Vietnam is drawing U.S. tourists since the country started promoting tourism in early 1987. Round-trip air fare from the U.S. East Coast: $1,500 to $1,600.

China

Phu Yen

Laos

Khe Sanh

Thailand

Vietnam

Cambodia

Haiphong
Pop. 1,200,000

Hue

Da Nang
Pop. 1,000,000

South China Sea

0   200
N   miles

Enlarged area

My Tho

Sa Dec

Cam Ranh

Largest city
Ho Chi Minh City (Saigon)
Pop. 3,500,000

Victory but no winners; wounds healing slowly

You probably remember pictures on TV or in your newspaper:

April 30, 1975: The last U.S. soldier lifted by helicopter from the roof of our embassy in Saigon (renamed Ho Chi Minh City). The USA had lost the Vietnam War.

Soviet tanks, driven by tiny but tough North Vietnamese soldiers wearing pith helmets, crashed through the gates of Independence Palace.

South Vietnam surrendered.

1988:

▶ The former U.S. embassy is now headquarters of the National Petroleum Board. The gun turrets surrounding it, that you saw pictured so often, are abandoned.

▶ Independence Palace, once a citadel of capitalism and democracy, now serves as the site for seminars on socialism, taught by Soviets.

THU: With wreckage of U.S. B-52 bomber downed during war.

VINH: With U.S.S.R. anti-aircraft missiles at ready.

Those who fought in what we call the "Vietnam War," but here is called the "U.S. War," harbor hard memories.

Major Nguyen Thu, 42: "My sweetheart died from American bombs. I narrowly escaped death several times. I'm tired of fighting, but if anyone invades my country, I'm ready to fight again," he says with a smug smile, while leaning on the wreckage of a U.S. B-52 in Hanoi's Lenin Park.

Capt. Trinh Quang Vinh, 34, is more grim: "You like wars very much. Now you are in Nicaragua, Panama, everywhere I turn. But you lost the war here," he says firmly in front of Soviet anti-aircraft missiles at the ready.

The cost of the war:

▶ 2.7 million U.S. military saw action here. Killed: 58,130. Wounded: 153,329. Missing in action: 3,537.

▶ South Vietnamese killed: 523,748.

▶ North Vietnamese killed: 731,000.

While MIAs are still a very emotional issue in the USA, Vietnamese shrug it off as a fact of war. They claim 100 times more missing than we do ... an estimated 300,000.

Except for an end to the fighting, life in Vietnam is not much different than it was in the '70s.

Then, it was a divided country. North and South. Hanoi and Saigon. Communists and capitalists.

Now, it's one country, but with two systems. In the North, struggling state industries and communist collectives. In the South, hustlers still profiting from the free enterprise system, albeit much of it illegal.

There are signs the South will prevail economically.

Foreign Minister Nguyen Co Thach, one of the government's most outspoken leaders, says:

"We have neglected the law of supply and demand, the law of value. Charity is not working. Without some capitalism there can be no socialism. We must learn from you." The Soviets, while still supplying arms, have done little to help build a base. The infrastructure — communications, housing, power, transportation — remains antiquated.

The personal aftermath of the war with which all sides sympathize is that of Amerasian children. Estimates of the number fathered by U.S. servicemen range as high as 18,000. Among those waiting and hoping to join their father-husband are **Tran Thi Quynh Huong**, 19, and her mother **Tran Thi Khan**, 39.

Says that mother: "He was a sergeant here in '68-'69. I got pregnant as a student in Dalat, where he was at the military airport. I still write to him, but he is lazy to write."

She pulls out a letter with the return address of **Edward G. Henderson**, Flint, Michigan. Dated November 1987. It reads:

"Hope the money gets to you be-

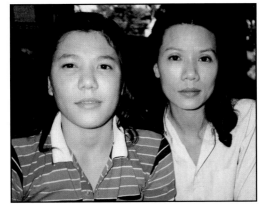

AMERASIAN DAUGHTER: Huong and mother; Huong's father is in Michigan.

fore Christmas and that you have a happy and more hopeful holiday." She hasn't heard from him since.

After we left Vietnam, we reached Henderson, a laid-off auto worker, in Flint by phone. He said: "This call is actually like a fairy tale. It's really great. I've been trying to get her out. There's no doubt in my mind she's my daughter." He says he's been "in a quandary" trying to get through the red tape.

U.S. State Department officials say they will grant entry to Huong if the Vietnamese give her an exit permit. USA TODAY is working to cut the red tape.

That's Plain Talk from Vietnam.

COUNTRY OF CHILDREN: Hordes of children clamor after visitors in Vietnam. While these children in Da Nang offer bright eyes and big smiles, others tug at sleeves and hold out their hands to Westerners.

CENTURIES-OLD METHOD: A Vietnamese peasant totes bundles of woven baskets in Hanoi.

HANOI: The capital of Vietnam reflects its French colonial heritage. The French divided the city into quartiers. In the second quartier, where the Vietnamese and Chinese were formerly the principle residents, pre-industrial Chinese architecture still stands.

CHIEF PRODUCT: Rice fields provide the basic food for Vietnamese farmers like this woman harvesting rice in a field in Da Nang. Hoang Thi Lam, 56, a farmer in Phu Yen Village, east of Hanoi, says: "We just grow enough rice for ourselves. This year's weather conditions are not favorable. We have just enough to eat for the year."

BATTLE SITE: Vietnamese emperors built the Hue Citadel — Palace of Supreme Harmony — in the 19th century. Located near the U.S. Marine command post, the Citadel was the scene of a major battle during the 1968 Tet offensive.

Tran Van Than, 62
Government liaison
Da Nang

"The war was fierce. Even five to seven years later, when people tried to reclaim their lands, they were killed or wounded by mines. You can't find a family that doesn't have someone killed."

Yo Van Giap, 45
Rice farmer
Hue

"Because of the weather and pests, we didn't get enough rice. My kids don't have enough to eat. We haven't had any help from the government. They don't give people pesticides or fertilizer."

Tran Thi Phuong, 52
Jeans merchant
Hanoi

"I cannot sell jeans quickly. They are fashionable but expensive — 75,000 dong ($25). Mostly the Soviets here buy them. People who go abroad bring them back and sell them to me."

Mai Chi Hai, 33
Tour guide
Ho Chi Minh City

"Tourism has improved. Americans like to go to Ho Chi Minh City or see the tunnels of Cu Chi. Tourists often stay in Vung Tau on the coast for one night. I was an interpreter before 1975. As for me, it's a better place than before."

Communism won't work without capitalism

Thirteen years after the fall of Saigon, Vietnam's new reform-minded leaders say they want to bury the hatchet with the USA — and borrow some of its capitalist ways.

Several members of the ruling elite made clear:

▶ They want to establish diplomatic ties with the USA — "so we can sleep with both eyes shut at night," as **Foreign Minister Nguyen Co Thach** put it. Like Fidel Castro, they're miffed the USA has gotten cozy with the Soviet Union and China, and not with smaller Marxist countries like Cuba and Vietnam.

▶ They openly call their communist-bred economy a failure. An infusion of Western-style entrepreneurship and profit motives is needed, they feel.

Most outspoken was Thach, an assistant to the legendary North Vietnamese General Vo Nguyen Giap. A top negotiator with Henry Kissinger in the 1973 Paris peace talks, Thach is sometimes mentioned as a possible candidate for prime minister.

His response on relations with the USA:

"We must put aside the war and look to the future. ... Both countries have been victims of war. Please tell Americans we are very grateful to them for joining with us to end the war. It is very uncomfortable to have enemies. If you have an enemy, you sleep with only one eye shut. It is the wish of the Vietnamese to have peace and friendship with the U.S."

On unresolved issues with the USA — servicemen missing in action, Vietnamese troops in Cambodia:

"Both sides must move on MIAs. Vietnam has taken responsibility. The American government has handed over responsibility to non-government organizations. In Cambodia we have withdrawn half our forces. We will withdraw totally by 1990. But why is the United States so concerned about the Vietnamese presence in Cambodia, and they do not concern themselves with China, which has supported the Pol Pot regime's genocide? Because we are small and China is big."

On Vietnam's economy, hit by food shortages, low industrial output and 700% inflation:

"We have taught that everything from capitalism is corrupt. This is false. Without capitalism there would be no socialism. We are very good dreamers but very bad economists."

The architect of reforms is **Communist Party General Secretary Nguyen Van Linh**, 72, an admirer of the restructuring in the Soviet Union — Vietnam's close ally.

To Linh, party leader less than two years, "renovation in the socioeconomic field is an urgent demand of the country and must be based on Vietnam's practical situation and must obey objective laws."

His chief aim: more food, consumer goods, exports.

General Secretary Nguyen Van Linh

Foreign Minister Nguyen Co Thach

Ho Chi Minh City Mayor Phan Van Khai

Economic Adviser Nguyen Xuan Oanh.

Foreign Minister Thach, 65, met the JetCapade news team in a large room, with no air conditioning, across from his foreign ministry office. During the interview, the power accidentally shut off three times but Thach and his staff continued in the dark without flinching.

Ironically, to help achieve that, the regime has named as its top economic adviser a Harvard Ph.D. who was a high official in the old U.S.-backed South Vietnam regime — **Nguyen Xuan Oanh**, "nearly 70." "Most of the reform today comes from my ideas," he said.

His recipe: local autonomy and perhaps profit-taking. Especially in what used to be South Vietnam, "where we encourage joint ventures and private ownership."

It is in the formerly capitalistic South that the regime is concentrating its revival effort. Spearheading it in Ho Chi Minh City — formerly Saigon — is the local mayor, **Phan Van Khai**, 55.

"This city has a very important economic role. We are producing 40% of the country's consumer goods. We have the best industrial infrastructure in the country, and a huge labor potential," he said.

This comes in part from the help of "re-educated" Southerners, Khai says. "We are using their skill and know-how to reconstruct our city."

There are problems: unemployment and population. But "people are coming here from the provinces," Khai says. "Ho Chi Minh City is very attractive."

WEST GERMANY

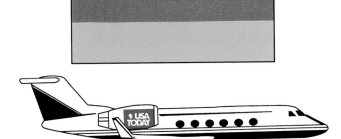

Featured in USA TODAY: Aug. 5

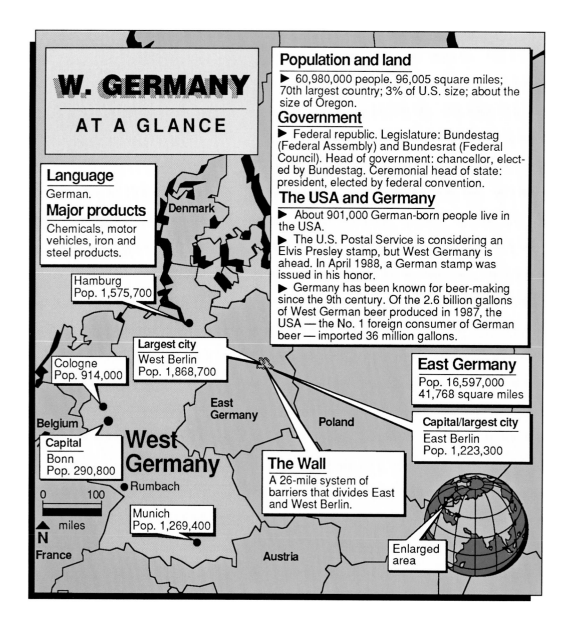

W. GERMANY
AT A GLANCE

Language
German.
Major products
Chemicals, motor vehicles, iron and steel products.

Hamburg
Pop. 1,575,700

Largest city
West Berlin
Pop. 1,868,700

Cologne
Pop. 914,000

Belgium

Capital
Bonn
Pop. 290,800

West Germany

● Rumbach

0   100

▲ miles
N

France

Munich
Pop. 1,269,400

Denmark

East Germany

Poland

The Wall
A 26-mile system of barriers that divides East and West Berlin.

Austria

Population and land
▶ 60,980,000 people. 96,005 square miles; 70th largest country; 3% of U.S. size; about the size of Oregon.
Government
▶ Federal republic. Legislature: Bundestag (Federal Assembly) and Bundesrat (Federal Council). Head of government: chancellor, elected by Bundestag. Ceremonial head of state: president, elected by federal convention.
The USA and Germany
▶ About 901,000 German-born people live in the USA.
▶ The U.S. Postal Service is considering an Elvis Presley stamp, but West Germany is ahead. In April 1988, a German stamp was issued in his honor.
▶ Germany has been known for beer-making since the 9th century. Of the 2.6 billion gallons of West German beer produced in 1987, the USA — the No. 1 foreign consumer of German beer — imported 36 million gallons.

East Germany
Pop. 16,597,000
41,768 square miles

Capital/largest city
East Berlin
Pop. 1,223,300

Enlarged area

U.S. roots in Europe; a reunion at Rumbach

Nearly 200 million of the USA's 243 million citizens have their roots in Europe. Here are the leading countries from which we claim ancestry (based on 1980 census):

▶ England — 49,598,000.
▶ Germany — 49,224,000.
▶ Ireland — 40,166,000.
▶ France — 12,892,000.
▶ Italy — 12,184,000.

The next 10 in order: Scotland, Poland, the Netherlands, Sweden, Norway, Czechoslovakia, Hungary, Wales, Denmark and Portugal.

My roots are in Rumbach, a tiny, hilly, farming village of 524 people. It's located two miles from the French border in Southwest Germany.

Midway through JetCapade in Europe, we paused here for a Sunday reunion with remaining Neuharth relatives. This was my second visit. The first time I simply drove around the town, visited the cemetery, talked to no one. Memories of World War II were still too fresh in my mind.

I had passed near Rumbach with our 86th Infantry Division in Patton's Third Army as we moved through the Frankfurt-Mannheim-Heidelberg areas in the spring of 1945.

My brother **Walter**, 70, of Long Beach, Calif., has traced Neuharths in this village to the year 1140. My great-grandfather, **George Neuharth**, then 38, arrived in South Dakota in 1874 with his wife, **Barbara**, and 1-year-old son, **John**.

Walter and his wife, **Irene**, 69, have made frequent pilgrimages here retracing their European roots. They urged me to come back and visit with my kinfolk. I'm glad I did.

On this visit, the war was a bridge, not a barrier. We talked of their feelings in fighting for their country. I talked of mine. We agreed that it must not happen again — that wars produce only wounded on both sides, not winners.

The wartime wounds among Rumbach's Neuharths were deep: **Edith**, 8, and **Karola**, 4, killed by American bombs aimed at

PERRET, 84: Ex-mayor who wound church clock for nearly 60 years.

a train. **Erick**, 16, and **Rupprecht**, 15, killed when they played with an unexploded bomb that detonated. **Richard**, 20, and **Karl**, 30, killed in action.

Fredrich Perret, 84, calls himself the "living dictionary" of this village. Mayor for 25 years. Wound the clock in the 1,000-year-old church steeple every day for nearly 60 years. Turned the task over to his son, **Werner**, 49, four years ago.

Perret spent most of the war with the German army in Italy. His sister-in-law, **Elizabeth Neuharth Perret**, who died four years ago, led women and children to the nearby caves of the Pfalz Mountains during the heavy bombings before U.S. troops took this town in early 1945.

"When Hitler first came through here, people were divided. Some who thought he was for the little people joined the army. Most of us were later drafted," recalls Perret.

Like all of West Germany, Rumbach has changed dramatically since the war.

Heidi Neuharth Koslowski, 43, first woman elected to the Rumbach village council, clings to the past while fiddling with the future. She and her husband, **Walter**, own and run the 21-room Haus Waldeck Inn.

HEIDI NEUHARTH KOSLOWSKI, 43: First woman on Rumbach village council.

Almost modish in her Frankfurt-styled hair and clothes, Heidi says:

"We see the fashions and hairstyles in the newspapers and magazines, so we go into Frankfurt to shop and have our hair done. But then we come back to Rumbach as soon as we can. I was born here. I will stay here."

A tiny village, slowly changing in a world that is becoming a huge global village. Reacting like folks in:

▶ Eureka, S.D., (pop. 1,350), my birthplace, talking about Sioux Falls (pop. 95,700).

▶ Or any small town USA, eyeing a bigger neighbor with both caution and imitation.

West German **Chancellor Helmut Kohl**, himself a native of the Pfalz mountain country, had this message when we met with him in Bonn three days after the Rumbach reunion:

"Tell those millions in the U.S. with German ancestors that we shall never forget how they came to our aid in 1947. We had lost the war. We were literally at the end. But the Americans with the Marshall Plan held out their hand and said 'come on.' Now we are doing quite well and you should be quite proud."

That's Plain Talk from West Germany.

DEATH CAMP: Visitors tour Dachau, Nazi Germany's first concentration camp. Set up by the Gestapo in 1933, the camp near Munich held more than 206,000 prisoners; at least 32,000 people died. Some of the prison's original barbed wire is still in place.

WOODCARVER AT WORK: Thomas Steidle, 30, finishes a model of Noah's Ark in his shop in Oberammergau. He attended the town's woodcarving school.

PROUD TRADITIONALISTS: Hans-Jacob Ueck, 34, and his wife, Martina, 27, conduct tours of their farm and orchards in Jork. Visitors also can stay in their house, designated a historic monument.

FANTASY PALACE: Linderhof is one of three palaces built by eccentric King Ludwig II of Bavaria in the 19th century. The retreat near Oberammergau was inspired by the style of Louis XIV of France.

BAVARIAN VILLAGE: Oberammergau, southwest of Munich, is famous for its Passion Play, the oldest festival in Germany. Villagers performed the first play showing Christ's Way of the Cross in 1634 and promised to hold it every decade out of gratitude for deliverance from the plague. Performances last more than five hours and employ 1,400 players. The next performance will be in 1990. An estimated half million people attend the festival — two-thirds from the USA.

Hugo Mayer-Norton, 49
Artist representative
Munich

"We look like a small country on the map, but when you read the economic indicators, you see the statistics that make us a leader of the industrial world. We're a surprising little country."

Uwe Paulson, 55
Beer company executive
Hamburg

"Germans can't go through a day without beer. We call it liquid bread. It provides nourishment without the trouble of chewing."

Maria Boomgaardner, 26
Print shop owner
West Berlin

"It's not more difficult or easier than anywhere else for a woman to open her own business and be her own boss. Women are getting ahead in Germany and getting good positions in business."

Sue Hepner, 42
Teacher
West Berlin

"Americans give people here a sense that life is not all serious, that it's not wrong to be patriotic, naive, or to like to wear make-up. Americans gain depth, open-mindedness and appreciation of the USA by being around Germans and being exposed to The Wall."

'You gave us a hand; we are your friend'

On Mikhail Gorbachev's glasnost policies:

"You have to remain sober here and have no illusions. Gorbachev doesn't want to do away with communism; he wants to make it more effective. I don't want to discuss with you whether that is possible. Today, the Soviet Union is one of two military superpowers. They have enormous economic problems and these problems have increased."

On the need for the West to remain strong enough to negotiate:

"We as Germans have made a substantial contribution to this. We have compulsory military service. We have prolonged the military service from 15 months to 18 months. Nobody else has done this. And I did this before an election. Of course, it's a sacrifice for young people to serve at the age of 18 or 19 for 18 months."

On a new U.S. president:

"I can only say that I have been very grateful to Ronald Reagan for his support. I think no matter who becomes president, we will continue this relationship."

On whether Europe will have political, as well as economic, unity after 1992:

"(French) President Mitterrand and I are of the opinion, and a number of others are too, that we also would like to bring about political integration. . . . There are some differences when we talk with Margaret Thatcher about political unity. What matters, however, is that right now I aim at 1992."

On U.S. aid to West Germany after World War II:

"The Americans came to our aid. The Marshall Plan was initiated. The money connected with the Marshall Plan was not that important, although it was a large sum. What was important was that someone extended a hand to us and said 'come on.' For many, that was a very personal experience. You know that I am the one in Europe who was attacked the most from within the Soviet Union for his pro-American position. But why do I do this? Because it's correct. When we were starving, the Americans helped us."

On relations between West Germany (the Federal Republic of Germany) and East Germany (the German Democratic Republic):

"(East German Chairman) Erich Honecker has not torn down The Wall, but he has opened a few more gates. Last year, 3.5 million people from the GDR came here to visit. We're expecting 4 million people this year. The trend is upwards. Of these 3.5 million, 1.5 million were here for the first time."

On how he would like people in the USA to perceive West Germany:

Helmut Kohl, 58, became chancellor of West Germany in 1982 after Helmut Schmidt was forced out of office by a vote of "no confidence" in parliament. A member of the Christian Democratic Union, Kohl won general elections in 1983 and 1987 and will be up for re-election in 1990. Kohl, who lost a brother in World War II and vividly recalls the war's devastation, has taken a leading role in disarmament efforts. But he has balked at suggestions that the number of U.S. troops in Western Europe be cut. The chancellor was interviewed in his modern, austere office in the German Chancellory in Bonn by the JetCapade news team. He spoke forcefully, but often jovially, through an interpreter.

"Our American friends should know that they have friends here. They should not mistake demonstrations against the U.S. for the opinion of the Germans in general. The Germans don't say: 'Americans go home.' "

On the status of the North Atlantic Treaty Organization:

"When I assumed office, the main thing was to make it clear to the leaders of the East that the Western alliance was coherent and standing firm — that there were no signs of dissolution of NATO. I think that NATO, compared to five or six years ago, has been strengthened."

CONCRETE CANVAS: Portions of the West Berlin side of The Wall are covered with layer upon layer of graffiti.

The Wall: Reminder of a country divided

The barriers that divide East and West Berlin were called the "wall of shame" when barbed wire and sandbags appeared overnight on Aug. 13, 1961.

Those barriers have long since become a 15-foot-high concrete obstruction that slices through the heart of Berlin. The name has changed, too. It's simply "The Wall" — a stark fact of life that's heavily fortified on the Eastern side by armed guards, dogs, barbed wire, electric alarms, mines and trenches.

WHERE EAST AND WEST MEET: If you enter East Berlin by car, you must pass through Checkpoint Charlie.

Since Erich Honecker, then security chief, but now chairman of East Germany, first started presiding over The Wall's construction, cars and trucks have rammed it, explosives have ripped holes in it, miniplanes have sailed over it, tunnels have been gouged beneath it. There are even cases of East German soldiers making a break for the other side and risking the bullets of their comrades. To date:

▶ 74 people — more than 40 the first year — have died trying to make it across The Wall from the communist East to the capitalist West. The most recent: February 1987.

▶ 5,000 have made it.

Visiting The Wall, says Maureen Paulley, 31, a teacher at a British army camp near Hamburg, "shows the vast difference between East and West." Looking over at East Berlin, she's struck by "the sense of freedom they must feel they lack. It's horrific."

Wilhelm and Gaby Bodewig of Koblenz, West Germany, brought their two children, Christian, 14, and Julia, 7, to East Berlin recently. "We came," Wilhelm says, "to show our kids what it means that there are two Germanys. It is sad. Very depressing."

Winfried Bartscat, 35, accountant in East Berlin, puts it this way: "I grew up with The Wall. When I became old enough to think, it was there. I realize now that I have a problem going to the other side to see what is there."

And Ragna Trierenberg, 14, a student in West Berlin, says: "The Wall is a prison. I have friends in East Berlin. Without The Wall, it would take 10 minutes to visit. With The Wall and the checkpoints, it takes two hours. It's really silly."

Army Capt. Scott Johnson, 41, Hutchinson, Kan., one of 6,500 GIs stationed in Berlin, wonders "what would happen if we suddenly tore The Wall down?"

Every East Berliner, he suspects, "wouldn't necessarily come running over. They have a guaranteed job, a certain security. And they could be scared of being able to cut it in a democracy."

TRAINING DRILLS: Air Force pilot Maj. Chase Johnson, 33, of Delavan, Wis., signals he's ready for flight while Army Specialist Eric Ruring, 22, of Selah, Wash., tries out an anti-chemical warfare mask.

GIs practice war to help keep the peace

The U.S. military presence seems to be everywhere: Green Army trucks rumble down highways; jets roar over the Rhine River.

West Germany is the heart of the U.S. military mission in Europe. The critical task: readiness.

Of the 325,000 U.S. troops stationed in Europe, 250,700 are in West Germany, where world crises take on an urgency because East meets West.

More than 56,000 GIs and their families live within 25 miles of the southern city of Kaiserslautern — in villages between the French border and the Rhine River. They are the largest community of U.S. citizens outside the USA.

The area is headquarters for a dozen Army and Air Force installations. Eastern bloc troops are less than 150 miles away.

If war came, Kaiserslautern would be the pipeline for supplies and troops. It's the largest logistics center for U.S. forces in Europe. Throughout the sprawling expanse of installations, people are readying for a day they hope never comes.

The practicing has become a career for many.

More than 350 of K-Town's GIs discussed their career concerns during a military town meeting held by USA TODAY. Pay, training, leadership and women's role in combat were top issues.

Many like being stationed in Germany. Capt. Dan

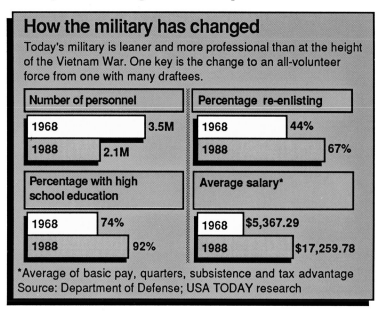

How the military has changed

Today's military is leaner and more professional than at the height of the Vietnam War. One key is the change to an all-volunteer force from one with many draftees.

Number of personnel		Percentage re-enlisting	
1968	3.5M	1968	44%
1988	2.1M	1988	67%

Percentage with high school education		Average salary*	
1968	74%	1968	$5,367.29
1988	92%	1988	$17,259.78

*Average of basic pay, quarters, subsistence and tax advantage
Source: Department of Defense; USA TODAY research

the largest community of U.S. citizens outside the USA.

Owens, 25, an Army typist from Mercer, Pa.: "Even when you're not out in the field it's real hard. You work until 6, 7 at night sometimes. You're up before 4."

Also, results of spending cuts are souring some. Terry Hurd, 38, a specialist from Los Angeles, plans to leave the Army: "Our (computer) system will be phased out ... and promotion in our group is non-existent."

The most controversial topic discussed was women in combat. Air Force Captain Rebecca Meares, 27, of Reeds, Mo., defends women's role. "I'm as willing to die for my country as anybody here."

Salvador Lopez, 21, an Army specialist from Martinez, Calif., differs: "Women should not be allowed in the battlefield because they would not be able to handle the stress and the pressure."

Drejza, 33, a pilot from Utica, N.Y., knows he could make more money flying commercially, but he's not leaving: "Money is not the primary reason people stay in the Air Force . . . (it's) patriotism, a feeling of self-satisfaction."

Still, some like the pay:

"In four years I've saved enough money to purchase a home (in the States) and to travel," says Air Force Sergeant Richard Palmer, 23, an electrician from Pittsburgh.

But the long work hours don't leave time for other things — such as evening college classes — says Specialist Judith

MILITARY TOWN: U.S. soldiers and airmen are a common sight throughout the Kaiserslautern community. Here, Army 1st Lt. Robert Kovacs, 26, Hampton, Va., and Pfc. Loyal Rowland, 22, Fort Collins, Colo., (carrying banner) lead a unit of the 66th Maintenance Battalion on a drill in nearby Landstuhl. They're preparing for a 100-mile endurance march in the Netherlands.

Leonard Booker, 32
Sergeant
East Orange, N.J.

"The Army is just like any other corporation. It just takes a little more discipline."

Frank Parriott, 24
Airman first class
Los Angeles

"I understand the need for order. But it's (no one) else's business how I fold my underwear."

Bruce Powell, 26
Sergeant
Ravenna, Ohio

"I like the military. You get to paint your face, run in the mud, jump out of aircraft. It's different."

Kelly Garrett, 23
Senior airman
Port Sanilac, Mich.

"I'm in a combat role. I'm the one that carries the (M-16). I'm a security specialist."

BACK IN THE USA

Featured in USA TODAY: Sept. 16

We are not yet united, as in the United States of America (USA), but we are nearly one world in most respects.

Allen H. Neuharth

Eureka! I found it, all around the world

In the beginning, I kept thinking over and over: This is a long way from Eureka (the South Dakota town of 1,300 people where I was born and grew up).

Toward the end, I realized more and more that it really wasn't.

Inescapable impressions from JetCapade:

▶ The world has indeed become a huge global village.

▶ There are no more mysteries, even in the most remote gully of the globe.

▶ We are linked electronically, country to country and continent to continent.

▶ We are not yet united, as in the *United* States of America (USA), but we are *nearly* one world in most respects.

On the last day of JetCapade in Moscow, I started with a 45-minute jog around Red Square and Alexander Garden behind the Kremlin. Thinking about the fact that this is where Lenin put Marx's Communism to work. And Gorbachev is trying to save it by adding a touch of Capitalism.

That's my daily routine. Early morning exercise, combined with sorting out thoughts, about yesterday, today, tomorrow.

I'd done the same thing in Mexico City's Chapultepec (Grasshopper) Park in February 1988 on JetCapade's first day.

And in Uhuru (Freedom) Park in Nairobi, where monkeys playfully mix with people.

The Royal Botanical Gardens in Sydney, Australia, in the shadow of the Coat Hanger Bridge, where Crocodile Dundee worked as a rigger before he went off to LaLa Land.

Yoyogi Park in Tokyo, where the homeless are as polite and proper as other Japanese. Beds are neatly made of newspapers or plastic. Shoes are neatly placed at the foot of the "bed."

The 2,224-acre Bois de Boulogne Park in the heart of Paris. A lovers' paradise. More used condoms scattered per square mile than anywhere else in the world.

Hyde Park in London. Pretty and proper. Where old-line Brits walk stiffly in English-made suits and ties and young Yuppies romp in USA-made jeans and T-shirts.

There, and everywhere, the "Made in the USA" label is what makes you feel close to home.

We've exported our food . . . fashions . . . films. Almost without exception, those are being gobbled up globally.

We are also exporting our philosophy . . . what's in our minds and our morals in the USA is making its mark around the world.

Results of those "Made in the USA" labels:

▶ Pragmatism is the politics that pilots today's world, prevailing over both capitalism and communism.

▶ Materialism is the medium of the rich and poor, the young and old, mastering most spiritual and intellectual values.

▶ The media, thanks to instant satellite communication, is the harness that hitches it all together.

Because I make my bread money in the media world, moseying through offices of newspapers and broadcast stations was one of my JetCapade favorites.

Nowhere did that bring more revelation or revelry than in the U.S.S.R.

Last time I visited Moscow, in 1979, the mood at *Pravda* and *Izvestia* was morose. Now, glasnost (openness) has those two giant newspapers beginning to practice our journalism of hope and opportunity.

Viktor G. Afanasyev, 66, editor in chief of the 11 million circulation *Pravda,* recalls: "Back then, you could not criticize anything."

Ivan D. Laptev, 52, editor in chief of the 11 million circulation *Izvestia,* says: "We have made this a newspaper for the people, not for the bosses."

Not too different from the 5.3 million readers of USA TODAY . . . or the 1,900-circulation weekly *Northwest Blade* in Eureka, S.D.

Small world. Nearly one world.

IZVESTIA EDITOR LAPTEV TO NEUHARTH: "Our newspapers must be for the people, not for the bosses."

The JetCapade news team interviewed 37 key leaders. Here's what some of them had to say about us and the country we live in:

▶ "The U.S. is such a fantastic country and to get to know it better would be extremely valuable."
Wojciech Jaruzelski, 65, president of Poland

▶ "Some members of Congress often say things which irritate the Chinese people, and some of their statements are . . . actions interfering in China's internal affairs."
Zhao Ziyang, 69, Communist Party general secretary of China

▶ "When we were starving, the Americans helped us."
Helmut Kohl, 58, chancellor of West Germany

▶ "The U.S. is concerned more about internal policies than with external ones and political issues."
Jose Sarney, 57, president of Brazil

▶ "This is a small land and so there is sometimes tension with military bases. But we have great affection for the people of the U.S. military and their families."
Noboru Takeshita, 64, prime minister of Japan

▶ "What did strike me in discussions I had in the States with all levels of the administration and members of Congress, was a very evident concern about the possibility of a pro-isolationist movement."
Ciriaco De Mita, 60, prime minister of Italy

▶ "There are large numbers of people in the U.S. who have a proper appreciation for South Africa. I receive many letters from people who express their good will toward our country."
Pieter W. Botha, 72, president of South Africa

▶ "If you look at our constitution and (the U.S.) constitution, there are a lot of similarities."
Rajiv Gandhi, 43, prime minister of India

▶ "Please tell Americans we are very grateful to them for joining with us to end the war. It is very uncomfortable to have enemies. If you have an enemy, you sleep with only one eye shut."
Nguyen Co Thach, 65, foreign minister of Vietnam

LOVE AND POWER: "Americans want to be loved, and that is much more difficult if you are powerful," Felipe Gonzalez Marquez, 46, president of Spain, told JetCapade. Gonzalez, shown here with Jet-Capade director David Mazzarella, is holding one of the crystal globes given to the world leaders.

▶ "We all owe an enormous debt to the U.S. and the way she defends freedom."
Margaret Thatcher, 62, prime minister of the United Kingdom

▶ "The U.S. is the only country that can be the negotiator, an honest broker between us and the Arab countries. We trust the U.S. There is a mutual confidence."
Yitzhak Shamir, 72, prime minister of Israel

▶ "U.S. citizens are not the most knowledgeable people in geography. Until (I won the Nobel Peace Prize) no one knew where Costa Rica was located in the Western Hemisphere."
Oscar Arias, 46, president of Costa Rica

▶ "Korea was devastated in the 1950s during the war. The U.S. came to our aid. We are allies forged in war."
Roh Tae Woo, 55, president of South Korea

▶ "I understand that there are public opinion difficulties in the U.S. (regarding normalizing relations with the U.S.S.R.). I think this trend can be overcome."
Eduard Shevardnadze, 60, foreign minister of the Soviet Union

▶ "(U.S. Secretary of State George) Shultz is un-American in that he is not arrogant."
Daniel arap Moi, 63, president of Kenya

▶ "You have been left behind in the chemical, steel, automotive and electronic industries. You are no longer No. 1."
Fidel Castro, 61, president of Cuba

▶ "I think that Americans and Mexicans do not always think alike, but we have grown used to respecting our differences and to trying to expand cooperation."
Miguel de la Madrid Hurtado, 53, president of Mexico

▶ "Canada is indispensable to the economic well-being of the United States, and vice versa."
Brian Mulroney, 49, prime minister of Canada

VIEWS ON THE USA: OUR GLOBAL NEIGHBORS

▶ "We Russians always thought of American people as our friends. We would like to open arms to the American people and show them our Siberian hospitality and that we are all the same."
Galina Berillo, 52, factory manager, Siberia, U.S.S.R.

▶ "Royalty is the basis of our tourism industry and our dignity. You Americans love our royalty more than most Brits, only because you don't have any."
Stephen Beattie, 22, constable, London, England

▶ "Americans think there are no roads in Kenya and they must have a four-wheel-drive vehicle. First they buy the safari suit, the big boots and the helmet. They want to carry a gun."
Jyoti Sharma, 62, manager of auto sales, Nairobi, Kenya

▶ "Typical Americans seem to be loud, but really nice blokes. They're usually appreciative of what you do for them. In other words, they're loud, but nice."
Rod Jackman, 35, cruise skipper, Tasmania, Australia

JetCapade talked to more than 2,000 "ordinary citizens" of foreign countries. Here's what some of them said about the USA:

IMPORT FROM THE USA: At Disneyland in Tokyo, Japan, JetCapade reporter Martha Moore talks with a Japanese Mickey Mouse.

▶ "You like wars very much. Now you are in Nicaragua, Panama, everywhere I turn. But you lost the war here."
Trinh Quang Vinh, 34, army captain, Vietnam

▶ "We don't like America in Greece because Americans are only interested in themselves. Period. The people we like but the politics we hate. The USA is never for us. They are for Cyprus."
Tegogiannie Theodoros, 52, retired civil servant, Athens, Greece

▶ "Do you know what it's like to live with your windows shaking, with nuclear weapons in your back yard? No more (U.S.) bases here. We've been too nice too long."
Aurora Jordan, 54, homemaker near the Torrejon Air Force Base, Spain

▶ "U.S. teen-agers are more superficial than Israeli teen-agers. American teen-agers care more about what they look like and what party they are

▶ "I've just written a book of fables to be published soon. I like to describe countries in terms of colors. Poland is gray. The U.S. is blue, like infinity. The possibilities there are endless."
Zeno Zegarski, 30, writer, Wroclaw, Poland

▶ "There are (many) women here who wear the veil, but they go to work. There are women in the U.S. who don't work. It's the veiling of the brain that's dangerous."
Nawal Saadawi, 55, feminist activist, Cairo, Egypt

▶ "You have more prejudices and problems. You have a limited view of the world. Canadians tend to take a broader view."
Vera Drobot, 33, supervisor, Fort Edmonton Park, Alberta, Canada

▶ "People talk about the love/hate relationship. I'd add jealousy. Americans have so much; Filipinos have so little."
Johnny Green, 42, airline employee, Manila, Philippines

going to on Friday night. We care more about what's happening in our country and the world."
Rubi Cohen, 16, high school student, Jerusalem, Israel

▶ "I don't think there is much difference between your country and mine. We have all the same things that you have. Except you can't walk anywhere, Americans have to drive every place. I imagine the U.S. even looks the same."
Asa O'Connor, 28, secretary, Stockholm, Sweden

▶ "American people appear to be very optimistic. Everyone seems to be sure that they can be successful in a lifetime. Even the people who live in poverty believe that they can change their lives."
Hans Ochsner, 28, stockbrocker, Zurich, Switzerland

▶ "You Americans eat soup at the beginning of the meal. This isn't good. It leaves no room for other food."
Wang Yong Lu, 54, business executive, Xi'an, China

▶ "Everybody wants to be Irish in America, especially on St. Patrick's Day. For us, it's just a bank holiday."
Maria Cotter, 22, clerk typist, Dublin, Ireland

The people behind the scenes and up front

MARY ELLIN BARRETT
. . . reporter

KATHLEEN SMITH BARRY
. . . photographer

RAMON BRACAMONTES
. . . reporter

STEPHANIE CASTILLO
. . . reporter

LIZ DUFOUR
. . . photographer

TOM FENTON
. . . reporter

MIREILLE GRANGENOIS GATES . . . reporter

MARILYN GREENE
. . . reporter

GWENDA IYECHAD
. . . reporter

LAURENCE JOLIDON
. . . reporter

DON KIRK
. . . reporter

PAUL LEAVITT
. . . reporter

KEVIN T. McGEE
. . . reporter

DAVID MAZZARELLA
. . . director

MARTHA MOORE
. . . reporter

LARRY NYLUND
. . . photographer

DAN NEUHARTH
. . . reporter

JOHN OMICINSKI
. . . reporter

KEN PAULSON
. . . managing editor

PHIL PRUITT
. . . page editor

JOEL SALCIDO
. . . photographer

CALLIE SHELL
. . . photographer

CATHERINE SHEN
. . . reporter

JOHN M. SIMPSON
. . . advance team editor

JUAN J. WALTE
. . . reporter

GAYNELLE EVANS
. . . reporter

JACK KELLEY
. . . reporter

WILLIAM NICHOLSON
. . . reporter

BILL RINGLE
. . . reporter

CHRIS WELLS
. . . administration

JetCapade was primarily a USA TODAY venture, but it would not have succeeded without the support of hardworking people at Gannett's corporate headquarters, broadcast stations and 88 other newspapers.

Visiting 32 key countries in seven months required extraordinary efforts by newsmen and women, circulation and promotion staffers, flight crews and others — many others. It was an exhilarating adventure but, in many cases, it meant exhausting weeks away from home.

I am grateful to all of them. Those who were with me throughout the trip, those who helped on specific segments and those who stayed home at USA TODAY and edited and published the JetCapade reports.

I especially want to thank David Mazzarella, 50, president of USA TODAY International and JetCapade director, and Ken Paulson, 34, my chief of staff and special assistant. Mazzarella coordinated JetCapade on the road and was the key person in arranging interviews with national leaders around the world. Paulson, JetCapade managing editor, started planning our global journey in September 1987, recruited the staff and followed through by coordinating newsgathering efforts.

Phil Pruitt, John Simpson and Chris Wells also played special roles. Pruitt, 37, was page editor and maintained contact with the embassies in Washington, D.C. Simpson, 39, was advance team editor and was the point person for our visits to China and the Soviet Union. Wells, 40, handled the day-to-day logistics of making the trip come together.

Other key JetCateers, their JetCapade roles and their Gannett units:

▶ Kathleen Smith Barry, 29, photographer, *The* (Nashville) *Tennessean.*

▶ Liz Dufour, 29, photographer, the *Pensacola* (Fla.) *News Journal.*

▶ Gaynelle Evans, 36, reporter, Gannett News Service.

▶ Marilyn Greene, 43, reporter, USA TODAY International Edition.

▶ Laurence Jolidon, 50, reporter, USA TODAY.

▶ Jack Kelley, 27, reporter, USA TODAY.

▶ Martha Moore, 28, reporter, USA TODAY.

▶ William Nicholson, 44, reporter, Gannett News Service.

▶ Larry Nylund, 37, photographer, USA TODAY.

▶ Callie Shell, 27, photographer, *The* (Nashville) *Tennessean.*

▶ Juan Walte, 48, reporter, USA TODAY.

Other reporters contributing: Mary Ellin Barrett, Ramon Bracamontes, Stephanie Castillo, Tom Fenton, Mireille Grangenois Gates, Dan Greaney, Gwenda Iyechad, Don Kirk, Paul Leavitt, Kevin T. McGee, Dan Neuharth, John Omicinski, Bill Ringle and Catherine Shen.

Assisting on photography: H. Darr Beiser, Rob Brown, Robert Deutsch, Frank Folwell, Kathleen Hennessy, Jason Johnson, David Leonard, Scott Maclay, Bob Roller, Joel Salcido, Carol Flaker Simpson and Paul Whyte.

Providing graphics help: Bill Baker, Richard Curtis, Elys McLean-Ibrahim, Marcy Eckroth Mullins, Dash Parham, Lynne Perri, Julie Stacey and Sam Ward.

Special thanks to the Gannett New Media staff, which designed, edited and published this book, especially Nancy Woodhull, Gannett News Services president, and editors Phil Fuhrer, Emilie Davis, J. Ford Huffman, Bob Gabordi, Randy Kirk, Lark Borden, Theresa Barry, Rebecca Conroy, Carolynne Miller, Mary Demby, Kent Travis, Larry Wheeler, Theresa Klisz Harrah, Bill Beene, Shelley Beaudry, Stella Pena, Celia Russell and Beth Goodrich.

Also, for their support for JetCapade throughout, thanks to Gannett President and Chief Executive Officer John Curley, USA TODAY Editor in Chief John C. Quinn, USA TODAY Executive Editor Ron Martin, USA TODAY Editorial Director John Seigenthaler, USA TODAY Publisher Cathleen Black, USA TODAY President Thomas Curley, Gannett Vice President/News Charles Overby, and Gannett Vice President/Public Affairs and Government Relations Mimi Feller.

And thanks to the following additional contributors:

▶ **Administrative support:** Thomas Bates, Kimm L. Boyle, Barbara Dutchak, Suzette J. Karelis, Juanie E. Phinney, Maria C. Pressley, Andrea L. Redding and Kirsten Sales.

▶ **Circulation/operations:** Hans Brunner, Hugh Graham, Anne Hillis, David Jones, Marcus Keller, Teddy Lim, John Rutland (deceased), Lee Webber and Sally Young.

▶ **Composing and systems:** Gerardo Escano, Tom Espinas, Guido Gomez, JoAn Moore and Jim Peters.

▶ **Flight attendants:** Laurinda Cameron and Ruth Chandler.

▶ **Flight engineers:** Ed Bohn and Gary Sanders.

▶ **Pilots:** Joe Hallahan, Chuck Hanner, Glen MacGregor and Chuck Thomas.

▶ **Promotion:** Sheila Gibbons.

▶ **Research/editorial assistance:** Melinda Carlson and USA TODAY/Gannett News Service Library staff and Laura E. Chatfield.

▶ **Television:** Jeanne Bowers, Sandra B. Butler, Byron Kelly, Ronald Ling and Michael Trammell.

▶ **Travel support:** Dr. Bernard Brody, Randy Chorney, William W. DeShazo, Katherine Lynn Friese, Joseph Varga and Dr. Joseph Von Tron.

Allen H. Neuharth

Other sources

Additional Photographs: Associated Press, Bettmann Newsphotos, Bisson-Sygma, Black Star, David Hume Kennerly-/Liaison Agency, Tim Dillon and United Press International.

Population figures and other data: Martha A. Bargar and Frank B. Hobbs at the Center for International Research, U.S. Bureau of the Census; Immigration and Naturalization Service; Population Division (Ethnic and Spanish Statistics Branch), U.S. Bureau of the Census. Also, press officers at foreign embassies.

Financial figures: External Affairs Department of the World Bank.

Flags: Flag artwork used in this book copyright 1987 Flag Research Center, Winchester, Mass. 01890.

Allen H. Neuharth, chairman of Gannett Co. Inc. and the founder of USA TODAY, also is the author of three other books: *Truly One Nation, Plain Talk Across the USA* and *Profiles of Power: How the Governors Run Our 50 States.*

When Neuharth was 11 years old and living in Alpena, S.D., he got a job delivering *The Minneapolis Tribune* — and never looked back. He found his life's work in the newspaper business.

His college career was interrupted with a four-year stint in the Army during World War II as a combat infantryman in Europe and the Pacific. When he returned, he majored in journalism and minored in political science at the University of South Dakota, where he graduated cum laude. He also served as editor of the college newspaper.

Neuharth joined the Associated Press in 1950. In 1952, at age 28, he launched his first newspaper: a statewide South Dakota weekly called *SoDak Sports.* It went bankrupt two years later.

Neuharth spent the next 10 years rising through the ranks of the Knight Newspapers in Miami and Detroit. He joined the Gannett Co. in 1963. That started another rapid rise. He became president in 1970, chief executive officer in 1973, chairman in 1979.

Along the way, Neuharth launched *Today* in Brevard County, Fla., in 1966 and, on Sept. 15, 1982, USA TODAY, now the nation's most-read newspaper.

Gannett is a nationwide news and information company that publishes 89 daily newspapers, including USA TODAY, 35 non-daily newspapers and USA WEEKEND, a newspaper magazine. It operates 10 television stations, 16 radio stations and the largest outdoor advertising company in North America.

Gannett also has marketing, television news and program production, research satellite information systems and a national group of commercial printing facilities.

Gannett has operations in 41 states, the District of Columbia, Guam, the Virgin Islands, Canada, Great Britain, Hong Kong, Singapore and Switzerland.

Its latest venture is GTG Entertainment, a partnership with Grant Tinker, which produces television programming, including *USA TODAY: The Television Show*, a daily program based on its namesake newspaper and featuring segments on news, business, sports and lifestyles.

OTHER TITLES AVAILABLE FROM USA TODAY BOOKS

USA TODAY Books is the imprint for books by Gannett New Media, a division of Gannett Co. Inc., with headquarters at 1000 Wilson Blvd., Arlington, Va. 22209.

For more information or to order, write to USA TODAY Books, P.O. Box 450, Washington, D.C. 20044, or phone 800-654-6931. In Virginia, phone 703-276-5985.

Truly One Nation
Allen H. Neuharth
With Ken Paulson and Dan Greaney
Pages: 144. Hardbound.

A journalistic journey that took a team of reporters to all 50 states in six months. It found a nation of diverse people, philosophies, politics. But above all, a nation united. Examines everyday life in the USA, from religion to recreation, politics to patriotism, civil rights to charity. Retail price: $19.95, includes shipping. ISBN: 0-385-26180-2. Publisher: Doubleday (New York, N.Y).

Profiles of Power:
How the Governors Run Our 50 States
Allen H. Neuharth
With Ken Paulson and Phil Pruitt
Pages: 256. Hardbound.

Today's governors are no longer back-slapping "good ole boys." Today's governors — men and women — are modern managers. With profiles and interviews of each governor. Retail price: $9.95, includes shipping. ISBN: 0-944347-14-2. Publisher: USA TODAY Books.

Plain Talk Across the USA
Allen H. Neuharth
Pages: 320. Hardbound.

Full color throughout with more than 500 photographs and interviews with people in all 50 states. Features details on all 50 states and conversations with all 50 governors and notable personalities from each state. Retail price: $16.95, includes shipping. ISBN: 0-944347-00-2. Publisher: USA TODAY Books.

And Still We Rise:
Interviews with 50 Black Role Models
Barbara Reynolds
Epilogue by Coretta Scott King
Pages: 224. Paperback.

A celebration of success and accomplishment in the USA. Features conversations with 50 men and women who share their insights and offer examples for success. Retail price: $14.95, includes shipping. ISBN: 0-944347-02-9. Publisher: USA TODAY Books.

USA Citizens Abroad: A Handbook
American Citizens Abroad
Pages: 128. Paperback.

A usable guide to living or traveling outside the USA, written by U.S. citizens living overseas. Tips on taxes, voting, going to school, personal finance, customs and how to get help. Retail price: $9.95, includes domestic shipping. ISBN: 0-944347-13-4. Publisher: USA TODAY Books.

The Making of McPaper:
The Inside Story of USA TODAY
Peter Prichard
Pages: 384. Hardbound.

When USA TODAY was launched on September 15, 1982, many journalists laughed at it and called it "McPaper," the titan of "junk food journalism." Now it is called No. 1, the USA's most widely read newspaper. A candid look at the ups and downs along the way. Retail price: $19.95, shipping extra. ISBN: 0-8362-7939-5. Publisher: Andrews & McMeel (Kansas City, Mo.).

The USA TODAY Cartoon Book
Charles Barsotti, Bruce Cochran, Dean Vietor
Paperback

Cartoons from the pages of USA TODAY's Life, Sports and Money sections. Funny, but filled with insight into our lives, our work and our play. Retail price: $6.95, shipping extra. ISBN: 0-8362-2077-3. Publisher: Andrews & McMeel (Kansas City, Mo.).

USA TODAY Crossword Puzzle Book
Volumes I, II, III and IV
Charles Preston
Paperback

A series of puzzles from USA TODAY's crossword puzzle editor. Each volume contains 60 puzzles never before published in book form. Retail price: $5.95 each, shipping extra. Publisher: Putnam (New York, N.Y.).

Portraits of the USA
Edited by Acey Harper & Richard Curtis
Pages: 144. Hardbound.

Glossy, high-quality coffee-table book. Features photos taken for USA TODAY, many of which are award winners. Photos are portraits of life in the USA, seen through the eyes of USA TODAY's photographers and selected by USA TODAY editors. Retail price: $29.95, shipping extra. ISBN: 87491-815-4. Publisher: Acropolis Books Ltd. (Washington, D.C.).

Tracking Tomorrow's Trends
Anthony Casale with Philip Lerman
Pages: 268. Paperback.

Features charts and information based on USA TODAY polls and news research. Information written in USA TODAY's light, easy-to-read style. Trends and what is likely through the 1990s. Retail price: $8.95, shipping extra. ISBN: 0-8362-7934-4. Publisher: Andrews & McMeel (Kansas City, Mo.). Audio cassette interview with the author: $8.98, shipping extra. Publisher: Listen USA (Greenwich, Conn.).